CIRCLEWORK is probably many peo[...] the Arts and Crafts of modern w[...] seekers of the Old Ways have be[...] book which tells them exactly h[...] what circumstances they can learn to work their magic. This is it!

Shan has turned her many years of struggle and learning into valuable material for anyone, in a coven or alone, who wishes to master the skills and call themselves a 'witch'. From casting a circle to rededicating a house, from lighting a candle to creating an inner temple, all the instructions are there. All you, the Reader, have to do is apply the years of effort, the dedication and long hours of hard work to turning the ideas in this valuable instruction maual into reality in your own life.

The Craft is extremely ancient and its gifts have always been free for all who truely seek, to find. The path to that source of wisdom, however, has been hidden, the Gods and Goddesses of the Old Ways have veiled their faces in our all-electric modern world, yet the path has not been destroyed. If you have the courage to walk in the Moon-light, drink from the well of wisdom, and hone your own goddess-given powers, then here is the guidance you seek.

No arts of magic are instant, no power can be gained over the will of others, but ways to make the world we all share a better place can be gained, and those desires to know, to change and to empower are at your finger tips. The way of witchcraft is not easy, it is not short, and you cannot buy it at any price. If you devote your life to the service of the Gods and Goddesses freely, and for many years, the rewards you will gain will limitless. Shan has spelled out the patterns, shown you the arts, described for you the rituals, all you have to do is to create the Circle, and step out beyond time.

May the Great Ones Bless you,

Marian Green.

Without other priestesses before me
I could not have done it.
I am especially indebted to the work
of
Dion Fortune
Doreen Valiente
Olivia Durdin Robertson
Merlin Stone Robin Morgan
Marian Green
Starhawk
&
Marija Gimbutas

My other major source of learning is
my counselling clients
whose courage, tenacity, suffering and wisdom
give me the gift of knowing I do something useful.

My skill with words is useless to
thank John and Taliesin
for their generosity day by day
I do hope they like this book.

Written, edited and illustrated
By
SHAN

Foreword by Marian Green
Editorial support: John H T Davies

Photographs: Pam Haas LRPS
Models: Cath, Marijka, John & Tal

First edition 1988   Second edition 1994
Published by House of the Goddess ISBN: 1 869973 06 2
33 Oldridge Rd London SW12 8PN
Financed by John H T Davies
DTP support courtesy of Daniel Cohen (Wood & Water)
Printed by Intype/ Input Woodman Works Durnsford Rd SW19
Trade Distribution: Airlift Books, London.

Also by Shan of House of the Goddess
WHICH CRAFT? An intro to Paganism & the Craft (1985) £3.99
THE PAGAN INDEX The Directory of Pagan Britain £3.99
THE PAGAN SONGBOOK (+ tapes in preparation) £3.99
PAGAN HALLOWEEN FESTIVAL 2 hr video by Shan & John £9

House—of the Goddess ™

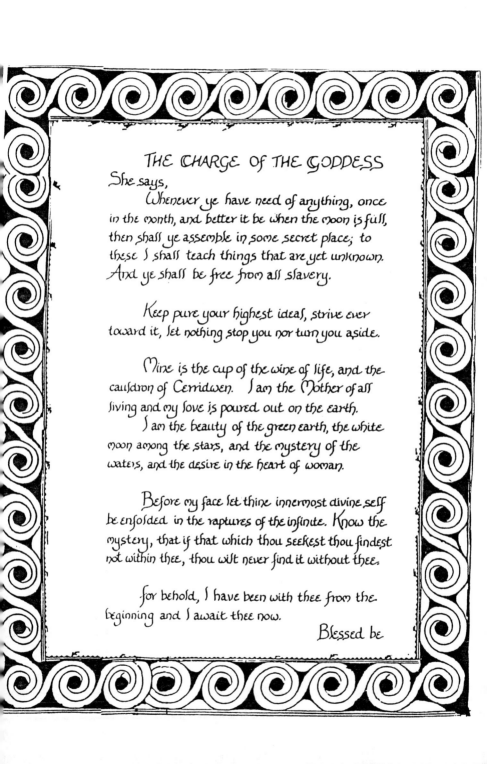

THE CHARGE OF THE GODDESS

She says,

Whenever ye have need of anything, once in the month, and better it be when the moon is full, then shall ye assemble in some secret place; to these I shall teach things that are yet unknown. And ye shall be free from all slavery.

Keep pure your highest ideal, strive ever toward it, let nothing stop you nor turn you aside.

Mine is the cup of the wine of life, and the cauldron of Cerridwen. I am the Mother of all living and my love is poured out on the earth. I am the beauty of the green earth, the white moon among the stars, and the mystery of the waters, and the desire in the heart of woman.

Before my face let thine innermost divine self be enfolded in the raptures of the infinite. Know the mystery, that if that which thou seekest thou findest not within thee, thou wilt never find it without thee.

For behold, I have been with thee from the beginning and I await thee now.

Blessed be

CONTENTS

1

WHY ON EARTH RITUAL ?

A preface for the intelligent cynic.

Why on earth spend precious time and energy learning to make rituals? It's only primitive superstition after all - people doing embarrassing things like talking to things that aren't really there - by candlelight to make it spooky as well. Whatever for - in this day and age?

Many people come to ritual work by way of an instinct that insists on it somehow, and then they find out how good it feels, what it can do, so even if it still seems odd, it works for its keep as it were. Some discover ritual as a much needed language for the deeper parts of the self within, which were unable to speak before, and now gladly does so.Some of us are not so instinctive; either we have been taught to be thoroughly wary of anything we can't explain sensibly, or we do respect our instincts, but we want intelligent explanation too.

Fair enough: here's a sensible list for these readers.

1) Although 'primitive' people do odd, and sometimes rather grubby things in their ceremonies, most anthropologists agree that such people are mentally healthier, more able to cope with life's ups and downs than civilised, rational people who don't indulge in such dubious practices. It would therefore seem rather foolish to dismiss a proved technique because it requires us to bend some of the stuffier codes of behaviour we are used to. .

2) Techniques from ancient sources in ritual work are often found under other names among people who handle a lot of challenge, for example:- Stress management in business & politics.

Creative arts (acting, writing, dance, etc especially inspiration blocks and performance anxiety).

Sports training uses stress management and creative development techniques.

Systems theory (patterns of energy flow).

Therapy, Humanistic Psychology, Psychosynthesis (concept of the subconscious, subpersonalities, trance, dreams, catharsis, sexual counselling).

Assertiveness (go getters, achievement, confidence).

Medicine (placebo effect, bedside manner, supporting the natural capacity of the body to heal itself).

2

3) After the Nazi holocaust Abram Maslow and other psychologists interviewed some of the survivors and found that the people who were more likely to survive great suffering were those who had a strong belief in something. It didn't have to be part of organised religion, or even come under the name of a religion. But as long as people had something to hold on to inside themselves beyond a clockwork universe, they had a much greater chance of survival, and of making a new life.

Such beliefs can exist without rituals, but ritual deepens them, makes them clearer, surer and stronger. It also works to help us shed beliefs that don't work well, but get us stuck and unhappy.

4) Although ritual was originally a mystical adventure which followed naturally when I found the spirituality that suited me at last, it rapidly became much more. It taught me to be more careful and efficient! in all important tasks. It taught me to be practical about tools, available time, and my own health and energy. It taught me how to work in a group, and how to really enjoy solitude. It taught me to trust my own inner good sense. It taught me to do practical things out in the woods. It made it possible to cope with many frightening interviews, the dentist, and an appalling birth labour.

5) Finally, when I came to the task which I firmly hold is the most enormous and challenging of all - being a mother - ritual had me well prepared. I knew by then to trust the wisdom of my own child self, so I could trust my son to do and grow as he wished. But I had also learned to accept certain basic limits which actually enlarged my freedom. So I had little trouble imposing similar basic discipline on my son. The ultimate essence of ritual, as in any key skill, is to balance spontaneity against discipline.

These personal testaments I have seen repeated in other people's lives hundreds of times over.

Having said all that, if ritual doesn't appeal, don't do it. It's not the answer to everything, just one of them; so you'll find what you need elsewhere if not here.

WRITTEN DOWN STUFF LOOKS
MORE IMPORTANT THAN IT IS

WHO HAS THE POWER ?

If you want instructions for the best ritual, the essential, the most effective, workable, meaningful, authoritative ritual in the the most sacred tradition - then you'd better write the instructions yourself! You probably will - and definitely will if you use this book. Because, you see, the first lesson in ritual I have for you is that YOU are a priestess, or a priest, (a priest/ ess).

As soon as you begin working ritual you are yourself in charge of your own personal sphere, and it's up to you how it is shaped and used.

You need no expert authority to do it for you, or 'correct' you. You hold in your own depths all the knowledge you need to directly key into power and divinity. A lot of people have made a lot of money, and created high positions for themselves in the world, by insisting that only some people (them) can be priests. They say that these special people (themselves) have the job of 'doing it' for everyone else.

Not so. You, and you only, can create the rituals that really work for you.

If this is so, you can rightly ask me, then what is this book for? Surely if the knowledge lies in your depths you don't need me in order to dredge it up and use it. Well, I stay faithful to my principle that in fact you don't need me. If you wish you could experiment carefully by yourself, and bit by bit uncover that deep knowledge within. In fact, you will still have to do a lot of that anyway. Intuition and independence are the keys.

However, as with learning to cook, it helps a great deal to benefit from someone else's experience to gain some basics plus a few tips. Vegetables get soggy if cooked over their time - that timing can be learnt from someone who cooks a lot, although your own common sense will get you there too after several tries. But no doubt you have already found how tedious it can be to struggle to learn something without any help at all, and at least if it's something like cooking you know what the result is expected to look and taste like to show you if you've got the hang of it.

So although I champion your individual quest, I also think it's sensible to use   other people's experience to get started, providing you check each suggestion against your own common sense and feelings as you go.

This little book is like a first cookbook with lists of pots, bowls, spoons, common herbs, hygiene guidelines, timing advice, how to balance a meal into a tasty combination, and a few useful recipes. It's an outline to get you started. You'll still have to adjust to your own individual taste, decide how plain or elaborate your style needs to be, and choose among the Celtic, Saxon, Wicca, American or Native Shamanic, High Magic or Nordic cuisine.

Most of us already work personal rituals without necessarily calling them that. Whenever you settle to write an important letter, choosing your time, clearing space on the table, selecting pen and paper with care and so on, you are instinctively ritualising it. You may already be familiar with Buddhist or Christian or other rituals. Whatever rituals you already know, Circlework does not demand that you sacrifice them. Your existing rituals can stay separate, or they may naturally weave into this new structure.

This is not the authorised version: there's no such thing. Circlework is a just a stripped down basic version of Craft ritual with my own style of teaching. It suits most people well as an introduction. It has served me for many years as friend, teacher, counsellor and entertainer.

The Craft is one of the traditions of the Pagans. You are welcome to use and benefit from our style of ritual without becoming a Witch, a Shaman, a Magician or taking any special initiation.

However if the fact that this is Witches' stuff makes you uncomfortable, I suggest you find out a bit more of the truth about Witches before you take and use our knowledge. I do not see why you should benefit from our work if you don't like us. My book 'Which Craft?', the ones by Starhawk, Doreen Valiente, or the Farrars can help you make up your mind.

Do not use Circlework or any other of our resources unless you have freed yourself of vicious propaganda about the Craft. Magic is a powerful mirror and amplifier. Your own fears and fantasies of evil and Satan will rise up to frighten you if those are the beliefs you bring into the ritual Circle. This is what is really behind all the warnings not to meddle irresponsibly with magic. But go into the Circle, or pick up the Tarot with an open mind, or in trust, and they will return your openness and trust back to you.

If you know that your background has left you with some feelings of distrust or tension about magic or Paganism, (and few of us are left free of it) use the chapter on Purification very thoroughly to bring out all your attitudes and feelings into the open. Do several Purifications about it, before going further with any other work in this field. Talk it over with someone you trust, even a Christian priest if necessary. (You can worship Christ in the Circle too!) Finally, take it slowly, step by step, checking each thing I suggest against what you believe in. If any item I describe worries you, change it a bit to suit your own inner guidance.

On the other hand if you feel that in due course you would like to train fully as a Witch, a Druid, a Shaman etc. then this is an excellent first step on your way.

There is nothing dangerous here, although there is power. If you try the technique, get muddled and forget bits at first, the worst that can happen is that nothing happens! Or you could end up feeling rather confused and tired like you do after the first day in a new job. The power you are learning to use is your own. Magic is natural energy, your own natural equipment. You already use it to some extent. These techniques have been worked out by others before you to help you use more of it.

I am well aware that many books on magic begin with dire warnings of disaster for the unwary and that what I have said here is not like that. You will only cause events to happen that you can cope with. It's your own power that creates what happens, so you can't bump your head until you get strong enough to stand up. If you're strong enough to stand you're strong enough to handle a bump.

Someone once telephoned me in some distress having bought a crystal ball. 'It's taken me over, I feel terrified, sick, dizzy, my head's going round....' The fledgling clairvoyant continued to use very dramatic terms like 'It's taken me over.' I asked her if the energy that had 'taken over' had made her attack her friend with a carving knife or vomit on the carpet. 'No, no,' she said sounding rather taken aback, nothing like that had happened. Once she could see her symptoms were not worse than what she'd suffer from a cold in the head, and she calmed down. Now I don't mean to imply that this was a silly woman; she wasn't. We have all grown up in a society that is mostly ignorant about magic and spiritual power. The feel of a good dollop of it can be frightening because it is unfamiliar and we have no guidelines.

The best possible guides are your own feelings. It wasn't silly for the girl with the crystal ball to panic. Fear is a useful protector, so respect its voice. But look clearly at what the fear would have you avoid, and it may change shape as you look.

WHAT IS RITUAL LIKE ?

by the fly on the wall - or on a tree

1) She puts out candles in each corner of the room, leaves them unlit, but lights incense. The delicate smoke curls blue in the space around her, hinting of other places. One candle in the centre of the room she does light, the first flame pale under modern lighting, but still pretty. The room is empty looking because several things have been pushed back to the walls, leaving open space.

2) She takes a bowl of water, sits comfortably, sprinkles salt in it. Holding it in both hands she begins to speak, looking into the water. Her voice continues, slows down, stops, then goes on again. She sighs, gestures, speaks once more, hesitantly. A second time she pauses, for longer than before, then rushes into words again. Finished, she puts the bowl aside, leans back with a relaxed curve to her body.

Now she takes the bowl outside and comes back with it empty; puts it with the salt back on the table with other things. There is a tall graceful cup, one of the unlit candles, a dish of bread, a pottery figure with an ethnic look, some green leaves, a taper, and a shell.

She begins to move round the edge of the cleared room, as if warming up for dance or exercise. She swings her arms, and kicks her feet, claps and shakes her hands, makes a soft grunt or two as her breath deepens. Now she slows and walks quite decorously all round the room. Slowing even more, she moves like a hunting cat, placing each foot with great care, and making each step an even flow from one to another.

Her face glows from the warm up, and its shape looks simple somehow like a classic drawing. She is ready.

3) The light is switched off and the room covered in shadows. Now the candle at the centre comes into its own and she stands for a moment watching its yellow flame. Then she takes the the taper from the table and lights it from the flame. She walks purposefully to one corner, raises her hands, and speaks. But now her voice is different, stronger, with a slight singing to it. She lights the candle and moves as if dreaming to the next. Here there is a special atmosphere around her like a smoky bubble enclosing her in something that is very much her own.

4) She breathes slowly and deeply and after a while begins to sway a little as if listening to music. And then she hums it, still moving a little with it. Words come, and the sound is a strong rythmn impossible to resist. She is no singer, and does not seem to be trying to perform, yet as the sound repeats and repeats, over and over, there is the seduction of all music everywhere. Odd, that an ordinary person in her own home stands swaying and singing by candlelight, yet she doesn't care, so it doesn't matter. She is clearly enjoying a private and peaceful task, a kind of craft.

Her singing strengthens a little. The telephone rings, and her face notices it but she does not stop her work. She makes a step to one side and the other, walks round the candle, still singing, then twirls round on the spot and - laughs.

5) She sits, very calm. There is no sign at all of the whirling woman who finished her strange little dance just before. She looks immensely serene, rather pleased about something. She makes some gestures, cups her hands. She looks expectant, a little worried, then her face clears and she nods, apparently relieved.

She touches her head, her chest, her stomach and her feet, quickly and easily so it is hard to see exactly where her fingers do touch.

6) Then she rises and fetches the cup and dish. Raising the cup in a toast to someone, she drinks, and eats a small fragment of bread. After drinking some more she curls up beside the candle and seems to daydream, staring at the flame. All seems deeply peaceful.

7) She gets up a little stiffly, and goes to the table. She speaks a little, puts out the candle. She does the same for the other three in the corners. Back at the centre she stands silhouetted against darkness.

Her work is done and she puts the lights back on and blinks. She sits down in a comfortable chair. She dials, and begins to talk to a friend. 'Yes, I thought it was you' she says. 'But I was in the Circle, you see....What? .... Oh, well .....no I didn't get what I expected, but it was very good. I know what to do now. Shall I come over tomorrow or are you busy?'

Meanwhile on the same evening, not far away, there is a bonfire in the woods, and the circling is noisy. Young vigorous bodies are leaping and dancing enthusiastically around the hot flames. Yet these too, stop and speak seriously and quietly at intervals. A crate of beer waits glinting at the edge of stamping feet. Piles of sleeping bags and blankets are ready for tired celebrants to sleep it off. The next day there will be no sign of their presence except some carefully earth covered ashes.

In a high rise flat, on the ninth floor, an older man sets out the candles. A huge plate glass window overlooks the great city spread out glittering in the night. He prepares carefully, then he slips off the robe he wears. Naked, his body is a little softened by age, with a distinct belly, but he moves with a grace that comes from long held health.

He works his Circle, and at one point turns to look out of the big window. He is far too high for anyone to see him; he looks over his city with a loving glance, then turns back to his special place.

A small group is drinking and laughing, colourfully dressed and excited. Most are wearing silk robes, both women and men, with a good deal of intricate jewellery. There is a lot of fuss going on 'Anyone got a safety pin?' 'Oh for heavens sake, where on earth is John?' 'I do hope I can remember my bit - I only got my script last night!' 'Doesn't Sarah look sweet in that veil, even if she's hardly a very virginal Maiden!' 'Don't forget to bring those cakes.' 'I'd better go to the loo now while I can.'

Everyone troops into the next room; as they go the door bell rings and a man is let in. 'I thought you'd have Cast by now and I'd have to wait for you in the pub.' But all is well, all gathered together at last.

The altar is elaborate here, draped, with a tall black candle and a tall white one. There are thick cords lying coiled, and gleaming knives. A brass disc is cut with the sign of a star. Here too there is a cup, a figurine, and a dish of cakes. Incense already fills the room with sweet smoke, and long velvet curtains along one wall aid the dramatic image.

They are very controlled with set moves, and speeches given as if in theatre. The figures move in their long robes like dream people in the smoke, voices rising and falling in a way that shows a skill at their craft. Dramatic images focus and dissolve; a woman walks

9

solemnly, barefoot soft, sprinkling water around the circle, then she marks the air with firm symbolic strokes watched carefully by the others; they all stand arms raised, deep sleeves fallen back, hands grasping the up pointing knives, a strange word repeated vehemently. The shining cup is held in his hands; he kneels, as she holds a knife in it, faces rapt in some shared understanding.

Afterwards, they stay on, drink together, eat cheese, biscuits, crisps ... the conversation is about children, cars, jobs and unemployment, clothes and cats. If it were not for the robes it could be any suburban party.

At a huge gathering in a public hall the finale of a whole weekend festival is about to happen. An expectant hush more or less holds a crowd of several hundred. Children are playing at the front of the crescent of space, or dozing on laps. At the back of the hall some workers are packing up their gear, but quietly out of respect.

The four quarters are called, two by men and two by women. One is obviously pregnant, dressed all in red. Two stand at the centre, a young girl with fair hair in white, and a solid, older woman veiled in black, with a wig of long black and white strands.

There is some singing and swirling dance; more people join the actors, then return to the edge. The veiled one embraces the other two women, and they pass to the rear. As they go by the three men who are crouched waiting, each man stands up, cloaked darkly and hooded. Their faces are masked dead white.

The veiled one speaks and sometimes the audience laughs, and sometimes answer her. At one point they all lean forward as she says something important. She repeats it, and then retires to sit.

Three emerge from the audience, and argue with each other, pointing at the dark figures of the men. Although the males look ominous enough, the three before them clown about and there is more laughter at obvious in-jokes. Finally one goes past the guardian men, to where the pregnant woman and the young girl have lit lots of tiny candles around a big black pot. The others follow and suddenly there's a fizz as they turn with sparklers spitting in their hands. More people from the audience go forward past the motionless men, and sparklers keep flaring and dying.

A big circle forms; everyone is singing, something easy to follow with a strong feeling to it. They all begin to move round in a stately way, singing still. The sound is full of power. A priestess leads them in a spiral pattern in and out. Faces are gleaming, open with confidence in a shared pleasure.

The drums beat together, deep and heavy. Faster and faster the people spin, until the pattern goes crazy wild and laughing they are swooping under each other's arms in an insane sewing dance that at last pulls them together still stubbornly singing that song.

Silent, damp, panting, they stand like that a little, enjoying the exhilaration, then gently separate back into the big open circle.

Sitting, they are shadowed shapes, actors and audience merged long before. One goes to the centre, another too. They hold up the cup and say something with smiles. They drink, gratefully, and pass it to others. More bowls are brought out and passed. Bread is given too, and then suddenly the black pot is carried forward, emptied over the floor, giving apples, brightly wrappered biscuits and sweets. They are shared out amid a buzz of talk and giggles.

A drum starts again and more singing. The power of it builds, sinks to almost finish, then rises again. Someone is playing a skitsy violin, someone else an acoustic guitar with sexy chords. A young man in black leather jumps forward and dances, and a fierce young woman with a mane of hair joins him. More dance, but many are content to watch and let the sounds flow through them. A child cries at the noise and is taken to the back for special cuddles. On and on the celebration goes as if it would never end, but it does, slowing to a peaceful, softer sound as the dancers sink to the floor.

Four of the original actors go to the four quarters to say thanks and farewell. There is a general exchange of kisses and hugs. An hour or so later all is packed away and the bare hall is locked up for the night as exhausted happy Pagans stream home in all directions.

In a candlelit circle, two embrace with increasing passion. They have set all ready, and the incense swirls around their bare skin. The age old dance happens once more with cries of joy, and a falling back into utterly relaxed abandon.

After a while, one reaches for the cup, and they drink, speaking the familiar words gently. They pull a soft blanket over their cooling bodies and eat the bread. The tenderness between them is obvious, and the candlelight makes them something a little more than they usually are. Finally they get up to make their farewells to each quarter, a little hurriedly, and snuggle back together in their nest of cushions.

'The Circle is open, but unbroken.'

11

a ritual creates a change from

you before	to	you after
LOOKING FORWARD TO		GOT STARTED
CONFUSED		CLEAR, GUIDED
WEAK		STRENGTHENED
LOST		FOUND
AFRAID		FACED FEAR, CALM
STRANGER		BELONGING
OLD SECURITY		NEW ADVENTURE
GIVING UP		RENEWED ENERGY
JUST MOVED IN		MY HOME
YOU AND I		WE
WE		I IN MY OWN WAY
APPRENTICED		INITIATED
SEARCHING		DEDICATED
APPROACHING HAPPINESS		CELEBRATING

You need to become aware of the full extent of your own sphere of power, which surrounds you like a great bubble several miles big. Within this you create your own reality.

Magic is, first of all deeply and thoroughly selfish. You need to understand your self, and you need to build a strong healthy self before you can think much about giving to others. The concerns of the first level of ritual are the immediate matters of everyday life - home, money, work, self confidence, love, sex, personal creativity, health, basic energy.

The second level of ritual is about the cycles of power beyond this, like the cycle of the seasons. We can control our comfort by using heating, but we can only adjust to the seasons' passage, not change it. To work against what is greater than we are would be folly.

It is important that the first level of ritual not be confused with the second. You have far more choice and power than you usually think, even if the options available to you are not ideal.

The third level of ritual is about a sacred exchange between self and Divine.

Circlework starts with the first level of ritual; the others follow naturally as you practice if that is your wish.

Ritual: a set of words, actions or symbols that make or accept change

1. Preparation

Decide what this ritual is for. Make all necessary practical preparations. Check you have all you need to hand.

2. Purification

Prepare your outer self (bathing, clothes) Prepare your inner self by getting rid of any unwanted distractions. Relax & focus.

3. Casting the Circle

Create magical space. Call the powers of Nature: AIR FIRE WATER & EARTH. Speak to the Centre of your beliefs.

4. Raising Energy

Time to awaken.
Breathe, chant, move. Wake up!

5. Working

Take the raised energy and put it into the work you want to do.

6. Communion

Relax, give thanks, connect with the everyday. Celebrate.

7. Opening the Circle

Bid farewell and thanks to your powers. Unwind your Circle.

Shan '94

The order that these stages take one after the other does matter. but 7 stages need not be crucial. Once you're familiar with all this you may prefer to think in terms of 3, or 9, or any number of stages that makes sense to you and which holds power for you.

THE TEMPLE

A Temple can sound like an elaborate place with lots of heavy drapes, massive pillars, statues, chanting crowds, flights of steps, gongs ... In fact a temple is any sacred place; anywhere we make special in order to go within ourselves.

During the days of persecutions by the Christians it was very dangerous to do anything that others could observe which would indicate that one was a Witch. We survived by giving up our public gathering places, which had mostly had churches built on them anyway. We went back to our earliest forms of ritual, meeting secretly at night in wild groves. We had to vary the places we met so that we did not get found out. Under these conditions we could not have complicated sacred geometry, crafted furniture, laid floors and the security of a familiar building. We learnt the hard way to create a Temple ANYWHERE with a few props.

What that means for us now is that we have inherited a working system in which you do not need big imposing buildings, or a lot of money. A Craft Temple can be made anywhere, and after a little practice, with no more than a few minutes preparation.

Having learnt the simple basics about it you can go on to work out your own special way of doing it. Although some Pagans dream of having a public Temple as our focus I think this would inevitably bring an unwelcome control and influence by those who were the caretakers of such a Temple. As it is, because each of us makes a personal Temple at home, and there are no central public Temples against which our personal choices can be compared, each in our individual way is the equal of all others. Which is how it should be.

Ritual need not necessarily be worked at home in a domestic setting at all. Outdoor rituals are an important part of Pagan life because we find the heart of the divine in nature, under the open sky, by tree and water, on the earth.

But I have found it best to learn how to do it first indoors where getting there, finding the chosen place perhaps in the dark, wind, rain, bumpy ground, cold, etc are not issues you have to handle. You may not always be working ritual in your own home, eg, if you are working a housewarming, or welcoming a baby. If you are the most experienced at ritual - and that could mean just that you've read this book and tried it out four or five times - you could easily find yourself the most responsible for what's going on.

A Craft temple is built from the five Elements of Nature:Air Fire Water Earth and Spirit.

Each are represented by a colour.

Air: Yellow   Fire: Red
Water: Blue Earth: Green
Spirit: White/ Black.

There can be any personal variation on this you wish   Coloured candles are placed at the four quartered points at the Circle's edge.

The SPIRIT candle represents the combination of the other four, put in the Centre, and is black, white or all colours.

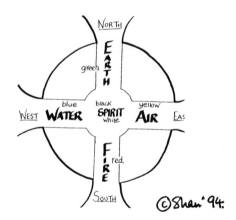

Memory aid

Yellow AIR + EAST   both begin with vowel sounds

Red   FIRE + SOUTH   go South for hot sunny holidays

Blue WATER + WEST   both begin with W

Green EARTH + NORTH listen to 'earth' and 'orth'

You can try to put all the candles except the Centre candle on the same level. Or AIR should be high (but with 2 feet clearance of the ceiling or it's a fire risk) and WATER low. If there's very little choice, don't worry about it.

Your Altar

Your Altar is your store for all the things you need for ritual, as well as special things you hold in honour. You may already have found that certain things almost 'find' you at times of intense experience, such as a shell, a plant, a stick, a picture, a statuette or almost any small object. You want to keep them and honour them but our practical way of life allows little space for them. These guides need an altar in order to complete their work by staying with you, reminding you, and often bringing more messages by the way they feel to you at a later time.

Your Altar is where you keep everything you need to hand. While you should treat your altar with respect you don't need to be stuffy or solemn about it.

You might like to drape your altar with cloth, adorn it with herbs or flowers, or choose a particular candle to be your Altar Candle. This is not to be confused with the Earth Candle which also has its place on the altar.

North

The small table or stool for your altar is put at the North point of your Circle. This is how I was trained, as a follower of the Earth religion. Some Witches put their altar in the East and a few focus on the West or the South.

My instructions assume that your altar is in the North like mine, so if you choose otherwise some of my instructions will be difficult to untangle. I suggest you begin with your altar in the North to make your first attempts, then listen for your feelings as to what suits you, and if necessary change later.

You find North by first finding West. Sunset is the West, sunrise in the East. Face sunset/ West and North is to the right. Face sunrise/ East and North is to the left.

The shape of your room, or the way big pieces of furniture are in the room, can make placing the altar in the precise North difficult. It doesn't have to be exact. It is convenient to have the altar and the other three Quarters placed either in the corners of the room, or in the middle of each wall, to make a regular pattern, if you can.

Setting out the Temple

1) Mark the Circle with ribbon, string, chalk, a rug etc.
Put your choice of a BLACK or WHITE candle
in its bowl in the centre of the Circle, for Spirit.

2) Set your tray or table, as altar, in the North.
The GREEN candle goes at the back of the altar (Earth).
The YELLOW candle goes at the right hand side, or East,
of the circle (Air)
The RED candle goes opposite the altar in the South (Fire).
The BLUE candle goes on the left hand side , or West
of the circle (Water).

3) Your altar is your own personal affair to arrange as you wish,
but here is how I do it if you would like a guide for now.
First, put anything personal on the altar as it pleases you.
Place the ALTAR CANDLE if you want to have one.
The SALT and DISH of BREAD go on the altar beside the Green
candle, for these are creatures of Earth.
The BOWL of water and your Chalice CUP of wine go on the left
side of the altar, the West side for Water.
The INCENSE materials go on the right side of the altar (Air).
The MATCHES/ TAPERS go at the front, opposite Earth and the
green candle.

4) FIRE SAFETY Put candles on steady surfaces, the floor, hard
chair seats, small tables, away from curtains, and 3ft clear of
ceilings.

A temple is a playroom for grownups.

PREPARATION

PREPARATION

Preparing for any important task is much the same. It means

deciding what I want to do

and

putting together whatever I need.

Unless you're fairly experienced, plunging into unprepared work is a recipe for a mess. Even the experienced usually need to prepare.

In Circlework, the first four stages, out of seven, are all different kinds of preparation. The actual work in the centre of the sandwich can be simple enough, and last no more than five minutes, yet need 45 minutes preparation.

When a photographer takes a serious photo, the actual 'click' takes seconds. Before that can be hours of setting backdrops, fiddling with lighting, arranging the items in the picture, and adjusting camera controls. It's all that fuss that makes good photos in magazines so striking.

Or consider a kiss. Compare a goodbye peck at the door in the morning, with the one that follows a carefully prepared dinner by candlelight, music, the pair concerned specially bathed, dressed, taking the time to enjoy each other's presence, waiting for the right moment.

Planning a ritual can be remarkably simple. A few practice ones from this book, and if your kit's in good order, you can plan a straightforward one in five minutes.

At the other extreme, planning a Sabbat festival for 60 people means setting the date well in advance, sending invitations, organising transport/ maps, food, first aid, childcare, a ritual drama expressing both the season and these particular people's feelings ..... and it can take weeks.

Your chosen tasks can be done as elaborately or as simply as you like. Some people respond powerfullly to robes, masks, artistic paraphernalia, impressive music, special effects and drama. Others feel smothered by that. It's your Circle.

A separate ritual need not be created for each thing you want to do. You can consecrate new equipment, carry out meditation, and invoke a special power, all in one ritual. But don't overload. More than 3 or jobs to do means you need more than one ritual to carry them.

Once the ritual has begun don't replan it

After the planning is done it is not a good idea to change your mind. You need to feel that anxiety about what exactly to do in what order to get the effect you want, is left behind. The best feeling is that of having a list of simple steps; all I've got to do now is follow them through.

Decisions involve tension and anxiety. Magic arises from a relaxed, playful mind. Decisions and organising are necessary, but only at the start. After that, let go, into the sacred dream. After some practice working alone, you can certainly be more flexible, to allow your intuitive wisdom to develop and instruct you what to do next.

But at first for at least a few months, even working alone, observe this rule so as to create as predictable and safe atmosphere for your work as possible. When you feel that this technique is familiar and you're remembering what to do easily and comfortably, then you can open up and allow more spontaneity to guide you.

This guideline is essential if you are working with anyone else so that none of you suddenly introduce anything that might not be what someone else wishes. It's awkward to stop the flow of action with disagreement so all must be decided and agreed beforehand.

Once planning is done, and all is laid out, accept how the ritual unfolds. It will happen as it happens.

No more fuss. If anything unexpected happens, you'll manage somehow. If it doesn't exactly follow the plan but that just sort of happens; if an important item was forgotten so you have to make do and improvise - that's exactly how this ritual was meant to be.

In the circle you can't do it wrong
(GREAT LAW OF CIRCLEWORK)

Things you need

The other part of Preparation is to put together all the practical things you need.

This is exactly like getting the food, putting out the plates, glasses and cutlery, and any special flowers and candles you choose, for when you have guests round to eat with you.

Eastern spiritual work is often less concerned with objects than we are. You may feel uneasy with the idea of a lot of objects. Or perhaps you are attracted to Pagan jewellery and crafted tools, but are not sure why.

The reason why we use material objects is because we are physical. We are so made that what we do in the material world usually seems more real to us. If I tell you to drink deep from the sweetness of the cup of life, you will experience that far more richly through drinking your favourite drink from an actual cup of beautiful design, as candlelight casts its gentle glow around you. Western people are far more inclined towards the material outside world, so the Western Way of the spirit takes and uses our practicality as a strength instead of condemning it as a weakness.

For the same reason, you need to try to get accustomed to speaking your thoughts aloud. We think much faster than we speak, so speaking brings a slower, more thorough experience. What you voice aloud holds more power and reality than what you only think, unless you are doing an inner journey or meditation. This applies as much to working alone, as to working with others.

You have very likely already used the magic of charging objects with your power. Are you in the habit of wearing a particular ring, a pendant, or a bracelet? Does this thing help you feel stronger sometimes? Or does it link your feelings to someone dear to you? Then you have discovered how to put personal power into an object by keeping it in contact with your body through time, so that when you are afraid or tense you can think of it, or touch it, and find comfort.

Magic is a language that the deep mind understands, not a language of sentences and logic, but images, colour, smell, sound, gesture and symbol. You can invest beautiful things with your power, and they will store and return it to you.

Because the great depths of feeling respond best to the language of the senses (think how a smell can bring back intense memories) magical objects are chosen carefully with regard to their colour and shape. Colour is especially individual in its effect, but most of us find red stimulating, blue reassuring for example. Incenses provoke the oldest part of the brain into action through the first of the animal senses: smell. Sound hardly needs comment now that music is universally used to direct mood.

Symbols are rather more mysterious, but there are simpler ones that are obvious such as square shapes for security, circular ones for sensitivity and creativity, sharp triangles for active power. In spite of our individuality we are all equipped with a subconscious language that advertisers and politicians study thoroughly in order to get what they want from us. We can learn this language of power and use it for ourselves.

The basic Ritual Kit for Circlework is:-
bowl of water,
salt,
5 candles,
matches,
incense,
cup of wine/fruit juice,
dish of bread

It's an excellent idea to learn this list off by heart, so you feel quite comfortable and confident about it. It will help a great deal if you don't have to panic when trying to remember what you need but just recite it off to yourself.

You may never feel the need for more than the basic list of necessities listed in the Basic Ritual Kit. Or if you do, collect together your own set of equipment and make it as elaborate as you like (athame/ knife, wand, pentacle, cauldron etc). Never forget however that these, however sacred they become to you, are only aids to your inner power. Enjoy their beauty, there is no need to worship it.

Witches are Craft in more ways than one, skilled at making beautiful things of wood, metal, fabric, pottery, paper etc. Male Witches have an especially proud reputation for practical craft.

Our tradition tells us that what we use for magic is best if we ourselves make it. Our love and care that goes into the making charges our tools as nothing else can. So wherever possible, make what you use yourself. You might find an unexpected pleasure in a new craft skill. (see chapter on Craft p. 101)

If you don't make it yourself, it must be at least hand made; preferably by someone in the Craft. Choose carefully what feels right to you. It is your power that will use these things, so make sure of a good 'fit'.

Some things will 'find' you, turning up just when you want them. You may realise that the right thing has been among your possessions for a long time and you never realised why you were keeping it. Some things come to you as gifts.

Our custom if buying an item for magic, is, once you realise it is what you desire, to pay the price asked.

Cherish your magical equipment. The state of your magical tools reflects your attitude to your work. Some schools of magic teach that magical tools should be kept apart and used for no other purpose (High Magic). An object kept for one purpose gains an aura of special power.

Others advise you to make magic very much a part of your everyday life, including your tools (Kitchen Magic/ Circlework). Decide what suits your temperament, in line with how you treat other things which are especially personal in your life.

Whoever shares your home - animals, children, flatmates or family who don't share your interests - may affect how you treat your tools a lot. Many people like keeping their things in a special box. It means you don't have to dash round the house finding everything each time.

Never allow someone else to handle or come near your things unless your intuitive reaction about it is completely comfortable. You have a right to as much privacy as you want for the things you care about.

The Bowl
needs to be of a size comfortable to hold in both hands, big enough to put at least one hand in easily.. I started with a small pudding bowl. It's wise to keep a delicate bowl, cup, or incense burner out of other people's hands unless you know them well; for groups use sturdy gear of wood, metal or heavy pottery.

All Salt is a good friend. Sea salt is especially good. A separate small dish for the salt is a graceful addition - I have been known to grab the salt packet from the kitchen in passing.

Incense is far more delightful than joss sticks, as it leaves its pure smell behind instead of a salty aftertaste. But if it's new to you and you are reluctant to tackle it stay with joss sticks. Either way you'll need a proper holder, or a dish of earth/ sand. (For instructions on using incense see Crafts).

Candles represent the four elements, traditionally YELLOW for AIR, RED for FIRE, BLUE for WATER, GREEN for EARTH, WHITE or BLACK for SPIRIT.

Matches are easier to find by candlelight in a large box size. You may like to have the elegance and convenience of TAPERS as well as matches A taper once lit can be taken round to mark the Circle, and saves scratching away at the box at moments of beauty. Incense charcoal lights better from a taper.

The Cup needs to be big enough to drink as much as pleases you. Fill it with wine, beer, cider, fruit juice, spring water to taste according to the needs of who's drinking.

The Bread or CAKE represents our basic staple food so it should not be sweet. Crusty rolls, fancy breads are nice.

Your Altar needs to be at least as big as a good size tea tray. A small table, stool or a tray serves well.

The time needs to be checked beforehand. You need at least one hour for a solo rite, one and a half hours for a group. That's minimum.

The space required is room to sit, if alone; but preferably 9ft. I find 13ft ideal, especially for groups. It is comfortable for a few, but can hold up to 30 at a pinch.

The Circle is laid out to the four directions. Unless you know already, think of where the sun sets (west) or rises (east).

PURIFICATION

PURIFICATION
getting rid of what you don't want

This means clearing the mind of any unwanted preoccupations so
you can focus very clearly on what you're doing. It has nothing to
do with sin, or making you somehow better quality and therefore
fit to enter ritual space. It's more like the feeling of settling down
to write an important letter.

There are usually tensions and anxieties when you're about to do
something important. Some are about things in your surrounding
circumstances 'Did I remember to feed the cat? Heavens! the
dentist tomorrow morning!' but also about the work you are about
to do 'What is all this hocus pocus anyway? Maybe nothing will
happen? Help! Maybe something will happen! Is there enough
time? But I'm so tired.'

Perfect love & perfect trust

A conflict or resentment with someone in particular may be
preoccupying you. This needs to be set aside to clear your mind.
Alternatively you may choose to include this in your actual ritual
work, giving time to expressing your feelings about it and working
to understand and heal it.

In the Craft we speak of the Circle as being a place of 'perfect
love and perfect trust.' I find this is an ideal that cannot always
be made completely real, but even coming close to it is doing
well. And it's surprising how often that love and trust really is
there, whether you're alone or with others. The powerful magic of
Purification itself is the cause. Groups naturally produce conflicts
among their members. These too need attention during
Purification. The problem must be admitted before the ritual goes
further. The two concerned may need to go apart for a session of
argument and settlement, or you may prefer to stay and use the
help of the others to work it out.

This is not necessary if you can at least put the problem aside for
the duration of the ritual. However, it is extremely destructive to
put on a peaceful face and pretend. Forgiveness comes of its own
free will, not when you demand it. So if that time has not yet
come, both persons must stay out of any Circle worked by their
own group. They may make their own independent Circles of
course, or work with others.

Some groups only exclude one person; to me this is unfair,

because how can others judge who is to 'blame'? It can too often look like the fault of one, and later come clear that the other, or more usually both, are involved in the problem.

To decide whether setting aside the conflict is possible, or staying out completely is necessary, test by asking for a kiss (on the cheek) of friendship. If this is strained, uncomfortable, or faces go very blank, then it is a time to stay out. Do this after doing the Purification.

Purifying delight

Purification can involve setting aside recent or anticipated delights! If you're Purifying in order to tackle the chores around the house then last night's fun, or tomorrow's treat is an unwanted distraction. Contrariwise, if you're Purifying to get yourself in the right mood for a party, then chores and responsibilities are now the unwanted distractions.

Widdershins & deosil

All Purification work is done widdershins which means anti-clockwise, against the sun. As the sun circles into our day it brings light, warmth and life. So to move against the sun is to cast out or banish. Work done in the Circle to banish or cleanse anything is also done widdershins; we Open the Circle widdershins at the end of a ritual to dissolve it.

If the words 'widdershins' and its opposite 'deosil' don't appeal to you, don't bother with them. 'Clockwise/ anti clockwise' are just as good.

Some teachings detest any widdershins/ anti- clockwise action. It is seen as 'black magic' or similar. This is a Christian idea, based on the all-good God and his nasty partner. Powers of nature are neither good nor bad; consider electricity, wind, water etc It is their effect on us that we call good or bad from a personal point of view. The cold rain that chills you is welcome to the farmer.

My own way is very similar to Taoism. All things have a mix of dark and light. To work always one way is to go to extremes, which is where things usually get painful. To accept life in cycles of up and down, and to work with both seems very realistic to me. The simple Salt Water Purification I give here allows a gentle, but profound awareness of how life generally has its problems. This is respected and given its place, so we may then move on to create brighter feelings and powers.

This was the first Purification I learnt from the Dianic Craft; many people over the years have said it is my most powerful teaching.

Salt Water Purification

Put SALT in the bowl of WATER.

Stir it widdershins/ anti clockwise until the Salt dissolves in the Water. The Salt dissolved in the Water, is a symbol of how our fears, anxieties and tensions can too.

Salt and Water are the oldest cleansers known to humanity. They were used by our foremothers in the time of the caves.

Let your body relax, slow your breathing.

Speak your tensions, preoccupations, worries and fears into the bowl - plus any particularly distracting delights.

Hold the bowl in both hands.

Look into the bowl: Don't look up.

For example **"I want to put into the water..."**

ALL MY TIREDNESS, MY FEELINGS OF NOT BEING ABLE TO COPE. I WANT TO PUT IN MY WORRY ABOUT MY MOTHER WHO IS NOT WELL. I WANT TO CONCENTRATE NOW WITHOUT BEING DISTRACTED BY THIS EXCITING INVITATION I'VE HAD. I WANT TO PUT INTO THE WATER MY ACHING BACK....

Voicing your feelings out loud releases them, puts them outside you. What is seen or heard or experienced outside in 'reality' holds far more impact for us. So get used to hearing your own voice on your own, and speak in as much detail as you possibly can. After all, in ritual space, you're the one in charge.

In groups you may wish to keep something private of course but as much as you can should be fully voiced. As each hears the vulnerability of others any fears about each other are much reassured. Speak your fears about each other as openly as you can.

You can refer to something without using people's names saying e.g. 'A FRIEND OF MINE', or without describing fully what happened e.g. 'A DIFFICULT CONFLICT THAT'S GONE ON FOR MONTHS'.

Speak personally and specifically, whether you are alone or with others.

People new to Purification, and particularly people who pride themselves on their intelligence, often say things that leave themselves very guarded.

'I put into the bowl any negative things that will hold me back from being fully here' could be said by anyone at all and means little. 'I put into the bowl all the distrust and anger and war I feel around me' sounds rather superior - does this person think they are really free of these human realities?

If a particular world tragedy is really affecting you a lot, then by all means Purify it. But I'd bet that an unpaid bill, an achey back, or a squabble at home is lurking around too. Life's like that.

Strong feelings

Sometimes Purification can seem a bit much. Someone in one of my Circlework groups will sometimes take the bowl, get quite tearful (salt water) and bring out a whole lot of misery or crisis. This is because many of us are walking about holding a lot of bottled up discomfort inside - because we are trained to be heroic and polite. We're not used to the idea that others sympathise, or we think we'd be weak if we let on.

Being given the symbolic bowl can be someone's first real experience of permission to express their woes freely. Up come the suppressed feelings, followed by considerable relief. Once someone does Purification from time to time, or something like it, the worst gets cleared, and after that there's a lot less to deal with each time.

You can use the Purification bowl both before ritual, and as a meditation on its own. It can be a great and powerful healing in times of stress or shock.

Law of Purification: Hold the Bowl for longer than you feel the need.

The magic of Purification can only work fully if you observe the Law. No matter how many times you practise Purification something will prompt you to end it - I can't do this any longer, there's the supper to get - I feel silly I want to stop now - Surely that's enough. Although you may feel it as boredom, tiredness, anxiety about other tasks, this is at its root fear, the Guardian of the Threshold. Often I have found myself saying 'Ah, that's everything' then I wait, in order to obey the Law - and something comes up in my mind that I was unaware of before.'

When you have really finished you say to yourself
'MAY I BE FREE OF ALL DOUBT & ANXIETY'

In groups pass the bowl widdershins, (to the person on your right) saying *'MAY YOU BE FREE OF ALL DOUBT & ANXIETY'*

As the bowl passes, you may feel that it's all very depressing, boring and pointless to sit through all this petty personal muck. It isn't a pleasure. But it does create pleasure, that is, a tranquil, trusting, sensitive, and relaxed state of mind.

Purification is about honouring both sides of life. We also do a mild form of Purification in large groups of people who don't know each other, called a Darklight Circle. Each person in turn mentions one thing from the dark side of their life, and something from the light as well. This allows the dark to be briefly honoured, but keeps the Circle lighter by referring to the light as well.

Give it to the Earth In a full Purification, you can deal with the unease which builds up as you hear a list of drearies unfold by letting it all drain into the earth. Put one hand up to your head, resting your chin on your hand, perhaps. Put the other on the floor. Imagine what is going on is caught by the upper hand as an antenna or aerial, and cast through you and out the other hand into the Earth.

Threefold walking Circle Finally a walking circle widdershins loosens up your body and attends to the tensions you may have pushed down into the muscles.

1) During the first Circle move easily and vigorously shake out arms and legs, have a good stretch.

2) During the second Circle slow down, carefully relax from top to bottom. Attend to slowing your breathing.

3) During the third Circle slow right down as far as you possibly can - then slow some more!

(see Earth or Walking Meditation p **69**)

Don't forget The used salt water must be cast into flowing water that will take it to a river and from there to the sea. There it will join the great oceans, be drawn up into the sky and return new formed as rain.

For us city folk who lack running streams it means putting it down the toilet. This water has taken all the psychic debris from us, so if it is left in the room it will taint the atmosphere.

Chakra Purification

For a solitary Purification, you may like a Purifying of your 7 Chakras. After Purifying with the bowl, touch each chakra or energy centre, in turn.

(see Self Blessing p124 for explanation of Chakras)

CROWN = top of head.

MIND = forehead.

COMMUNICATION = lips/ throat.

HEART = centre of chest.

STOMACH = solar plexus/ centre of waist.

SEX = triangle at top of legs/ genitals.

BASE = feet/ anus.

Say *'I PURIFY MY CROWN ...'* etc.

Some people work bottom to top (more conventional, and masculine). Some people work top down (less common, feminine).

The power of Purification

The most striking example I remember of how Purification works was when my first two Circlework groups met to plan a Spring Equinox together. It all seemed straightforward; well trained by Circlework, enthusiastic, together in my familiar temple. But half an hour of a precious 2 hours dribbled away in foggy talk.

One student suggested doing a Purification to clear the air. But many felt that eighteen people would take almost an hour to do it, leaving only 30 minutes for the vital planning itself. Yet as the awkward, foggy, aimless chat seemed likely to continue and spoil things anyway, we went ahead.

And of course, it emerged that while everyone did feel confident and eager, they also felt shy and strained about dealing with the 'other Circlework group.' Once voiced together with all the other very human attitudes around the circle, this dissolved in friendly laughter.

After that in half an hour flat we created a full and complex ritual drama with different people responsible for bits of equipment, to be held in Richmond Park , on an agreed date, with a car convoy, local guides, picnic catering for 20, tea at a rest house afterwards to follow.

It's remarkable what people can do when they're relaxed and free of fear.

CASTING

THE CIRCLE

CASTING THE CIRCLE

creating magical space

THE CIRCLE
flows eternally, one Circle continues into another.
THE CIRCLE
puts everyone in it on a basis of equality.
THE CIRCLE
provides you with your own place of safety.
THE CIRCLE
holds energy for you as you generate it,
concentrating it by confining it like a cooking pot.

The Pot   Some Magical teachings speak of the Circle as a protection against what you fear. Certainly it is that, a sanctuary.

But I prefer to emphasise its meaning as a container, in terms of the positive nature of what it holds within, rather than what it keeps out. It can be understood as a kind of pressure cooker which speeds up natural processes, and 'cooks' ingredients put in it. This is a modern image of the Celtic Goddess Cerridwen and her cooking pot or cauldron.

Many people vision the Circle as blue light or fire. However it appears to you, as blue, white, golden fire, as flowing water, as a rainbow, as an earthen wall ..... the inner work of your imagination and feelings is what really casts the Circle.

Marking the Circle   You do need to mark out the Circle in some way to make it real to you. You can do it by chalking it out on the floor (try using the ancient engineers' method of tying string to something heavy in the middle and knotting the other end round chalk - still the best after thousands of years).

Or you can lay out cord, tape or powder. Some people make a circle of cloth or carpet specially for their rituals.

Some like to carry the four Elements round the Circle first to bless it. You can do this by carrying round the Incense to represent Fire and Air, then salted water to represent Earth and Water (here salt = Earth). Puff the incense and sprinkle the water as you go (careful of how salt water bleaches wood and fabric though - I once left pale marks on a parquet floor.).

The Spirit Candle at the Centre is first to be lit, the first act of the rite before you Purify.

Unlike Air, Fire, Water and Earth we cannot invoke Spirit. For Spirit is everything, so it's already here in us and among us. Yet Spirit is the most elusive of the Elements. Body, emotions, raw energy and even the quick mind we can identify when we know them to be present.

But Spirit, though everywhere, is nowhere.

Spirit is change, transformation, transition, the essence of Magic. Spirit is the only eternal truth, which is change. Everything we know is in flux. Everything, even the great burning Stars, comes into being, has its season, and passes away; to return in a new form.

Power to the Pagan, is of two kinds. One is found in tornado, conflagration, tidal wave, earthquake, and in armies, the scientific elite, the huge multinational corporations, the bigger, stronger individuals we meet in everyday life. This is power as Control.

The other kind of power is not so obvious. It is found not by exerting power over others but by generating it within so that you can move in harmony with greater powers to create what you need in the world.

This power of Capacity is the birthright of each one of us. It will not dominate the will of another, so it cannot make a loved one return who does not want to. Neither will it bring money and status in the world by easy instant methods. What it will do is ensure that you in your own way can face any experience you have, surviving the painful ones and enjoying the happy ones to the fullest.

Are you unhappy? Then take courage for your struggle, for this, like all else, must pass away. And the power to speed its passing lies in you. Accept Change.

Are you happy? Then open and enjoy this experience in depth, for this like all else will pass away. Take what you want, and then let go. Accept Change.

Change is invisible. All we can experience are its effects so we know change has happened. This is why we say that Spirit is nowhere, although also everywhere.

The symbol of the Centre candle is that by lighting it before we do anything else we create the illusion that it is always lit. Then we extinguish it last, as we leave the room when all is done.

Black is the colour of the Spirit because black is the colour of inward, dark space. Black is the no-colour of void, nothingness, mystery and potential. All things come from darkness, where dreams are born. People wear black when they are making personal transitions: mourning, descended in depression, lacking identity, in retreat, even sexy black is trying to make a transition! So to Pagan folk black is our sacred colour.

Black has frequently been associated by Christian beliefs with evil. This was partly a political trick to persuade people that the old Pagan beliefs which honoured black were dangerous. But on a deeper level, religions like christianity need a devil. A completely good god cannot have created pain so another secondary god must have. This leads to the useful device of persuading people that they need professional priests to free them from the devil and its evil. Make people feel guilty, and they'll buy from you, to make themselves feel better.

Black is the colour of the earth, richly moist, full of life and renewal.

The Quartered Circle is found all over the world, as
part of the native or shamanic faiths of each land. While everyone nowadays agrees on a geography with North at the top, East on the right and so on, each culture has its own pattern for the Elements.

For example, we here in Europe look West and see the Atlantic Ocean, the great waters, so to us Water is in the West. We go South to find heat for our summer holidays, so it's natural to put Fire in the South. But in America, the same Elements are in different places, as they are again in India, Australia, and China.

The Craft is earth based: that is, we work with the land, with our surroundings wherever we are. We work with respect for those ancestors who lived here before, and for the children who come after us.

Invocations

An invocation means to 'call in' so invoking power is to call it in. We call in or invoke Air, Fire, Water and Earth.

Invocations can be long, short, spoken, sung, silent, gestured, danced, expressed through gifts. They can be very formal, or extremely informal, even a bit rude.

In group rites, one person can cast the Circle; or one person can cast a Quarter each; or in a big gathering two can do each Quarter together.

Traditionally, casting is female work: after all, the Circle is a female womb, the original container of all. But do listen to your own intuition about that. (In Canada I understand Craft Circles are customarily cast by men, perhaps because of the recent pioneer experience of a defensive wagon circle.)

Similarly explore how you feel about men invoking Air & Fire, women doing Water & Earth, or doing it otherwise entirely.

The person who actually speaks or acts the invocations is only a speaker for the rest. S/he is not the most important in the group at that point. The most important work is done by those who are silent, standing close behind the speaker, visualising the Element invoked.

Begin

from the altar in the North.

Take your taper and light it from the Centre Candle, OR just pick up the matches, to use at each Candle.

Mark out with your arm and hand extended the edge of the circle from the North/ Earth altar round to the East.

Try and make it a curved shape, or else you'll be casting a diamond!

If you're not using a taper which marks a Circle of flame in the air, you'll need to have marked it some other way, as above.

The quarters can be named as Guardians (Guardian of the East, Guardian of the South), Watchtowers, Ladies, or Lords, whatever you like best, perhaps by trying out each in turn.

Begin invoking in the East

Say hello or give greeting, calling them by name, and ask for them to be present. You can be very informal, speaking from the heart, or very formal, using prepared speeches.

What you are invoking is as much a power in you as outside you. So as you invoke, think of the powers you are calling in as either your own qualities, or as great Energies in the universe. This will seem less and less odd as you do it.

End by saying *'BE HERE NOW'* and light the candle.

End your invocations at the Earth/ North Altar.

Having done Earth, you can put out the taper/ matches and put them back on the altar.

Go to the Centre

We do not invoke the Centre, for it is everywhere but nowhere at once. We honour it. You can do this in silence, or we have customary words:-

THE CIRCLE IS CAST

I AM BETWEEN THE WORLDS,

BEYOND THE BOUNDS OF TIME:

WHERE NIGHT AND DAY,

BIRTH AND DEATH,

JOY AND SORROW,

MEET AS ONE.

The correspondences of the Elements

Each Element, Air, Fire, Water and Earth has its colour, its personal power, season of the year, time of day, animal, angel, jewel .... It's an endlessly fascinating language of power.

If you were training as a Witch you would spend a full month studying each Element in turn in depth. The ones I show you on the chart come from my Initiation study. Yours will be a little different to suit you. To begin with you are welcome to use mine until you create your own. Other books such as Starhawk's , Valiente or Green give slightly different descriptions. which can help you compare them.

Some experience the Elementals as personal companions, like

great, awesome, but simple personalities. To others they are not personal, but tidal forces.

Once they become familiar friends, which happens surprisingly fast, because they are so natural, these Guardians can help you a great deal in difficult situations. When facing anything frightening or painful you will find that calling them around you evokes the safe, strengthening feeling of being in the Circle. My dentist was very interested the first time I did it there.

Air and Fire are conventionally thought of as masculine, while Water and Earth are feminine. But they can be all feminine, all masculine, or each having both masculine and feminine aspects.

You might find it helpful to copy the qualities on to four cards, putting them beside the Quarter Candles to help you when you make your invocations.

Air	Fire	Water	Earth
East	South	West	North
Yellow	Red	Blue	Green
Mind	Will	Emotions	Body
Dawn	Midday	Evening	Midnight
Spring	Summer	Autumn	Winter
Beginning	Moving	Deepening	Ending
Decision	Action	Struggle	Completion
Knowledge	Willpower	Courage	Silence
High flying	Fast moving	Diving	Still Spider
Bird	Cat	Fish	

The Law of the Cast Circle:
Once Cast none may leave it.

This is very sensible, as anyone who has struggled to concentrate on a meeting when people bustle off to piddle or smoke knows well. It sharpens the ability of late arrivers like me to be more courteous, and generally ensures everyone starts together and stays together for the work.

Working alone, too, it helps me to settle seriously to what I'm doing.

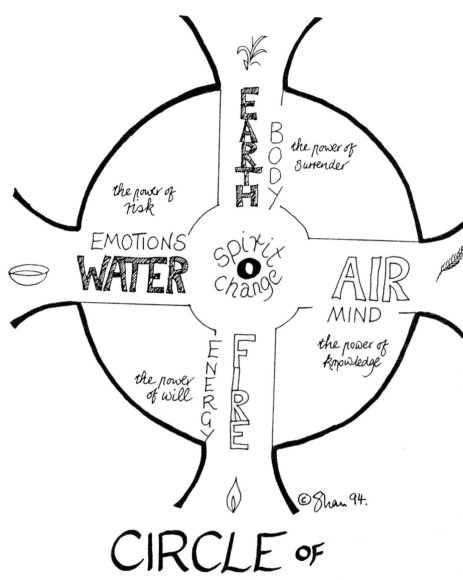

CIRCLE OF
THE ELEMENTS

If you need to go to the toilet go before the Casting. Any forgotten equipment must be improvised. The phone or the door bell becomes irrelevant. No one may leave and then return, because this seriously disrupts the focus. This Law allows you to fully relax into deep concentration.

EXCEPTIONS to the Law are children under 13 and animals. These may come and go as they please, joining in where they wish and staying apart as they wish also.

Emergencies such as signs of fire hazard, children's

accidents and so on must of course mean breaking the Law. In this case, trace a 'doorway' with your hand as you step out. You can 'close' it if all is well and you return.

A Circle may not be witnessed

Never allow photographs or recordings of your rituals, although you can pose before or after them in 'ritual like' positions, or make a special piece of tape separately. No-one should observe your rituals. They should either join them fully or stay apart. Someone present with a half-hearted attitude dilutes the energy, makes you self conscious and not fully focused on the inner work. If that same person prepares and purifies with you, then they will find they overcome their nerves and unsureness because of the ritual process itself.

THE EXCEPTION is a ritual done in the open air, in a public place, especially in daylight. Druid circles for example, sometimes accept, and welcome observers, photos, or tapings, partly as a public teaching and celebration.

In the Circle you can't do it wrong

RAISING ENERGY

RAISING ENERGY

Even though you've Purified and created a magical Circle around you, you are still not far removed from your everyday level of energy. Think of moments you have known of really high energy: shouting with enthusiasm; dancing with abandon; taken out of yourself by drama or music so that you feel elated; when you're uplifted by love; expanded by joyful sex; plunged into an angry rage; excited and sustained by a great ideal. These are experiences of energy in its purest forms, and you need some of that stuff to do effective work.

Raised energy is not a state well understood or respected by our society. We are trained from childhood to hush, to play quietly, to restrain our natural energy. Some of that restraint is quite necessary if we are to succeed in living crowded together.

Once it was different. The Celtic warrior went naked and screaming into battle and was praised for his or her courage. Folk dances recall some of the wildness we once expressed under the open sky, but now hide away in basement discos. However, if we are to key into our own true personal power it's no good keeping everything polite and controlled all the time. That way we die inside, a stifled kind of dying while the appearances are preserved.

There are three simple steps to Raising Energy -

Breathe, Sound, Move

We raise energy gradually. Even those of us who are less hampered by reserve can't just give a whoop and away into instant energy. So we begin gently, and let the energy build in its own time to whatever is its natural peak on this occasion. You will find fears of not reaching enough energy, and fears of uncontrolled pandemonium are both equally groundless. You will create as much energy as you need, and go as far as your personal temperament allows. Trust your guiding Spirit.

Breathing is the first key to energy. Most of us think very little about our breathing, and yet it is the first essential for life energy. Increase that life supply of oxygen and our brains, hearts, blood and nerves can all work more happily, making us warm, alert, intelligent and confident, with rich inner fuel tanked up and

ready to go.

Many teachers make a big fuss about special breathing until it all sounds very mysterious. If you have trained in yoga or any other form of breathing control, by all means, use what you know. But if not, the essence of it is very simple, yet very powerful:

CONCENTRATE ON THE OUTWARD BREATH, pushing your breath out a little more than is usual. That's all there is to it.

Most of us, if told to breathe deeper, immediately heave in a big breath then wonder why it feels pressured and uncomfortable, and we can't seem to get a really good deep breath. This is because we're trying to pull a lot of air into a pot that's not empty, so we actually can't take a full breath of new air.

There's an important teaching here about how emptiness is more powerful than fullness. The negative is understood to be more powerful than the positive in magic. If you've done a Purification by now you will have discovered how deeply quiet and potential you are when you've emptied out, and how very magical that feeling of readiness is.

You never need to think about the inward breath at all, as once you've breathed out and emptied your chest nature will quickly take over and you'll breathe in without any effort at all.

Once you've done some breathing, it's an excellent time to stop and listen. Open out your awareness to encompass the whole Circle. Listen and feel towards everything that is around you, little noises, smells, influences. If there is more than one of you, keep your eyes closed but open your awareness as clearly as you can to the other(s) present.

Sound grows naturally out of enriched breathing.

A soft humming on one or two notes is an easy start. Try staying on a higher note, then come down on to a lower one as a 'stop.' Pause. Do it again. 'MMMMMMMM Ah!'

Chanting is something many of us feel uncomfortable with at first. It's well worth pushing through the embarrassment. Ritual chanting is often very beautiful - but it doesn't have to be. Some of the best ritual chanting is raw sound, not especially musical as we normally think of music.

Begin when the breathing is well based, with simple humming, as softly as you like. Take deep breaths, and keep it up. Then open your mouth and try AAAH or O sounds. Use any note, stay on it, or change it. Chanting can be slow and solemn, or playful and silly.

If you find yourself laughing then that too is sound, isn't it?

Keep it up. Eventually you'll make your own natural kind of music. Whatever comes, let it out. (You may need to tell the neighbours you're studying Chinese opera!)

You will find your voice dies away. This does NOT mean you've finished chanting. It means a pause, or it means you need to open out into renewed effort. Think of it as something that expands and contracts. After contracting, open out again.

A POWER CHANT (one made to raise energy) is very simple and easy to repeat. It may have two or three words, or just a satisfying sound or two, like baby language. E.g. 'Bind us in One', or 'Power, power, power', or 'AAAYEEE OH!', 'DUM DUM DEE'.

There are lots of chants that Pagan folk pass on to each other and some have found their way into various self development groups, such as 'We all come from the Goddess...' and 'The Earth is our Mother..'

I call on you to make your own chants, whether or not you already know some of the existing Pagan ones.

Use a bit of a tune you like, sing it over and over, put some words you like on it.

Just repeat one simple sentence, or the same few words, over and over and over again; that's how a Pagan chant is made.

Sing a pop song, or a psalm, or any bit of music from anything at all you like.

It's in you. Bring it out.

CHANTING IS NOT ABOUT MAKING BEAUTIFUL MUSIC; it's just about making sounds with your body.

To get you started, here's one I made, to the tune of Three Blind Mice.

> 'GODDESS & GOD.
>
> GODDESS & GOD
>
> I AM THEIR CHILD.
>
> I AM THEIR CHILD.
>
> GODDESS & GOD.
>
> GODDESS & GOD.'

A Powerchant needs to be repeated lots of times, so you need to keep singing something like the above about 20 times or more to work up the energy. As you keep repeating it, it doesn't matter if you don't get it exactly the same each time. In fact, if you find the words or the tune changes as you go - that's excellent powerchant.

Try chanting it a bit faster and a bit louder.

Try clapping to it.

Don't forget that the power comes in pulses, so your sound will fall away, then return if you wait and begin again. Often it comes stronger after first dying away. Don't forget too that you're not performing for anyone except the Goddess, for whom every noise you make is music. Chanting is not singing.

Moving flows out of the rythmn of sound. If you get a Powerchant going it's quite difficult not to move.

It's a great energy builder. Many of us left a lot of vigorous movement behind in childhood, so now we turn to aerobics or exercise class instead. Again rather like breathing, if you know some yoga, tai chi, dance, then use it. Foxtrot, belly dancing, break dancing or ballet, whatever is yours, use. With or without training we need to free our movements.

SWAY gently as you chant. Or shift from foot to foot. That's movement after all.

CLAP your hands in time to your chanting.

Swing your arms as if to warm up - warming up is another name for raising energy.

Rub your arms and legs briskly to get circulation going.

Try a few high kicks or punches at the air!

With very little space you can still hop, or skip round your circle - clockwise (deosil) this time, because you're calling in energy.

SPINNING is a lovely energy raiser, excellent for solo work, limited space - or muddy footing - and you don't need to fall over. Twizzle to your right (clockwise/ deosil) for a few turns, then before you get dizzy, twizzle to your left. Then back to the right again and then more to the left. You are building energy by balancing it.

DRUMS and any other musical instruments are lovely if you have them. If not, why not consider a small bongo? Many Pagans have a special love for the bodhran, the Celtic drum in the Housewarming photo.

You can end up leaping, dancing, whooping, yelling, twirling and circling - and of course laughing - until you subside in breathless, panting excitement. If you're feeling seriously drained and tired you may manage no more than a brisk walk round the circle. But this will not apply every time you work a ritual.

You may feel that limits are necessary, because a) your lover/ spouse will be disturbed by the commotion b) ditto neighbours, flatmates c) ditto parents d) you aren't the kind of person who goes in for making funny noises or flinging yourself about.

Well the first three may certainly moderate how much raising energy you can do at first, out of consideration for others' feelings. But if after a few tries you find you like ritual work and you want to keep it as part of your life, it's time for them to consider your feelings.

Eventually you'll have to rearrange something to allow you more freedom to do as you wish. After all, you're not proposing to do anything harmful.

If the limit is in you, and what you think of all this, consider that in acting out energy you are being what you are, an animal. However sophisticated, dignified, or well behaved you are a lot of the time, that doesn't change the fact that you and I are by nature, animals.

YOUR ANIMAL SELF (the Horned One) is not bad or good. Animals are not better or worse than buddhas. They just are what they are. Most medical and spiritual advisers agree that in societies like ours a great deal of all illness comes from our continually controlled behaviour. We all need times to open up and be basic and natural.

When you raise your voice and move your body in the sacred Circle, you are being what you are in the company of no-one but the Goddess, the God, or your own most real Self.

However if you still feel you couldn't possibly do these things, then something is much more important to you than expressing your own natural energy safely and privately. As a key to self knowledge you need to be sure and clear what that important something is.

Focusing the Energy

After raising the raw energy we shape it, or it will spill about everywhere without being much use.

The Circle now comes into its true nature. It's not only a circular line on the floor or even a disc, but a beautiful, delicate, but powerful sphere. One half of it is a dome that rises up from the floor. The other half is a mirrored dome that matches it, downwards.

With practice you will feel and see the three dimensional Circle more and more strongly. You can begin by 'seeing' the tongues of flaming energy around the edge as you Cast. Then let those flames grow until they reach up and meet above the Centre.

MAGICAL 'SEEING' is not nearly as mysterious or difficult as you might think. Begin by imagining. Look at the edge of the Circle 'as if' those tongues of flame are there. With your ordinary physical vision they are not, of course. But with the eyes that see your dreams, or see cities in sunsets, they are. Magic, to the everyday, is a lie. Reality is what you expect, what you tell yourself to see. The flaming circle is real, if you say it is.

In the circle you make the law.

Many people see the flames as blue. But you can see them as white, sparky, red, yellow, green, multicoloured - whatever your mind tells you.

You could imagine the energy produced by your body as steam or smoke, rolling off you into the space around you. This is probably not difficult if raising energy has been thorough and you're panting and sweating! So close your eyes and see that smoky stuff streaming off you, until it has filled the Circle.

When the atmo-sphere is full of it, there are two classic shapes you can use.

SPINNING THE SPHERE
and
DIRECTING THE CONE

Spinning the Sphere

Build the idea and feeling of the Sphere out of the flat Cast Circle.

Experience the upper dome forming above you. It may seem like a delicate spiderweb tracery, or smoked glass, or the interlaced branches of trees. Or something else again.

When the dome is in place imagine it doubled, to make the underneath half. You are standing on a floor cutting halfway across it.

Now without moving your physical body, imagine you go to the edge of the Circle, where the wall of the Sphere curves above you. Now PUSH it - deosil/ clockwise - slowly at first, then let go as it builds its spin.

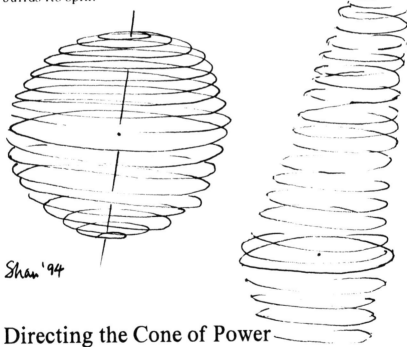

Shan '94

Directing the Cone of Power

Imagine a cone reaching from the base of the Circle upwards and upwards. Ideally this should be so intense as to make you shake or shiver a bit. The Cone of Power, or Vortex, as it is called, does not just reach up to the ceiling. It soars upwards to the stars. Finally let it go, sending it into the Whole.

WORKING

WORKING

The first level of ritual is the needs of the self. Denying the self only sets up a battle, but satisfying self creates a well fed self, strong enough to go further and work wider than immediate self.

Magic works through the intensity of desire. So you'll work best what you want most. What someone else wants will only work well if you can feel a strong desire for it to happen. This is very important and explains why a lot of people try to offer a Witch a lot of money to work magic for them. If the desire is not part of the Witch's world this is clearly the only way apart from terror to get someone to employ their own intense desire in your service. However, Craft custom forbids taking money to work a ritual.

Working for others may be both well meant, and an interference. I consider very carefully whether to work for someone else. Why do it for them, rather than encourage them, or show them how to do something for themselves? If someone wants something worked for them without being present, why? Is it because they don't want to be responsible for making it happen?

Even if someone is ill, if I really want to help, it would be a great deal more effective to work around their (hospital) bed - perhaps quietening the Raising Energy bit! Sometimes the suffering or deprivation a person bears is necessary; is it my job to affect it?

One, Two, Three pieces of work are enough for one ritual usually. More very probably is an overload, meaning you need to set up more than one ritual. Put quality energy into a few rather than spread thin for several.

With more than one piece of work in the same ritual, you are likely to need to Raise Energy again between each piece, or perhaps after two pieces are completed Just go into breathing, chanting and movement until you have built a stronger pulse of energy.

First rituals Dedicating chosen tools. Meeting the Elements. Meditation. Divination. Self Blessing. Sanctuary. Creativity.Self Knowledge. Sex (see Sex Magic). Self Healing.

For each, go through stages 1, 2, 3, 4 Preparation, Purification, Casting the Circle, & Raising Energy; finish with Communion and Opening the Circle..

Dedicating Tools.

Purify the object with Air, Fire, Water and Earth.

This means pass it through the smoke of incense, a candle flame, dip it in a bowl of water, and rub it with salt. Apply common sense to purifying a paper for example, pass it over the heat of the flame only, not through the actual flame, and pass it over the water slowly.

Hold the object close to the skin of your body; breathe deep and strong. Tell it what purpose it will carry for you, what you want to use it for. If possible, after the ritual, keep the object next to your skin, or in your bed for 3/ 7/ 9/ 13/ 28 days, as feels right.

Honouring an Element

Choose one and build a ritual around that nature. E.G. Water. Play a tape of water sounds; bathe your face/hands/body in special water; surround yourself with water colours; draw/ paint a picture of water things and shapes; enjoy a specially prepared drink in a carefully chosen cup.

Meditation see p. 69 Divination see p. 73

Self Blessing see p. 124

Sanctuary

Busy people like mothers or full time employees especially need to plan times for rest, quiet and replenishment. But everyone has times of stress, recovery from illness or grief, when extra care for the struggling self is necessary. Choose a time once a week perhaps when you take 1 or 2 hours just for you. If this seems impossible then your life is heavily overloaded and I'd recommend you really think seriously about changing things a bit so you can have this time. If you don't you could be very ill quite soon.

The work of this ritual is quite simply to do anything at all you feel like in the hour it gives you. You could prepare first with a Magical Bath and provide a favourite food for the end of the ritual.

Massage is a delightful replenishment. If you've never done massage, rub moisturiser, oil or talc into as much of your skin as you can manage. Have a manicure. Lie curled in a blanket and read your favourite type of magazine or novel. Try a game of Patience or Solitaire. Play favourite music. Dance (naked if you

wish). Dress up like you did when you were a child. Let your wise
child within live and play.

Self Knowledge

In your Preparation stage you need to provide four sheets of
writing paper, and a pen. Make the paper and pen special; even
plain inexpensive paper looks good with your own doodles round
the edges.

After stages 1,2,3,4 sit facing East and jot down your Air bits of
self (you as hopeful, planning, thoughtful, deciding self.) Then
move to face South and list your Fire bits (you making efforts,
pushing, laughing, picking up & trying again). Move West and
note West bits (you struggling with a fear, opening up to love,
sexual, angry, intuitive). Lastly face North and set down your
Earths (times of patience, quietness, listening, accepting loss,
responsibility, physical strength).

If you put negatives down each must be balanced by a positive.
Try to note specific events rather than general attitudes.

Creativity

Creativity is magic. Magic is creativity. Any kind of creativity
you like will be enriched and stimulated to new direction if done
in the Circle. Write, draw, sing, dance, massage, sew, play games,
martial arts, make music, study, put on make up, prepare food,
make models in wood/clay/paper, make masks/kites, talk myths.

Self Healing

Go to each of the quarters in turn and have a chat. Explain how
you feel at the moment. Take your time. Try to talk to each
Element as if to a good friend, an affectionate sister or brother, or
counsellor.

Ask each kind of strength to swell up in you and empower you for
what you need in your life at present. Stay longer with one or two
of the Elements if they are more necessary than the others.
Sometimes talking like this can get you upset and even tearful for
a bit. The Elements are quite used to that. They've been listening
to the troubles of us humans for thousands of years. If you do cry,
or get angry or upset this will quite naturally clear away after a
little while. Finish by going to the centre and having a treat you
especially like.

FINISH WITH A COMMUNION, & OPENING THE CIRCLE

COMMUNION

COMMUNION
celebrating thanksgiving earthing returning to the everyday

After working you need to relax and enjoy yourself. Pleasure is essential to Pagan spirituality, as well as accepting the difficult side of life. Happiness never needs justifying, so whether the preceding parts of the ritual have been merry or not, now is the time to serve a good helping of it. But as well as an important opportunity to celebrate and give thanks, Communion is an essential safety device.

After all the preparation, building, and the work itself, you have been in an altered state of consciousness. It is a shock to come from a sunlit garden into a dark house, and in the same way it is uncomfortable to snap out of the open, trusting, intuitive state, into the tighter everyday state. Communion protects us from this shock of transition, and ensures that we do it safely, before we face traffic, social challenges, and all the aggressive stuff our society routinely throws at us.

There are many stories current about people attending events where they stay somewhere for a couple of days or more, practising magical or therapeutic techniques; they then come away in a confused, inefficient, unsafe state. They tell of getting lost on familiar roads and driving around for hours before getting home. Some have accidents - thankfully not major ones. Some people find it distressing to come away into shops, garages, train or bus stations, where instead of kindly, enclosed space there are lots of rushing strangers, bright lights and noise. Other people seem hard, alien and closed, compared to the affinity and openness which may have developed over the course of the event.

It is not at all that these events are not helpful to us in what they do. We need times of withdrawal, with opportunities to open up deeper parts of ourselves. But just because these events are so effective at doing this opening up, we need definite attention to coming back into the everyday.

A personal ritual at home may seem small stuff compared to three to five days way out in the woods or closed off in a conference centre. But Circlework may be simple, and may take only an hour or two; it is still very effective at helping you reach beyond your everyday state.

There are meditations about white light, or being a tree, or gestures of touching the ground, often called grounding, or earthing. These are certainly soothing, and introduce a quiet, reassurance to the mind.

But I cannot see how I can come out of a mental state by using purely mental methods. The touching the ground is more solid, but still brief, and mainly symbolic.

My driving instructor years ago warned me not to try and eat when driving 'because with something in your mouth you can't think about anything else properly.' He was absolutely right, and I only break his advice now as an experienced driver if I'm on very familiar roads, and with an extra effort of concentration, remembering what he said.

Eating earths us wonderfully. The spurting of saliva, the sensation of taste, the activity of chewing, the solid stuff sliding down to the stomach all demands and takes our attention. The blood supply moves to the digestion system (which is why one often feels heavy and tired for a short while after eating). It also switches off mental activity by drawing blood away from the brain.

We are therefore completely naturally and fairly quickly brought out of rarefied mental states. The practice of fasting obviously uses the same thing in reverse.

If you ever attend an event where you do a lot of meditation, therapy, shamanic or ritual work which gets you in touch with sensitive, dreamlike states, it's worth bearing this in mind. If you're not offered food just before you leave and winding down time, create a kind of Communion for yourself. Go somewhere as neutral as possible: a quiet pub or cafe: an understanding friend's: buy a sandwich and drink and sit in the car or in a shelter for a while. Read a magazine or a light novel. Don't go and sit in a park and daydream. Don't eat sugar or drink alcohol right away.

A TEACHER IS A GUIDE NOT A BOSS

Take up the Cup

Hold the Chalice up above your head for a minute or so, in silence, looking up at it. Remember how Water is given to us to give us life.

So offer a sprinkle or three of the drink to the God/dess. This is a very ancient custom called a libation.

Then have a good drink yourself.

Give thanks for something in your own personal existence. I think that giving thanks for 'friendship' or 'inspiration' is poetic but not nearly as real as 'Victoria's hot bath and supper when I was so exhausted' or 'the guidance the Tarot gave me last Tuesday.' These specific things also give the Lady proper thanks for her gifts to me personally.

There may be things about the ritual you would like to give thanks for. Don't be afraid of speaking fully and openly, offering back some of the energy you have received to the Circle. In a group the sharing of happinesses is another building of trust and affection.

And even at dark times, there will be some glow of thanks possible.

Deosil

In groups the chalice is then passed deosil/ clockwise around the Circle saying

'BLESSED BE' or 'MAY YOU NEVER THIRST.'

I like to have one serious, and attentive, round of a Chalice at least, with each person speaking in turn.

And I like my Chalice to be plenty full enough for all to drink well. It is easy to get happily tipsy at Communion and this is only unwise if there is little time to be leisurely and enjoy it.

Drugs & alcohol

People who like dope or other drugs will enjoy them after the cup has passed round once. However, it is very unfriendly and divisive to take drugs among people you don't know well, without checking if this is acceptable. A quick check with the core group, or ritual priestess, beforehand, avoids any disapproval or embarrassment that could introduce strain at the end of a nice event.

If you have a reason not to drink alcohol you'll probably have been exploring alternatives for times when others drink. (I can recommend Aqua Libra and Norfolk Punch, which I used a lot during pregnancy.)

Whatever is drunk has a powerful effect when passed round a Circle deosil at the end of ritual when people are in a sensitive state. So although most Pagans enjoy drinking, I usually find our events are surprisingly light on alcohol. A little has a lot of effect.

It's worth providing two chalices if you have guests; one non alcoholic. Alcoholics or young children qualify for this, but sometimes someone on medical treatment does too, or just with a strong personal preference. Two Chalices are quite manageable; in fact I have used four at big rituals. Mineral water, spring water, fruit juice, even tea or milk or any drink you and others like, will serve well.

See chapter on Drugs p 92

Working alone you are not limited by practicality and can enjoy a fragile, beautiful cup of glass or porcelain if you wish. A shared Chalice will make people anxious in case they break it, so reassure them and keep them in their relaxed and happy state by using something sturdy. My first group ritual used a pudding bowl.

Witches vary in how pleasure directed they are. Some prefer to Open the Circle and so finish the more serious part of the ritual, and then go on to the Communion. Others feel that it is specially important to keep Communion clearly in the main part of the ritual, because so many other religions have destroyed the simplicity of joy in ritual. Moderates feel that a warm and friendly Communion is appropriate but dislike it developing into drunkenness. For those less moderate, drinking songs and joke telling and so on develop into a happy carouse.

Bread

Eat or pass the Bread/ Cakes after the Chalice. Give thanks again. This tends to evoke thank yous for simpler pleasures, material comforts, or physical things.

Feasting

Feasting can follow on after the Bread/Cakes have been passed. Whether or not to do so depends on several matters. After a long ritual of two hours or more you may want to pee. Smokers will often enjoy the feast more if the Circle is Opened so they can indulge. Heating food is difficult in the Circle, however an extension lead and a hotplate/ electric kettle is a great help.

The Feast can be enjoyed without losing all the Circle's beauty (but allowing for piddling and cigarettes) by Opening the Circle, then making a ceremonial farewell, but relighting the candles again and staying there. Some of the feast supplies arranged on the Earth altar look lovely.

Candlelight, good food, wine and relaxation as you sprawl on cushions is a sound recipe for satisfaction. Whether alone or shared these are pleasures that almost all of us can hold in common.

A BOOK IS A BOX OF SUGGESTIONS:
PICK WHAT YOU WANT

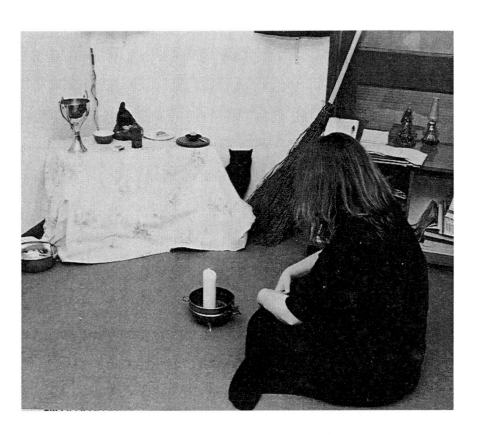

OPENING <small>THE</small> CIRCLE

OPENING THE CIRCLE

Any good hostess knows the feeling as the evening comes to an end. Attention wanders, voices slow and quieten, perhaps a yawn or other hint of fatigue shows up. The same feeling signals the time to end a ritual. Let Communion continue for a comfortable length of time, allow conversation (in a group) or daydreaming (alone) to have its way.

Some more chanting or drumming may develop here. In fact it may actually go into stronger, higher energy than when energy was being raised earlier. This is probably because the earlier stage was more serious in intent, about building the temple circle itself, so it involved effort. This time a second burst is celebratory, and comes from the satisfaction of the ritual completed.

This part may occasionally reach a kind of easy, steady energy, intense but sustained - but practicality may not permit an all night drumout unfortunately. If this happens, and you know that babysitters, transport, early commitments tomorrow, or the hours the room is available, mean it has to stop, you may have to gently insist. Use a slow drumbeat, a slower chant, or recite the Charge, or something else in slow words.

Opening the Circle reverses the process of Casting the Circle.

Start at the North
Go to each of the quarters, going anti clockwise/ widdershins to the four Elements, Water/West, South/Fire and East/Air, thanking them for their presence and their gifts.

Say '*HAIL AND FAREWELL*' and put out the candle flames.

But do not put out the Centre candle.

Come to the Centre
(Groups gather close in a ring.)

There is now shadowiness again lit only by the Centre candle and your special altar candle if you have one. As with the Casting, we cannot truly say farewell to Spirit for s/he is everywhere yet nowhere. So we say anything that comes from the heart.

Then there are traditional words for marking the end of the ritual.

'*THE CIRCLE IS OPEN AND UNBROKEN.*'

followed by a blessing, for example '*MAY THE PEACE AND LOVE OF THE GOD/DESS GO IN ME/US, AND FLOW*

Kiss of Peace

In groups the Witches' Kiss is usually exchanged. This is rather like a Continental kiss on each cheek, but ends with a kiss on the mouth or the forehead.

As you exchange it you say 'Merry meet' (first kiss on cheek) 'Merry part' (other kiss on other cheek), and finally 'Merry meet again!' last central kiss.

Obviously you only kiss on the mouth if that is something you have done with that person elsewhere, although I have seen ritual farewells clearly introducing a new stage of closeness.

Either pass the Witches' Kiss widdershins round the Circle, or at a Festival or high energy Circle have a general exchange where everyone does it with everyone else. It's a lovely symbol of human family.

Women and men in some traditions of Craft keep to strict alternative placing, so a passed kiss would go from woman to man to woman. However in a women's circle, or the recent men's circles this particular weave of energy is obviously not there. I also like mixed sex circles to experience accepting any other human being, so I do not direct people into patterns. The connection that has often caused the most surprise and amusement is when two heterosexual men face kissing their own type for the first time in their lives since childhood. Interestingly, there is far less hesitation and awkwardness about this than there was when we first held our circles nearly ten years ago.

It might at first look as if a solo rite loses out on the Kiss, but you'll find as you stand quietly saying the words by your Centre Candle, you will feel within a very personal and gentle feeling. This will be in no way less, just different. All Circles are one.

After Opening the Circle you may feel reluctant to leave, or dismantle your Temple. So take your time, if you can. Your plan may have included a Feast to follow the ritual, a quiet solitary walk, or a rousing party.

Be careful to put out the last candles before you leave.

SUMMARY

Ritual is for making or accepting change.

1. Preparation PLAN & GATHER KIT

THREE STEPS PLAN: free imagining, theme, the 7 stages
RITUAL KIT: Bowl of water, dish of Salt
5 Candles (4 primary colours, + black or white)
Bowl for Centre candle.
Matches. Taper if you like.
Joss sticks + holder. OR Incense, charcoal + holder.
Extras: whatever is necessary for the ritual.
Cup of wine/ juice etc.   Dish of Bread
Time: One hour alone, one & a half for a group.
LAW: Once begun do not replan.

LIGHT THE CENTRE CANDLE

2. Purification GETTING RID OF ANY DISTRACTION

negative/positive   SALT WATER PURIFICATION: Put Salt
in the Bowl, stir it widdershins (groups pass it widdershins)
Speak aloud even if alone. Say *'MAY YOU BE FREE OF
DOUBT & ANXIETY'*   Speak in personal, particular terms.
THREEFOLD WALK: 1) Vigorous shake out circle walk.
2) Easy relaxed walk 2nd circle. 3) Sl-o-o-w walk.
LAW: Hold the bowl for longer than you feel the need.

3. Casting the Circle CREATING MAGICAL SPACE.

Make a circle. Call the 4 Quarter Elements, honour the 5th.
Start in the East, call/ invoke working clockwise/ deosil.
Light the candle, say *'BE HERE NOW'*

At the Centre, say *'THE CIRCLE IS CAST*
WE ARE BETWEEN THE WORLDS
WHERE NIGHT AND DAY
BIRTH AND DEATH
JOY AND SORROW
MEET AS ONE.

LAW: Once Cast none may leave it.

4. Raising Energy BREATHE, SOUND MOVE

Breathe: Deepen the outward breath.
Sound: Hum, Chant, Open sound, Animal voices.
Move: Sway, walk, skip, dance, spin.
Don't force it, accept what you get.
FOCUS OR SHAPE THE ENERGY: Sphere, Cone.

5. Working Do not try to do more than 3 pieces of work in

one circle. Use raising energy whenever needed to refresh you.
The classic shape of ritual is to move from dark to light.
See in 'Working' first section, and 'Planning' next.

GREAT LAW OF CIRCLEWORK
In the Circle you can't do it wrong.

O

6. Communion THANKSGIVING RETURN TO EARTH.

Consecrate the Cup by holding it up in silence.
Give thanks for something personal to you.
Groups pass the Cup clockwise/ deosil, say *'BLESSED BE'* or
'MAY YOU NEVER THIRST'

7. Opening the Circle FAREWELL, DISSOLVING.

Start at the Earth altar, say what you wish and
'HAIL & FAREWELL' Go to Water, Fire & Air too.
At Centre say 'THE CIRCLE IS OPEN BUT UNBROKEN'
Blessing. (groups) Kiss of peace.

THREE STEP PLANNING

Once you've tried a few of the example rituals, and the seven stages are familiar, it'll be time to come back to this page and start on your own independently designed rituals.

It looks entirely sensible to tackle planning by going through the seven stages from start to finish, step by step. But I've found it doesn't work out well doing that. There are four preparatory stages (Preparation, Purification, Casting the Circle and Raising Energy) before the central work. After carefully planning each of these I get tired and start losing interest just as I get to the most important bit of all - what this particular ritual is all about.

It often feels slow and tiring too because the central work is the most challenging to plan, so that creates nervousness, and one tends to hold back and stay with the easier opening stages longer than necessary.

The way I usually do it is to plunge straight into planning the working stage right away; the rest of the ritual then falls into place quite easily to fit in with this part.

Without experience, it can be almost impossible to think of how to create something in an empty space. Even with experience, you need to feel sensitively what you need this time, not just sling in something you've done before. The circle is Being Here Now.

1. Image
Let go of trying to find exact, clever things to actually do. Let your mind float. Just throw up any words, images or feelings you have about this ritual - anything at all. Jot down words and phrases - call out words - a snatch of song - make a gesture - describe a picture - a messy pot of stuff. Don't try to be sensible or intelligent.

Let it be unconnected to the ritual - silly - useless any old rubbish. Keep doing it. Tape it. Scribble it. With another, or others, keep speaking out and sharing.

When there's some stuff to work with, try quietly to ponder what you've got. Try to see what it's telling you, what's in common between most of it.

Aim at a ONE OR TWO OR THREE WORD THEME. Can you see anything that most of this has in common? It takes a little while to see it sometimes. You're looking for a few words, or an image, that represents all this mishmash thrown up. If you really can't see anything that links as a theme, go back and do no 1 again.

2. Action

Having got your theme 'Playful children' 'Cold and weary' 'Guiding Star' or something, think finally about how to act it out. As far as possible, try to work out how to express your theme without using words, like a children's game. Is there a folk custom that would fit? A piece of yoga or taichi? A scene from a film or play? A symbol?

Try for one action that seems right. Then build some more bits round it. This can take a little time until you're used to the idea.

As ritual is about change, and we generally prefer to honour the Dark, but shift into the Light, you could think of two pieces of action. The first expresses the uncomfortable, limited, undesirable passive aspect of your theme. The second expresses a release from it and a joyful reaction.

For example, binding with wool, breaking the bonds; curled up as a foetally sleeping seed, unfolding upward; inner meditation, active movement or dance; frantic movement, stillness and meditation.

The Four Elements are excellent helpers. Doing one simple thing with each in turn a little differently, gives a powerful rite.

Use folklore, myths, bits from books, nursery rhymes, bits of theatre, stories, spells, jokes, art, poems ...

If a planning is particularly stressful, for a larger group than you're used to, or with unfamiliar people, a new style or place, you can always Purify to ease the stress, before getting back into the planning itself.

Remember to check for overload: 3 items of work is enough

3. Seven stages

Now you have the centrepiece you will find the rest is shaped by it. Kit can now be listed; Purification details become obvious (though it's normally best to stick to the classic style with salt & water).

For Casting the Circle, ask how the theme of the ritual affects how you need to call on the nature of the Elements.

Particular chants for Raising Energy? - don't script too heavily in this most free stage of the whole ritual.) The work planned next may affect where or how you finish up Raising Energy; eg you may need to try and end up by the North because the first bit of Working is a dark Meditation about Earth. Is Communion affected by the theme? Opening the Circle usually reverses Casting.

THE NATURE OF MAGIC

We are always in two minds about it all.

Everyday Self talks in adult language, plans, sets goals, checks details, makes lists, worries about sensible adult responsibilities. - Protects us from getting in too deep, or failing to take care of ordinary practicalities, or forgetting what's on the list to get done.

Deep Self dreams, inspires, weaves reality, makes love, makes angers, plays, mourns, reaches the source of being, finds meaning and purpose as we need it. - Communicates in odd words, song, dance, art, symbol, poetry, colours, smells, gesture.

The dominant idea in our society is that the Everyday Self (Starhawk calls it Talking Self) is the proper person to be in charge. After all, we do need to put food on the table, look after basic hygiene, and accept a few rules for behaviour here and there.

So our Everyday Selves tend to be a bit pompous, and feel they should be in control, and get affronted if they are not treated accordingly. They get very anxious about us wasting time and making fools of ourselves. To be anything but cool, calm, collected and sensible means being childish, weak, unsuccessful, a loser.

There is also a very influential alternative idea that the dominant way is too limiting, played out, and the source of a cold, callous science which is wrecking our lives. We are asked to look to the Deep Self for salvation to heal our world. This culture is full of signs, dreams, art mystery, drama and letting it all hang out.

But can we live in a dream? Is drifting around in a cloud of joss stick scented smoke babbling about blue lights, astral messengers, higher powers, and the healing of everyone and his aunt really going to create a satisfying life? I've never forgotten the idiot who 'kindly' offered to get her coven to light a candle for me when I had been bedridden and in pain for weeks. What I desperately needed was some shopping or washing up done for me.

I think that we need BOTH - I'm very keen on having both in lots of ways.

The Deep Self is essential for important life decisions, for healing illness and misery, for finding meaning over and beyond the everyday mechanics of life; and last but by no means least, for touching the peaks of joy itself.

The Everyday Self is essential for day by day living, for sorting and organising, for practical comfort. We need this Self in order to check the Deep Self stuff in case we slide off into fluffy craziness.

Everyday Self is very good for putting together the things and resources I need in order to carry through the vision of the Deep Self.

So I see my Everyday Self as a fine, high quality secretary: but not, definitely not the boss. Sometimes I think Deep Self is the boss. Producing the theme, or giving guidance looks like being the boss. But perhaps they are really partners, squabbling often, sometimes in painful disagreement. They work best when each of their voices is heard and respected. That sounds like I'm a third part of the team, the one who puts their two sides together in some sort of sense.

This can all clear up the classical definition of Magic. I said above that Everyday Self is very good at putting together the things I need to carry through the vision of the Deep Self.

'Magic is the Art and Science of changing reality according to the Will.' Aleister Crowley.

'Magic is the Art and Science of changing consciousness according to the Will.' Dion Fortune.

These teachers are talking about the Will as a deep Will, something rather more than impulse, or whim. They are speaking of the deep drives that shape our lives, what I call the Deep Self. If Magic is an art or science of expressing this Will, this Deep Self, then Magic must be how the deeper levels connect with the Everyday Self who can put things into practice for us.

And that has to be about creating a marriage between two minds, about exploring any method, with care, that can help these very different parts of me talk to each other and work together.

Now first of all these two actually talk differently.

Deep Self: dream of raging, beautiful fire, an inferno of gold, scarlet, orange, purple and silver roaring and dancing, exploding with pure life energy. Cut to quiet, dim stillness, and a shabby, iron stove, most unglamorous. Sense of shock, of an unwelcome ending, of being reluctant to accept the second part, and yet that it was not dangerous, but somehow helpful for me.

This was an actual power dream I had during my initiation year. I did not understand it at all at the time. Later my Everyday Self put it into words: 'Shan, you are exploding with energy and purpose. But you need to learn to contain your power, how to be practical, and to accept limits in yourself and others at least for a while.'

I often need to reassure my counselling clients, my brave voyagers who reshape reality indeed, that they can speak to me in silly ways, that nothing they say when speaking of their feelings is silly, that they do not have to use whole sentences, to present an impressive intelligent report.

I explain that there is a difference between being childish, and being childlike. To be childlike is to be an adult but to be capable of being like a child as well, to draw on hope, laughter, playfulness, courage, and simple self knowledge buried in our own feelings. To be childlike is to know.

But this may come out in broken words, between crying fits, with soft moans, or bursts of anger. It needs to be given what it likes, pretty colours, music, games and dances and toys. It needs silliness, cuddles, stories and treats.

And I myself often need to be reminded and reassured of all this when I am working on something of my own.

A temple is a playroom for grownups.

Sex is an excellent example of how magic works. Not so long ago the information about how our bodies work, and how they mesh with our personal feelings, just wasn't available. It got closed away in cupboards, prosecuted in courts of law, sold illegally in squalid circumstances. Much of what we now know wasn't even known at all 50 years ago in the last days of the guilt edged god.

So now we have books telling us openly about different kinds of orgasm, sex positions, what pleases her, him, at different ages, or different times of the month. Great. We can all, if we wish, try out different things and find out how to do the basics, and a few personal favourites, on our own or with a partner, just like any other craft.

Everyday Self can learn, make lists, remind us of all this when necessary. And many a stale relationship can indeed be revived by all this useful information on how to enjoy ourselves. In the middle of actually doing it, even, I can liven up a boring bit by shifting into one of the clearly illustrated positions in the book, or changing to faster or slower, according to what I've learnt.

Ah, but although this works fine up to a point, we surely don't want it all to be like that? What about romance? being swept away to the sound of violins and pounding sea surf? What about the burning storm of lust that just tears us up by the roots, shakes us, and shatters us into a sweaty tangle of flesh? Or what about the simple pure sense of the body itself just saying 'Do that now'?

Don't the books, the diagrams, the earnest efforts to do it right, don't these kill the essence of what it's all about? The answer is yes, they can, for a while. During a period of learning any craft well we have to be awkward, make some mistakes, actually enjoy it less for a time. But then the new knowledge slips into place, and we can call on it much more without thinking or worrying about it. The flow comes back. But there will still be times when a thoughtful check, a special effort to try to do it differently, or better, will really help.

The best answer then is to be able to move between the two. Sometimes if it's not working well the information and the diagrams (Everyday Self) can help a lot. Sometimes, bogged down with anxiety about paying bills, or what the diagrams say we ought to do, we need to float more into the more feeling world of the Deep Self. Listening carefully to what I really, really want (time to unwind, a touch of savagery or of delicacy) will be the right thing this time.

So all that stuff about Magic being all about sex is actually true all along. Welcome to the wondrous wedding and passionate bedding of Intelligence and Intuition.

MEDITATION: Something simple

There's a lot of complicated stuff blathered about meditation. My first experiences were boring, and uncomfortable to boot. It made me feel inadequate and extremely uncertain about the whole thing.

People who enjoy meditating speak of a refreshing sense of inner peace which is frustrating if all you've got out of it is a backache an a bore.

Meditating is noticing. Just noticing.

Notice each detail of how you wash up. You're meditating.

Notice every second of feeling and movement as you walk. You're meditating.

Notice totally every feeling in every part of you during sex. You're meditating. Also when the sex is shared, if you really tune into your own body completely you will begin to do naturally just the things your partner most needs as well! Now you're definitely meditating.

Notice how a plant grows, how a cat walks, how a sunbeam strikes the carpet. You're meditating.

Everyone meditates; some call it daydreaming. Lots of people do it when they drive a car, clean the floor, or first wake up.

You can if you like, choose a particular thing to centre on to make a meditation: a plant, an ornament, your own hand.

Don't try the lotus position unless it's fairly comfy. People from cultures who use it a lot sit like that from childhood so they're used to it. We're not.

Support your back, make sure you're warm.

Now just notice whatever you notice about your chosen focus.

You might look at it, smell it, touch it, watch it, think of things it suggests, look at it some more, touch it again ...

Notice what distracts you from staying with this thing. When we try to stay on one thing the brain jumps away. It's designed to, for survival. If you kept drooping over a flower in the jungle something large might come up behind you with unkind intent, without you noticing it. So the brain does a rapid scanner routine for us, and skips about too to keep us awake and aware. But under safe conditions, we can afford to let the scanner slow down, and go into the healing state of waking dream. We can't go into the still mind for very long though, because of the anxious, ever protective scanner. Even experienced meditators will skip into other thoughts every 3 minutes or so.

Because it is anxiety, and protectiveness, which pulls us away from our chosen meditation topic, it will tend to keep skipping towards whatever is our key needs or weak points right now. So noticing just what distracts me is an excellent fruit of trying to meditate.

BODILY DISCOMFORT: check carefully if this part of the body is unwell. Do something extra to provide comfort for yourself, some stretching, and shaking out, and an extra cushion or two, a drink, a piddle, a biscuit. If it still nags, try gentle discipline, asking your body to cooperate for 10 minutes, no more, or cut it to 5. You can always build it up step by step to longer.

FEELING SILLY: a little of this is a natural barrier but more than a few moments of it means you're quite nervous of what you're doing. Respect your wariness, talk it over inside yourself. Give yourself whatever reassurance you need.

RESPONSIBILITIES: accept each one (unpaid bills, ugh) as it occurs, noting it needs attention. Tell it you will be better able to manage to do the right thing if you relax for a little now.

PERSONAL RELATIONSHIP MATTERS:

quarrels, misunderstandings etc treat the same as responsibilities. Anything that comes up a few times in a meditation should not be avoided later, but puzzled through. confronted, counselled etc. Anything that rises up more than once in a meditation matters.

ALTERNATIVE IDEAS FOR MEDITATION: Means you want more control in your life. Take your own preferences more seriously. Choose your own focus for meditation, don't follow someone else's lead.

Don't try to meditate every day

Don't try to do it at all for a while if three tries are no fun.

Doing anything every day is a strict discipline that is best worked up to over about 6 months. 1) Start by doing it once a week. 2) After 2 weeks do it twice a week. 3) After 3 weeks try it every 3 days. Let yourself off if you're ill, or having big problems, or very tired. Go back to the previous step, and wait until that settles into something you can manage comfortably before going up a notch.

After 3 weeks of doing it every 3 days, try every other day. After three weeks of managing that comfortably, do it 5 days a week. And if you can do that for a month, you could ease it into 6 or 7.

Earth Meditation: (soothing) 1) Start by walking vigorously round in a circle, or back and forth. Shake your arms and legs. Make snorting, grumpy noises to loosen your breathing.

2) Walk naturally, easily for a bit.

3) Earth walk. Slow down. Bend the knees, curve your arms, relax shoulders - be a gorilla!

Put each foot down heel first. Take small steps.

Relax shoulders and belly. Don't forget to breathe! Notice the feet and their cycle.

This is a lovely meditation but it does take a little practice. Drop it if the third time is no fun, maybe try again in a few weeks if you like.

Walking on different floors, on grass or sand is interesting. Check for stones or twigs etc first.

Water Meditation: (creative) Sit well supported, relax belly and shoulders.

Look into a bowl of water in a dim light- candlelight or similar. The bowl is best made of metal, or dark pottery. Some people like to put a silver coin in the bowl.

You may see pictures in the bowl, or they may come into your head. Or you may get pure feelings. You get what you get.

Fire Meditation: (strengthening, inspiring) Look into a candle flame or a real fire. Very easy and delightful as a first try meditation. Most people like this, or they like the water bowl. Fire tends to stimulate pictures, and symbolic messages.

Air Meditation: (calming or informative, trains discipline) Sit very comfortablly with especially well supported back. Your task is to notice your breathing. 5 minutes at first only. Your attention will go all sorts of places every minute or two. Gently notice what distracts you, say inwardly 'I can see that's important, but right now I'm concentrating on my breathing.'

Five Elements Meditation (awakening, energising, balancing) Especially good as a gentle waking in the morning.0

AIR - face East, wave arms and hands slowly as branches in the air, turning fully round.

FIRE - face South, flat hands, rub belly really hard and fast until you feel the heat. Enjoy it, then shake it out of your hands. Do it twice more.

WATER - face West, kneel, slowly scoop up the water of life, raise it slowly over your head and pour it over your body, touching gently with your fingertips. Do it twice more.

EARTH - face North, stand still. Pat gently, slowly but firmly your own arms, face, shoulders, breast/s, tummy, legs, feet.

SPIRIT - face Centre, offer your energy forwards in your cupped hands. Shape it in imagination to your desire. Enjoy it. Let it go.

Meditation is difficult if you have eaten in the last hour; it makes you dopey and heavy. Enjoy that, don't destroy it with mental effort.

Visualisation is a frequent part of meditations in books but a large number of people can't visualise, or only a little. However they can meditate, pathwork, whatever, in their own way. Focus on the feeling, or you may get quick flashes of pictures. Few of us actually go to the cimema fully in these experiences.

MESSAGES FROM THE DREAM
DIVINATION: (Tarot, Runes, Dowsing etc.)

The closest idea to what it's like in the deep self, is the dream state. It's colourful, eventful, endless .... not quite understandable .... familiar, chaotic, poetic .... all in the present tense yet full of past and future memory... often gives guidance ... or just plays ...

We think of ourselves as awake during the day, asleep at night. It is the dreaming self, the deep self which does not sleep, is dreaming on as you read this now. It is only the everyday self which sleeps.

Power dreams, vivid, haunting dreams that come more than once; or come once but continue to nag at the mind for days or weeks or more, tend to occur on the borders just after falling asleep or shortly before waking. Such dreams always carry guidance, but do not necessarily come clear right away.

Coincidences make us feel dreamlike, especially when several happen together. Odd patterns of events tug at us, just like the power dreams, as if the dream has transferred into ordinary reality. As I was writing the section on practical crafts, wood and metalwork, my phone rang. It was a wrong number: a man was asking for the well known local specialist shop in DIY. As I wrote the summary of the book to go on the back cover, the phone gave me a journalist who had been asked by a publisher to write a book on rituals for people to do for themselves. To me such things are messages, encouraging me on, telling me I'm doing the right thing.

It's not just a fancy to me, the idea that the dream has moved outward and become solid in events. I have seen too many instances of how the shape of the inner mind imprints the shape of outer things. The simplest example is going out in a cheerful mood and seeing smiling faces; going out feeling low and seeing grim faces.

People often want magical help to get a lover back. It is hard to accept that spells or rites alone cannot do it. Not because they are not powerful, but because if there is a gulf between there are reasons for it. Sooner or later a magical ribbon will wear thin and fall away, with the gulf still there. Whatever all too human fear, jealousy, insecurity, resentment creates a barrier must be healed before any real bond can be reworked. By contrast, I have seen dramatic results come when the personal matters that hold people apart are dealt with. One woman's lost love, not seen for years, after her inner attitudes to relating changed after several counsellings, phoned her from Australia.

What we are inside, creates what we are outside, inner landscape paints the outer picture.

'How can I find a friend? or a lover?' we groan, in lonely states - surrounded by busy human networks, passing, almost touching hundreds of others every day. Once the inner gate opens, the right person is often already there all the time, unnoticed.

It's an odd idea at first. Does it mean that other people are no more than shadows in my dream, puppets of my mind? Am I no more than someone else's theatre prop too? Ugh. Perhaps so, but then if so, I am still an independent part of this mysterious dance, where we all act out each others' dreams. It is the weaving of the great web of fate, the great sacred dance itself: we each shape those around us as part of our chosen steps, as their movements in turn influence ours. It's as if through it all threads a shiveringly alive nervous system that can ensure that the same events that serve my will by reflecting it, can also mesh and interconnect with all the other wills spinning around as well. One hell of a database.

Even if this seems the mad fancies of an overworked priestess, I think some of it has to make sense. Inner feelings definitely affect outer physical events, as modern medicine is discovering more and more.

Psychic experiences, telepathy, poltergeists, warning dreams etc seem to come in bursts. Telepathy is commonplace between mothers and children at key points of a child's development; also between lovers, especially in the early stages of passion. But true to its root in feelings, with their rise and fall like tides, psychic experience comes and goes. A 'psychic person' often feels bereft when the tide falls, and all the exciting signs and visions recede.

The most frequent time for psychic stuff to rise is around personal change, decision points of life. The lifestyle gets stale, goes boring, then erupts into colour. It can be a bit dizzying by contrast. I often have to reassure people not to get too nervous about the stage effects, and just have a good look at what this is saying.

Then later, message received, and acted on, it all calms down, goes quite boring. In humdrum life after getting my temple going I wondered rather wistfully why the lady was sending no more intriguing events or silver visions. Had I lost it, that lovely delicate guiding thread? Then I laughed at myself, as I realised that all that happened to get me on track. So if it wasn't happening any more, it just meant I was actually doing the right thing, and didn't need to be nudged.

Years later I found the same idea in the Tibetan Book of the Dead. It speaks of 3 levels of reality, or 3 levels of experience. The everyday one shows us what we need to know by words, books, friends' advice and observing ordinary events around us. The dream as psychic or magical events comes in if we don't understand; don't want to, or can't because of conflict or fear. Finally, if the dream cannot get through to us, it turns to nightmare, bringing loss, pain, illness and suffering to teach us the hard way.

The connection often seen between illness and psychic experience has several reasons. One is that as just described, if we try to ignore psychic instruction or help, it will eventually get more insistent until it hurts and can't be ignored. Another is that times of deep personal change tire us and use up our energies anyway, so the immune system can be depleted leaving us more open to illness. We may also need the retreat that illness gives as its gift. In these two cases, the illness is happening independently as part of the needed shift; both illness and psychic stuff happen together because of it.

It can also occur if someone deliberately tries to stay heavily connected to psychic levels continually without breaks for robust, jolly, practical things. Insisting on staying with the modes of change, crisis and intensity is obviously not a good idea.

This rather changes the idea of psychic work as a superior level of living, or as creating an extra sensitive kind of person. Instead, it needs to be something that swells up in us at times for a while, to help us understand, but by no means a healthy thing to stay with continually. We may honour the guidance we need, and be grateful for its help, but there is a time to let go, get back to practical living, and not make this kind of thing an escape.

So a lack of psychic experience can actually be a very healthy sign of life unfolding as it needs to. Signs, dreams, visions have their season, like everything else. A frantic avoidance of anything psychic would also be unhealthy and silly - why completely waste a natural source of support? It would be like deliberately never using one hand, or refusing to look in mirrors even when there's something hurting in your eye.

Various methods and simple tricks have developed through our history to help us use this natural source of guidance and support. There's the Tarot, Runes, Astrology, Scrying, Palmistry and many more.

The marriage of the two minds already described helps to understand what we are doing.

This is an outline of dowsing for keys.

1) Set the goal. 'I want to find the keys' (Everyday Self).

2) Float dreamily about the room, going slightly ga -ga.
   'Hmmmm. Keys. Yes. Find the keys. Think about keys.'   (Deep self).

3) Resistance, tension. 'What do you think you're doing?'
   'You don't think this kind of mumbo jumbo can find keys
   do you?' (Everyday Self).

4) Dialogue to give the scandalised, disapproving, cynical Everyday Self reassurance or distraction.
   'I'm just mucking about.
   It's worked before.
   It can't do any harm to try.
   Other methods haven't worked.' etc.
   Everything's got to be somewhere.'

2) Float. 'Hmm. Keys. Um. Er. Keys ....' (Deep Self)

You may go backwards and forwards between floating and resistance several times before anything happens.

A variation on this is 'beginners' luck, when you play at divination a few times (1). It works (2). You panic! (3) It then doesn't work any more.

What is happening is that it worked at first precisely because you were playful and childlike - non-serious in your approach. But now it's worked, your everyday self is cross and argumentative, you are stuck in a major resistance/ tension stage. You need to work through it steadily and gently, allowing your doubts and fears and worries about being silly etc to have their season. What this can mean in practice is that you continue with half serious attempts to do it at intervals and wait it out. Can be boring! Don't push to hard, don't criticise yourself for failing, just accept it. It will come.

One teacher I worked with years ago asked us to tell her what was in a bowl she held - we couldn't see in the bowl. Someone said almost crossly 'Of course I can't tell you what's in the bowl - I don't know.'

The teacher said with great calmness 'Lie to me. Lies are very magical. Tell me a lie about what's in the bowl.'

The cross person was so startled they tried it, and told her exactly what was in the bowl!

It's your own personality that constructs the doubts and barriers. So you need to find ways that fit you personally to deal with them. One person loves the Tarot, another the Runes. Find the particular Tarot pack that appeals to you - just because you like it, you don't have to know why.

Some of the magic comes from the tool, the cards, the runic symbols, the water in the scrying bowl. These things have been proved over time to work for a lot of people. But much of the magic lies in you, in the dream you hold inside you, as we all do. Like the telephone and the electric drill, it depends how you yourself use them.

You can divine from matches, if you watch how they fall. Or with a handful of cuddly toys, if you got used to them. When you first practice with a dowsing pendulum, you ask it a simple question such as 'Do I live alone?' You know the answer, let us say it is YES. The line swings a certain way as you hold it. Ask more questions, which you know have clear YES answers. Notice what the line tends to do while you are working with YES answers.

Now practice with NO answers. Keep going till you can see a clear difference. Now you can practice a bit with questions from friends, with answers that can be checked.

By all means follow instructions from clearly written books that don't confuse you or make you feel nervous. But most of all, notice your own language, your own personal signs.

IN PERFECT LOVE
& PERFECT TRUST

How about going somewhere you don't know, with strangers, and doing a set of procedures new to you, which involves being in complete darkness some of the time - oh, and you're expected to take your clothes off? Not keen? I'm not surprised.

Something like this is at the centre of many people's fears about what witches do. Of course, there are a few centuries of church lies about us. Like the Jews, and the early Christians themselves, we have been accused of doing revoltingly cruel things to babies and animals. The latest round of this campaign against us exploded in the late'80's. Comprehensive enquiries by all the authorities have shown there is no connection between the child abuse scares and Pagans.

So why the sudden claims against us? It was a great shock when new and disturbing information about widespread child abuse throughout our whole society became known. It is especially difficult for us to deal with the idea that the men who do these things are ordinary people; in fact our own friends, lovers, husbands, fathers. For men it is hard to face the truly ugly side of masculinity as we currently know it.

Rather than looking fearfully at the people we know in our own lives, it is much much easier to point at another group and get angry because it's them who are doing it. The ancient rite of the (e)scape goat lives on still.

At the same time, there has been an impressive number of converts to Paganism. The church which has always tried to claim to be religion for all has understandably not been pleased, and its more nasty branches went to town.

Few real Pagans had their children taken away; and each case was eventually put right - but we lived in fear of it for years. It was a dirty tactic to attack us through our children, and we have yet to see signs of the churches putting their own in order about it.

The media don't always help matters. One recent shock expose story about Pagans in a naked orgy involving children was actually about a sweat lodge, a native shamanic technique which is like an outdoor sauna. Its cleansing effect through steam is very uncomfortable unless it's done naked. All the thousands of Scandinavians who do it regularly at weekends would be amazed to know they are holding orgies, or corrupting their children, as the idea is rather more to do with cleanliness being close to godliness. The parents at this one held in the West Country naturally did not permit photos, so the newspaper used photos taken forty years ago, of a completely different group of people with black boxes pasted over their private bits.

One can only applaud the implied stamina of the orgiastic pensioners involved. Sensible people can see a sensational press campaign for what it is, and understand that the explosions of hysteria are untrue (in the case of violence to children) or greatly exaggerated (the orgies).

Basic human needs

However it's one thing to try to set aside frantic fantasies and explore a new community. It's another thing to face experiences which are genuinely frightening because people are inconsiderate about basic human needs.

I think I have a good track record about making people feel safe and relaxed at my events for two reasons. One is that outside areas that I know well and feel confident in, I am myself quite timid; certainly very cautious. So I treat other people as I myself wish to be treated when I am new and uncertain, that is, with careful slow timing, and clear instructions, and room left for choice.

The second is that my work with Pagan groups developed during the child abuse scandals when the Press, social workers and fundamentalist christians were promoting us as dangerous people. I therefore expected people to be very careful in approaching me, and to need reassurance and time to make up their minds.

A young woman who has just begun working with me has pointed out that it was a nervous matter approaching me, because it very well might have far reaching effects in changing her life. She comments that change, even if it is for the better, is scary.

Fear and toughness

There is usually a tough way to do something, and a soft way. Myself, I'd rather take the soft way if I can. After all life throws enough hard knocks without me deliberately making it worse. I'd rather save my fighting strength for when it's really necessary.

Fear is not well understood in a masculine type of society like ours. As an amazon sort of woman I did not understand it much myself until I was coming close to 40. I knew how to dismiss it; how to shrug, take a deep breath and plunge through it and out the other side. I did not understand that it has its own gifts that are worth stopping for.

The warrior cult which glorifies toughness has its place. It can be a measuring of oneself against one's past capacities - 'I never thought I could do it, but I did.' There's certainly a place for this as it pushes us to achieve richer landscapes. In crisis, when there's not time to deal with feelings, we need our brisk, action modes. However, modern emergency workers like fire and police workers are discovering that 'post traumatic shock syndrome' (being very upset to you and me) means people can survive shock and disaster much better in the long run if they talk it through with sympathetic listeners soon afterwards. This applies to children as well as adults. Doctors, police and other workers who deal with ugliness and pain stay far kinder if they get support, doses of gentleness, themselves so they don't have to survive their work by switching off their feelings about it.

Going into our own deep inner places means trying to create 'perfect love and perfect trust.' It isn't instant, and once created it can falter, and need rebuilding.

I have come across ritual circles where I was being asked to do things that either frightened me, or made me very uncomfortable. I have always found it exceptionally difficult to relax in real darkness for example, and one ritualist wished us to do a meditation in complete and utter darkness. Another time, shortly after having a miscarriage, I felt extremely sensitive about being naked even with someone I loved and trusted, let alone anyone else.

Now I knew full well I could push through these fears if I really wished it. I have faced far far worse in my time in terms of 'ordinary' life experience. For example, like many other women, having a baby was an epic struggle of great pain and stamina. But that particular struggle was one faced in order to gain the greatest gift of all.

In contrast, when I was asked to go into a scary darkness, or work ritually naked when I felt sensitive about it, in neither case did it seem clear that I stood to gain a great gift. Certainly I could 'prove myself' and set my fear aside, but I had done that many times before.

Others might think I was silly, but balancing my fear of what others' think, against my fear of what they want me to do, is a miserable business.

Finally, as one of the others there tried hard to persuade me, why couldn't I just go along with it and see what I could get out of it? I wanted a better bet before making the effort. Basically I suppose I'm seriously against anyone else telling me what's good for me. I think my own feelings are the best guide on that.

It's not that I am always, always stodgy and careful either. I have felt swept up in a crazy certainty that I must do this thing that scared me a lot, because ... because .... well, I don't think at the time I could have explained. It was just a total mad certainty. Going self employed was like that. Getting married too, and then having a child. And my first sweat lodge done when I was quite ill! Creating the first national fully Pagan festival was another. These kinds of things have a sort of insane obviousness. As I leap into them I feel uplifted, dramatic, extremely clearheaded, and very sure that I must do it.

I have seen people come into my work affected the same way. They're scared of the step they're taking, but they gleam with excited power, and they feel strong in it, and sure of what they're doing. 'I don't know why, but I know it's right,' one says, and finds out later why. The brain is so much slower than the quickness of feelings. But we still sit together and listen to the fears even when it all starts in a blaze of passionate commitment.

This, however, is an occasional experience, not an everyday guide. Perhaps because it is exciting it can be easy to slip into the habit of confronting the edges of fear as a habit. Buzz. Buzz. I'm so brave.

Fear is a powerful protector and guide. Deep within, we know just how much we can handle. Fear sets out the limit as we approach our own boundaries. 'Where there is fear there is power' says Starhawk. Because here where fear speaks loudest is where we can go on further to open up new places we have not been before.

But who says we have to do it NOW? Where does it say I am wrong or worthless if I don't rush? On the contrary, if I respect my fear, sit with it, listen to it, at the edge of my world, isn't that brave?

Whatever I speed past I don't see clearly, don't feel very much. Anyone knows this who rips a plaster off fast, or has jumped quick into cold water. This is fine when a moment's unpleasantness such as these, is followed by immediate relief and comfort.

In the adventures of the soul, nothing guarded by fear is a minor matter.

A different courage

Allow fear to speak. The body will go still, and colder. I feel lost, cold inside. I panic, but let myself slow down and stay. The body begins to shake delicately. I moan, softly, jerkily. It's all very very unpleasant. I go still, then begin the shaking again. What I am afraid of flashes across my mind again and again. But then as I patiently sit with this deep visitor, the shakiness dies away, the flash images subside. I go limp and feel nothing at all. This can repeat several times.

Now I begin to warm up again, and a feeling of gentle power washes me. A peaceful, sensitive feeling arrives, and I know that very soon now I am ready to go forward, without fear, in new strength. And that I will not have to fight this fear again because this place has become a friend.

This takes more courage than shoving through fast. Sometimes the needs of life mean I must use the shoving way to get ordinary things done. But that has not dissolved the fear, only skipped it, so sometime later the work with the fear waits to be done. I've noticed people who make a habit of skipping fear are not kindly, because they have so little pity on themselves or others.

In ritual, we are trying to create 'perfect love and perfect trust.' We can fake it, and go through with doing things we don't like, or fear, or doubt. That will not reach the flowing, delicate power of the purest magic. It will bring us a feeling of achievement, and pride, which are good to feel, but not deep safety and trust.

So I am asking you to respect your fear as a friend, and not to do what it counsels you not to do, until you are at peace with it, and ready to go on. Some people, a lot of men, and women who have put much effort into their independence, are so concentrated on being tough, effective and sensible, that they actually get very disconnected from their fear. If you pride yourself on your strength and lack of wishy washy wimpiness, it would be worth giving yourself a bit of extra attention on this one. The list of common human tensions and fears below, like strange people, strange places, darkness etc affects us all, because we are all basically animals. We may have learnt to be strong and ignore them, actually not feel them, but they are still there and will generate tension in our bodies, and in other indirect ways.

To reach that really deep state of perfect love and perfect trust, where the power flows at its best, you may need to actually pretend that you are more sensitive to the flashpoints of fear than you actually are! Check the flashpoint list, and put in gentle reassurances in how you're doing things, AS IF you are more tense than you are. This way, the hidden crevices of you that you are not consciously aware of, will receive the reassurance, and you'll release even more power than the straightforward 'go ahead and do it, I can handle it fine' approach.

It follows that we have no right to ask others to ignore their fear either. In dealing with others' fear we cannot consult the sure guide of feeling, because others' feelings are closed off to us.

Flashpoints of fear

There are a number of basic things that so many humans share because they come from our most ancient past before we were human.

STRANGE (NEW TO ME) PLACES make us tense. I always give people extra time to get used to my temple, and as a guest I need the same. In a new place you are entitled to stay closed, and only open out gradually.

STRANGERS are a very basic fear. All over the world the stranger is treated carefully, with taboos and etiquette designed to help both sides move past their fear. Our Western custom of shaking hands goes back to showing that the knife hand is empty. Take as long as you like - and a bit longer, to assess new people.

NEW ACTIVITY is challenging and stressful so check if anything on your menu is not familar. Any new act needs to be introduced slowly, and time allowed for fumbling and awkwardness. If you're trying to get a friend to share an activity with you, show what is done yourself in a slow, exaggerated way, answer questions patiently, and always praise the first attempt. You can help them get it really right later.

DARKNESS of course, is a very common, ancient fear, which we share with most animals. Looking away from whatever light there is, helps the eyes adjust; it's surprising how darkness turns out to be just darker after a few minutes wait. But don't push your limits on it unless you wish it.

KNIVES although part of the influential Wiccan tradition, can sometimes cause problems. Among those who use knives for real, one never turns the back on a knife bearer. Although an athame (magical knife) is not supposed to be sharp, it may be pointed, and its shape suggests violence. An old Celtic tradition tells us a knife must never be drawn out without taking blood: its owner must give it a small nick of one's own therefore - a graphic reminder of the nature of a knife.

LOUD NOISE, though a joy to some, can terrify others. Those whose past holds a noisy bully will be sensitive to this. If your needs are for the gentler sounds, work with what works for you.

THE UNEXPECTED was already mentioned by way of the law of Preparation. Knowing what's going to happen as much as possible helps me relax about it.

TOUCH, except on hands, and lower arms, is stressful to some, especially anyone who has survived sexual pain. Men who wish to be considerate can ask clearly if their touch is welcome saying 'May I take your hand?', or putting out their own hand and waiting for the woman to take it. 'May I hug you?' is also very considerate, rather than assuming a liberated attitude to touch that crushes choice for the other person. And women can awaken men's sensitivity a lot, by treating them as the delicate creatures they are, even if they are hiding it all too well. Naturally I am not suggesting gentle treatment for some clumsy idiot who has bruised your dignity, unless you're in a very sunny mood at the time.

Anyone, man or woman, who does not respect your physical dignity, even in petty ways, deserves a sharp comment to help them grow up.

NAKEDNESS of course is ruled by taboos, and we're kidding ourselves if we say they don't matter. Working 'skyclad' is a genuine Craft tradition, representing equality and truth, but it doesn't suit everyone. I've seen earnest witches working skyclad with stiff armoured bodies that dare not touch each other in a relaxed way. It would be better to have kept their knickers on and felt more naked as people. A good witch is not necessarily a naked witch.

It's surprising though how rapidly the feelings of discomfort about being naked wear off if you're new to it. It usually takes about 15 minutes to get over the nerves and discover that it's all right after all.

If you'd like to try it:

1) Don't work your first rite naked, let the Circle become familiar first.

2) Have a Magical Bath to prepare, put on one loose garment afterwards you can easily remove without fuss. Hopping about on one foot struggling with zips doesn't help one feel relaxed and at

one with the universe.

3) Purify clothed, decide on a point in the preparatory stages when you will disrobe.

Working with anyone else women obviously feel sensitive about being unclothed. The Veto described a little further on should help. When menstruating you may feel an especial need to stay veiled, or you may like to reveal your splendour, blood streaked and all. A middle road is to wear a red ribbon or cord.

Men are often assumed not to have problems with nakedness, but of course they are sensitive too. Fears of having an all too obvious erection are common. It rarely happens; the mind is in a relaxed, rather different state. If it does, this is a sight well pleasing to the Goddess who created it; the worst you should get from companions is a friendly giggle. Under this fear lurks another - of not having an erection - for after all should not a properly red blooded male arise eagerly in the presence of nakedness? Properly red blooded males, in my own quite extensive experience, respond differently depending on tiredness, state of mind, what they feel is expected of them etc. A salute of the penis can easily be nervous politeness! A lack of one does not at all mean a lack of maleness.

Ultimately one of the finest penis teachings is they rise, or not, when they will, very much as free spirits.

DEEP WATER, CLOSED IN PLACES, DARKNESS, ANIMALS

Trancework needs to take account of these common fears. Check beforehand if anyone is sensitive to any of these triggers. If so, ladle out the reassuring language ('an underground place with a cosy feel to it, with a little draught coming in from above...' or 'friendly waters where you can see the pebbles clearly on the bottom' or use another pathworking instead. (see Trancework p 95)

These, then, are the flashpoints of fear.

STRANGE PLACE	THE UNEXPECTED
STRANGER/S	LOUD NOISES, BANGS
NEW ACTIONS	TOUCHING
DARKNESS	NAKEDNESS

IMAGES: DEEP WATER/ ENCLOSED SPACE ETC

WEAPONS, KNIVES

As a general rule, I think putting more than an absolute maximum of two flashpoints in one ritual is a recipe for trouble. Working alone, check your own feelings carefully for how comfortable you feel.

Even if you restrict what is involved to two flashpoints or one, it's a sensible kindness to check with those present if they are happy and consent to participate in what you propose. Fear not spoken will dull and drag on the energy you want to lift and fly on.

The Veto
At House of the Goddess I operate an absolute veto system. Where even one withholds consent, it is dropped. We try not to argue. Pushing and persuading someone to go ahead will only get a fake cooperation, and the inner levels of ritual know a fake and won't work with it. You actually have some chance of someone freely changing their minds if you instantly and completely respect their hackles. Given an absolute veto, a person feels strong, sometimes strong enough to give up the veto!

It seems unfair and frustratng to work hard on designing a ritual, carefully fitting it round the needs of those who are going to do it, only to have someone come up with unexpected bugs that tear holes in it. Try not to feel too hurt or annoyed. You can't possibly be expected to know all the sensitivities of those you work with, even if you know them quite well. Only they know their own limits, so all you can do is ask. By doing so you show your mature skill as a ritualist, and as an organiser.

Children
For years I have taught 'In the Circle you can't do it wrong,' and I still uphold that. However, I did not seriously expect people to throw the baby out with the bath water when freeing themselves from unnecessary inhibitions.

I was very upset by one particular Halloween circle I attended where everyone was asked to bring a sharp knife which turned out to be for carving pumpkins. This was a lovely idea, except that there were about five small children among us. I just managed to stop one little chap from picking up a knife by the sharp end.

By contrast I have fond memories of a children's Yule, where each child lit three small nightlights in honour of the newborn Sun/son. The blaze of many small flames on a silver circular dish lit a ring of entranced small faces. Each child was under five, one barely one year old. But each was held and guided by a protective adult guardian.

In fairness to the organisers of the first example, it is only in the last few years that we have as Pagans been learning how to include our children in our Circles, and celebrating our faith in families instead of as isolated individuals or adult covens. Some mistakes from inexperience were bound to happen, and helped later projects to be more sensible, like the Yule that was so beautiful.

The Halloween idea could have been fine; some kitchen knives could have been put in one place till needed, and then replaced. While in use, each knife could have been entrusted to a guardian.

The guardian idea is very important at children's circles. So is clear division of adult event, children's event or mixed event. It's the mixed event that is the hardest, because adults and children do have very different needs in some areas. Activities that both enjoy, like singing, drumming, dancing, invocations need to be emphasised, while meditations are kept short, and other work acted out rather than speechified. It seems peculiar to invite children only to shush them, so try to treat the children as honoured guests like anyone else. If a temple is a playroom for grownups, it would be nice if it could be one for children too. This may mean a rite of chaos, but this is primeval energy after all.

But if this all just makes you shudder, don't disrespect your own needs for a childfree Circle. Perhaps you could help towards the cost of the babysitters that others will have to provide in order to make you comfortable.

Safety must always be pinned at the child's level, with attention always to the capacity of the youngest present. Fire safety with candles and incense is the usual main worry; all that needs to go up off the floor, on steady surfaces.

The Yule circle referred to cast the circle with blowing bubbles at the Air quarter, a red fluffy dragon paraded about for Fire, toy fish splashed in a bowl of water, and trolls/ gnomes cuddled for Earth.

SAFE & UNSAFE MAGIC

When students of magic, or divination etc, ask me anxiously about the dangers of getting in too deep, I can usually reassure them that far from skidding suddenly into uncontrolled powers, the problem is overwhelmingly about coaxing our safety censors into opening the doors of perception just a tiny crack. The lifelong learned 'sensible self' in our society is so powerful that its protection ensures very effectively that fledgling adepts cannot run before they can crawl. They can get a bruise or two:- a headache, an unpleasant dream, a bit of dizziness. But this hardly rates the dire warnings current in some circles.

The reverse problem is frequent: the poor student must patiently stick at it, practising exercises while not at all sure if anything is going to happen, getting rather bored. Not quite the instant searing experience so beloved of popular drama.

While much of my effort goes into reassuring people that exploring a natural part of human experience is harmless, there are some situations of serious concern which can and do produce unacceptable risk.

Magical mirror

Where magical practice rebounds on the practitioner it happens because the methods of magic give us a faithful reflection of our inner states. Problems occur with a beginner full of tension, fear, nightmare images, and guilt, such as are produced by beliefs in sin and devil. These beliefs crash back on him or her, but amplified by the hypnotic power of the method used. Results can be fits of intense hysteria, depression, acute anxiety, hallucinations, poltergeists, even self mutilation.

Slow learning

The major protection against all this is that magical methods such as Tarot, Runes, Astrology etc require months to learn even the basics of how to use them. During this learning period the student has time to pass slowly and thoroughly through their fears and apprehensions, getting used to and familiar with what s/he is doing, so that by the time anything significant occurs, s/he is a relaxed and positive bundle which does not fuel the nightmare engine.

Those who believe in ...

On the other side, the major factor in a destructive experience, are those religious teachings which scarify about sin and hell. Those who believe in Satan and demons will meet them. Those who don't, don't. Near death experiences where people 'die' medically, or go into deep coma, but then after a short time return, have given us their reports of what happens immediately after death. Reports reflect closely the accustomed beliefs of the person concerned. The Christian meets Christ or the Madonna, the non-believer a loved one, a Buddhist meets Buddha; these persons act as guides across rivers, bridges, gulfs, through tunnels or gates.

Those who believe they will be judged and punished experience that; those who believe in self assessment experience that.

Many people who think they are free of demonic beliefs, still had them drummed well in during childhood. It is not enough to ignore such deep mind shaping. Such beliefs lie there, waiting to frighten us, just when we are feeling low, or when we explore deeper into our own minds. The detached cynic can suddenly find themselves thumped by unwelcome discoveries. The answer can only be to face one's inner programming with honesty and courage, and to rework it into a more nourishing spirituality. Denial alone ('I've rejected all that stuff from my background') is arid, and cannot offer a solid help in time of trouble. One way to effect this personal healing is in supportive therapy, or work with a gentle spiritual advisor, - or sometimes a devoted lover can provide inspiration and loving support. The more healthy meditation and ritual you can do by yourself, building your own way forward, the better. Exploring myths, images and symbols that do not tell you you are unworthy, is the key work you can do on your own.

Young people, of course, are closer to childhood bullying by the sellers of nightmares. When younger we have not yet built our own inner security to defend ourselves. Bravado is a pathetically brittle shield against inner fears.

Again, the necessarily slow training in most magical techniques allows teacher and student, or the student alone, to realise gradually that these terrors are there, just below the surface of our more 'grown up' beliefs. Step by step they can be gently but firmly reassured, and the bogies sent into leisure fantasy where they belong. The very tension produced by such beliefs will squash the early steps in magical work; the learner is thus kept safely neutralised until the frighteners evaporate, in their own time. Sometimes, this stage is so boringly unproductive that the student gives up in disgust - another natural protection!

The instant method

The obvious loophole is if a particular method is instantly easy to use. That means there can be no neutral period in which bogeys can be challenged and put to rest. Quickly learned techniques are variations on dowsing, (pendulums, some crystal work, ouija), candle magic, scrying and basic hypnotism, all knacks which can be rapidly acquired. But only hypnotism and ouija can really be seen as dangerous.

Dowsing, water divining, pendulums, crystal work, candle magic, scrying are all easy to learn in outline. But as my colleague Marian Green wryly comments "Most magic is easy to learn in one weekend - then go and practice for 20 years!" Getting any particularly challenging results only comes after skill builds up slowly with practice; allowing time to adjust one's attitudes if necessary. Also all these are usually solitary arts so the practitioner only has to cope with the product of his/her own skill.

Hypnotism is a whole field in itself; one hopes that regulation of its practice is imminent, as its misuse does not harm the practitioner, but an innocent partner. However it has become largely the concern of the therapy community, so is not my central concern here.

Ouija

Ouija is a remarkably easy technique to learn. But because it is typically done by a group it challenges each individual involved with the combined force of the group capacity. People in the group may not know each other well, with all the hidden human nerves that usually carries.

Moreover, the 'cop out' attitude a simple group mechanism promotes i.e. 'well I'm not psychic so if anything happens it'll come out of the others doing it' actually helps each individual into a prime state of relaxed expectancy - ideal for magic to occur. The fact that these sessions often take place in a non-serious situation, often a party, when everyone feels playful, also promotes the uninhibited attitude which stimulates intuitive power. Attempts are usually made late at night when darkness or low lighting has stimulated the hormone melatonin, another major aid for magical capacity.

Add in a frequent lead up of horror stories told with widened eyes, lowered voices, deepened breathing and collective frisson, and there's a good dollop of group hypnotism going on.

And last but not least, many such events are laced with alcohol and/ or potent modern designer drugs that would buckle most self respecting shamans at the knees!

To summarise, ouija is a crude, easy technique almost anyone can learn in minutes, allowing no adjustment period in which to release fears and fantasies. Unlike other easy methods which are mainly done alone, ouija is practised by a group, so each is flung into a pool of group power. Each can expect something to happen without the limits of their own capacity, so they are not restrained by their inbuilt cynicism about their own powers. Dramatic atmosphere through shared colourful stories, a relaxed 'silly' feeling reducing ordinary inhibition, late night melatonin hormone enrichment, and the underlying intense loosening of alcohol or drugs - it's hardly surprising some nasty ouija incidents happen.

And of course, among a group of teenagers, the sexual component is at its biological peak, mixing another powerful excitement and boost into an already volatile pot.

In a different society, less bedevilled by fundamentalist Christian teachings, we could perhaps leave our young people to experiment fairly safely with the contents of their minds. But there are those who make it their life's work to ensure that ghastly beliefs about sin, judgement, hell Satan and self hating guilt are well lodged within us. They are especially enthusiastic about infecting the young and vulnerable, our children.

In view of this we must do what we can to educate people about the function of magic as a mirror of the self within, the especial dangers of fundamentalist teachings, and of instant techniques like ouija. In doing so, it is important not to glamourise ouija, so as not to actually attract more people to it. It is certainly true that people of any age whose lives include friends, some natural sexuality, creative personal beliefs and some real self respect, are unlikely to be tempted by the sleazy lure of demons; it is the more pathetic, immature people who are the ones at risk.

DRUGS

To some drugs are anathema; no real Pagan would use any stimulant at all to assist magic, ritual or trance, they would insist. To others drugs are an ancient, honourable part of our traditions.

It is not for me to pronounce finally on the matter. In a community of spiritual adults, you must decide what suits your path for yourself.

What I can offer is a bit of helpful information if you want to try shamanic herbs; and a theory of exactly why drugs are either not a good idea at all, or need very sensitive, careful handling.

Peak experiences

All of us sooner or later have what Maslow calls 'peak experiences.' These are uplifting moments of pure understanding and oneness; or profound images which enfold us in total love. They can happen without fuss, while lying in a garden, or sitting by the sea, or doing something restful and everyday.

Drugs stimulate these feelings, or uncover them in our total perceptions. With the drug we are hurried, pushed or even exploded into the magical state. It would seem a helpful job they do to ensure we get over our obstacles to have these important experiences.

When the peak occurs naturally, we can usually look back and with hindsight see that it was the result of a long process building in our lives for weeks, months, sometimes even years. It's as if thousands of little cogs and gears, or pieces of our personal jigsaw, have fallen into place, in order that the peak can happen. The jigsaw makes a support web all ready for the peak moment to happen.

I use the same idea in healing when I spend a session or two, or more if necessary, preparing someone for an intense shift. Thoroughly sorting out thoughts about intense feelings, making clear exactly how they can be safe, even when allowed to explode, means a session which later erupts can be really and fully cleansing. Unfinished bits don't get left behind, neither does shame.

Without such a careful build up, a sudden peak can crash on to a personal base which is not ready and not strong enough to accept the experience without fear and shock, and then learn from it.

Drugs create a sudden peak, whether or not we are ready to have one.

This may help explain why we often can't remember what we knew under drugs; why we can panic under them; why their effects sometimes weaken us and sometimes strengthen us. It is worth considering that the blocks and barriers in our minds are always there to protect us from what we are not strong enough to handle. Nature is not stupid.

Fast, invasive methods of penetrating our barriers can cause great distress, particularly without knowledgeable, kindly follow up and support, as well as the same kindness beforehand. This applies as much to hypnosis as to drugs, and to any instant type of mental remedy. Even drums and chanting can be a too strong opener if someone is feeling fragile.

However, before you dismiss me as a stuffy expert and killjoy, I do think a sensible approach to such things can work well.

Shamans, shamanic herbs

Before using any shamanic herb or mushroom, check your health carefully. If you have the slightest tickle of a cold threatening, or any other physical weakness, leave it out. If you're upset about love, career etc and feeling low, best not, unless you want to be brave and use a trance to ask for guidance. In that case don't pretend you're doing anything else though.

Basically, only go ahead if you feel well in mind and body, so you're approximating that prepared web of strength which would occur naturally. Begin from strength; walk after that in sensitivity. The more delicate you allow yourself to be the more you will find.

Shamans the world over certainly use various herbs, mushrooms, even snake venom to induce the 'flying' or trance state. The risks which can accompany such aids are often seen as the challenge or price of the job. The shamanic task is sometimes, though not always, intended to be a journey by the shaman to the place of the dead. As the ancestors who observe all, the dead can guide us through difficulty. They can also be expected to feel parental and protective about their descendants. Travelling to the dead might be expected to carry a certain amount of risk of not coming back, so dangerous drug side effects are not considered to be unreasonable in these cultures.

However such practitioners spend several years building up their immunity to the poisons they take, by taking small amounts and increasing the dose bit by bit.

ANY SHAMAN WOULD BE DISGUSTED by anyone who just used shamanic herbs to make a cocktail to get stoned. This would be seen as someone being a sick child unable to grow up.

Where there is no trip to the dead involved there is still a shift or crossing to alternate reality; something to be as carefully prepared for as we would for a journey abroad. The shaman learns the geography of the other places from a teacher or from fellow shamans, together with warnings about the tricky bits.

If you wish to follow this type of shamanism, study the herbs involved carefully. They have very individual effects, so what has a mild result on your friend could have you hung over a toilet bowl in painful meditation for a day or so. Experiment with small amounts to start with, to find out how each herb affects you.

Don't mix herbs until you've tried out each one on its own and found it reacts well with your system. Don't mix them with alcohol, or any of the modern drugs.

Shamanic herbs are legal, and safe - they won't kill you. But they can make you violently ill if you are careless with them.

As you work with each one, make drawings of it, either realistic drawings of the plant, the crumpled leaves, or completely imaginative patterns which show how its spirit comes to you. Ask the spirit of the herb to visit you in vision and teach you of its nature. It may come as a person, an animal or a symbol. Treat it respectfully if you want to be treated gently in return.

Some excellent guidance, both practical and spiritual, can be found in the earlier Don Juan books by Castaneda. The classic 'Doors of Perception' by Huxley is also still useful teaching.

As well as shamans in other cultures, European witches had their own trance herbs. The most famous is 'flying ointment' which has several recipes. The commonly reported sexual experiences which arise in flying visions are very likely to result from using the ointment as a vaginal balm. What people meet and find in their visions generally though is heavily influenced by what they expect to happen. The inner world can only speak to us in a language we understand already.

High magicians such as Aleister Crowley have rather given the occult use of drugs a sleazy reputation. He became addicted to cocaine and other drugs through being given them as medicines for his acute asthma at a time when doctors made such mistakes.

He was also an outsider personality, many years ahead of his time in his thought, which is a stressful place to be. In the '60s and '70s he would have seemed unremarkable. However, those who now admire his drug excursions and try to copy him do not have the same justification.

In a group circle, agree beforehand if shamanic herbs, alcohol etc is acceptable to all. Nothing should be taken before the Chalice is passed once; and only after that if all present are happy about it. Drugs often seem to join us together, when in fact we have gone into separate bubbles. A shared circle is a mockery if we seal ourselves off from one another; it would make better sense to make separate individual circles, and more honest.

Yes or No?

For those who dislike drug use, speak your mind. Do not go into a circle with those who take them. Your mutual uneasiness will make shallow or unpleasant magic. Better to withdraw and find others in greater affinity with you, or work alone.

For those who wish to use drugs, experiment step by step with care. Respect your body and mind; check your health, mood and present company before taking anything. Take one thing at a time, in small quantities, until you know its effects. If mixing ingredients, and using drums or hypnotic techniques too, do so with people you trust, in familar surroundings. Work with each plant spirit with respect, getting to know them as people.

If using mushrooms, gather them with expert help only. The effects of the right ones are mild, but there are others which look very similar which can cause serious illness or death.

Cigarettes are drugs too. Smoking before a ritual effectively seals you off from some of its effects. Think about how much you want to be cut off.

THIS IS MY TRUTH; WHAT'S YOURS?

TRANCEWORK

Making journeys into other worlds, other realities, is a core
magical skill. There are many pathworkings, guided
visualisations, inner journeys etc in books and on tapes you can
use, but you can also make your own to use by yourself or with
others.
All the names mean much the same thing; light trance or
daydreaming is created, and a series of ideas or pictures suggested
to make a sequence intended to be healing, inspiration, guidance
etc.

Visualisation?

'Guided visualisation' has the unfortunate association that you've
got to be able to visualise in order to do this craft. About a third
of all people don't visualise, or not at all well. It doesn't mean
they can't trance. A non-visualiser, providing they've not been
tensed up by suggestions that they're 'not good at visualising' can
receive the sequence through feelings, sometimes noises, smells
etc. Often I've done a very alive journey - I saw little of what
happened but I could describe it quite clearly if asked.

Visualisation, or seeing, is the most dominant, hunter skill, linked
with scholarly work like reading. Perhaps this is why so much fuss
is made about it in our society.

Control

Some people have difficulty going into trance because their
experience of life has given them good reason to prefer to stay in
control. If this is you there are several things you can do to ease
the restriction your guardian self sets on you. One is to sit up, or
only recline comfortably. We all feel safer and more in control if
we stay upright. The other is to tell yourself repeatedly and firmly
that you are staying in charge all through this experience. Choose
a signal - moving your hand, or saying NO - and tell yourself that
when you do this you will immediately come out of any tranced
state.

As a matter of fact, people have efficient protectors in their own
minds that shut off the experience if something disturbs or is
likely to upset them. The problem is really to open the gates of
perception, not to keep them closed to protect us. People drift off

to sleep, or just don't remember what the trance guide said after a certain point. But if this happens to you, it can also be a much needed doze when you're tired.

Distress

Occasionally, someone will come out of a trance tearfully, or distressed. They may have some bad dreams, or a headache or some worrying emotional reactions for a while. This may be because the trance was designed carelessly, and has triggered a flashpoint of fear. But whether this is why or not,, I have such respect for the protective guardians of the mind, having battled with their stranglehold in so many people for so many years, that I judge that an upset reaction means the upset was very close to coming out anyway. The trance triggered something that was due for an airing. Unless you are determined to think that emotional states are a 'bad thing' this means a kind of healing release has been helped to occur.

However, the fact that people are fairly well defended cannot excuse a pathworker or trance guide being careless about people's fears. And always make sure you are able and willing to help people express their feelings fully, before you throw things at them as a guide. (A spot of co-counselling would help you a lot if you want to be a guide.) If people are stimulated into some release but then don't do it properly, they choke off and feel worse. They also learn to distrust letting their feelings out, because the incomplete release is uncomfortable. Such an experience makes it harder to reach a needed healing than when they started.

Some people respond well to group trances, where the shared experience helps to overcome doubts or lack of confidence. Others feel much more relaxed doing it alone.

Using tapes & books

When using a trance written in a book, you need to follow it several times until it's very familiar and you can go through its sequence without stopping to check the book. So book ones are only worth trying if they look really good.

Using a taped trance, listen to the person's voice a bit first before you buy it or use it. Does this voice make you feel good? Safe? Free -er? If not find someone else's tape. The trance works through your very personal instinctive reactions, so respect them. Would you get what you want more easily working with a female or male voice? older or younger? your own or another culture?

The whole art of a trance is to evoke your own independent, inner world responses, to the outline you're given. Avoid any that give you such a wealth of detail that there's no room for you to imagine what kind of .... what colour ..... they said ...... and so on.

The best trances give you skimpy information, with plenty of pauses to let your mind pick up what it's given, and use it. Once you relax and go into any trance state, you slow down a lot, so the trance speaker needs to give you a good deal of extra time to react, or else you're just beginning to when the next suggestion crashes in.

Many trancemakers confuse an inner journey with a storytelling. A storytelling keeps you fed with images without stopping, rather like a film. You can lazily let the storyteller create reality for you, and enjoy it. But just because it is someone else's reality, however attractive or clever, it cannot touch you as deeply as a technique that calls up your most private parts and weaves them into something beautiful and powerful. An inner journey, or trance, is not like a film; it's like a slide show with long silent gaps for you to fill with your own contributions.

A trance also usually gives you an introductory relaxation step by step. Soothing words help you drift into a safe, enjoyable mind state. If you use a book pathworking, it may not provide this on the same page.

A good relaxation sequence will take you soothingly through an almost boringly detailed 'relax your feet' pause, 'relax your ankles' pause, and so on. Once you find a relaxation sequence that you like, you could make your own recording. Then you can record a trance from a book or other tape following it. Reading it yourself, speak very very very very slowly! When you think you're speaking slowly, you're not, because of your own self conscious nerves, so slow down. Let your voice sway and sing a bit, as if soothing a child or an animal.

Without the important relaxation work, even a very powerful trance will have much less effect. This is the same thing as the slow careful build up in 4 stages for Circlework ritual, which transforms simple working into transcendence. I use about 15 minutes relaxation to 5 -10 minutes trance. A good return from a trance would be some kind of Communion - cup of tea or coffee and toast, maybe?

Drums

An effective alternative to the lengthy relaxation sequences through feet, ankles, knees, thighs etc is drumwork. You need any kind of small skin drum that has a note better than a short thud. The note should last a little.

Trying out a drum, if it's old, or the weather is dry, damp it a little with a damp (not wet) cloth, and it may sing better. If it's damp weather drums get soggy, and need holding near heat; right up to a radiator or over a fire. You have to try little bits of such treatment to get the timing of how much heat. Too much and the skin gets too tight and repeats of that will crack it.

You don't really have to know how to play it. Practise until you can keep up a steady bong! bong! bong! for a while almost without thinking about it. Then just relax and listen to the drum; you'll be away quite quickly. Use this by taping about 5 minutes of it at the beginning of a trance recording. Or do it live, then switch. Or just follow the drum on its own. People often like images of 'riding the drum' like a horse; or of going down into the earth.

DIY

1) If you do want to craft your own trances, don't forget those crucial pauses. And make your voice ridiculously SLOW. Do a full relaxation with pauses after every suggested station of the body. (Even if your central material is not brilliant, good preparation will ensure it has a good effect.) Go from feet to head, as feet are easier to relax first. Suggest that the outward breath go out more deeply.

2) Choose several comfort and safety words you like yourself, and sprinkle them all through with enormous generosity, such as 'safe, comfortable, gentle, pleasant, slow, supported, protected, kindly, lazy ...' Use them especially around any image that might be fearful on some level, like darkness, water (see Flashpoints p84).

3) Give a transition or crossing over image; walk in the woods; bridge; boat crossing; acquiring wings; or just go through the colours of the rainbow.

4) Make your key working very simple - don't try to be impressive because the deep self will just get bored with too much clever stuff and drift off. Choose one, two, three at most four images with grand pauses between.

5) Give a return warning - 'In a little while it's time to return' because one actually doesn't like coming back from these pleasant, relaxed levels.

6) Reverse your crossing over image. Say firmly 'When I say SEVEN you will be fully returned to ordinary consciousness, feeling relaxed and looking forward to the rest of your day.' Repeat this once more. Count slowly to 7.

Allow time for tea/ coffee, chat.

If you lead a group pathworking, if anyone is a bit upset at the end, let them talk about it, and try not to be too responsible. Your work was a trigger, their inner states are what it's really about. Respect that, don't let it guilt you.

The hardest thing about giving a trance is to keep going slowly to the end, with no reassurance that you're doing OK. (Are they polite & bored - or is it OK?) Sitting among silent bodies can be unnerving (Is anybody here with me?) One good sign is if they're not fidgety. But then some people just fidget.

Try not to feel rejected if someone says afterwards that they dozed off, or can't remember what you said. As above, that happens out of their own needs to curl up inside.

If you can, take a deep breath, and invite people to each tell you what they especially liked, and what they didn't like so much. This will give you far better teaching than I can about how things work. It's how I learnt how extraordinarily important the pauses are.

By getting nice comments, both you and the others feel more able to cope with the critical things. But these are the gold dust. Listen well, and learn from them to be good at your craft.

As you listen, breathe out deeply, and don't look at the speaker till they finish. Then, don't argue. Just say 'Thank you.'

DO WHAT I TELL YOU ONLY ONLY ONLY
IF YOU WANT TO

CRAFT (this section by Shan and John jointly)

It's not for nothing we call our particular kind of Paganism 'the Craft.' We're talking about a Craft attitude, a craftworker's way. That is, everything is a craft. Everything, no matter how enormous it looks, can be learned. Each craft has its guidelines or rules to indicate how to do it well. And most crafts benefit a lot from a personal teaching by someone who knows their stuff. Apart from being up on the dodges and practicalities, a good teacher helps one's confidence over the sticky bits.

Everything is a craft. Including sex, leadership, the very personal skill of the emotions, housekeeping, parenting, magic and healing.

Some of us have an advantage over others on a particular craft; family traditions and heredity or sheer personal talent means we learn something faster, and can go further with it, and maybe enjoy it more. But everyone can learn just the basics of anything.

The Wicca revived the Craft when it almost died out earlier this century. They then sustained it and developed it into a powerful system during 30 years, up to the '80s, when most other Paganism was comparatively inactive. Because of this proud record Wiccans have a regrettable habit of speaking of Wicca as the whole Craft itself.

This is a shame, as it makes Wiccans appear arrogant and immature; reluctant to give due respect to other strands of the Craft tradition which differs from their own. (I hasten to add that not all Wiccans do this.) It's also a shame because it lets go the powerful teaching of craftworker in the very name of the Craft. 'Wicca' is specifically Saxon, and claims to derive from 'the Wise.' This tends to imply elite, trained scholars, with access to superior wisdom, with recognised status. In fact, Europe lost its native priesthood, the Druids, to Roman persecutions. We have suffered a great loss of spiritual leadership as a result, with poor substitutions for it later bringing an aggressive, highly political type of priesthood into being. What survived of Paganism was not all uneducated; a few aristocrats and church scholars preserved fragments of lost teachings. However, the majority of Pagan lore has survived through folk custom, a mass of everyday beliefs and practices connected with work, the home and family.

The wisewoman or cunning man was skilled with their hands at things like:- herbs, cooking, massage/ healing touch, metals (smithcraft), animal care, childbirth, practical nursing and the care of corpses. They were also necessarily good at understanding human relationships (psychology) culled from careful observation of their own local community.

Today we are in danger of losing our hands' power and delight, together with other skills such as voice, and body movement. In a time of professional art and laid on entertainment that crushes us into passive bundles, we need to remember and sustain our capacity for craft. The practical 'hobby' crafts actually teach us how to tackle the big ones like sex, leadership, parenthood, and politics.

There's something else. I have watched my little boy emerge from his own passive bundle stage of existence into confident, competent childhood. He plays. This is clearly serious stuff, done with fierce concentration, considerable patience and effort. He's learning survival skills. He does it by mimicking us. Overwhelmingly what he wants and is driven to do, is mimic. He also makes copies and models of the overwhelming things in the outside world he has to one day take charge of. I honestly think that humans are not the animal that thinks, speaks, uses tools or any of those theories. I think we're the playful animal which mimics others' skills. Whatever we do cleverly, we have copied from some other animal, either the idea, or the actual design, or both.

If I'm right, our craft heritage is not just a sentimental matter 'what a shame about television, people used to sing round the piano after supper', and 'aren't country crafts pretty, so quaint.' It's our key to survival, teaching us to use what we have to make what we need.

A WITCH USES WHAT COMES TO HAND.

I certainly like practical people with craft training of some kind in any tight situation - they're better at coming up with solutions using whatever's available.

There is a Craft tradition that a trainee must make their own tools. Perhaps making everything you use in the Circle is a tall order. But I think honouring the tradition with at least one set of hand made supplies from your own efforts is essential to consider.

On my Circlework courses I ask each person to make something, or 'do something creative' on a given theme. Sometimes I suggest the Elements, sometimes Goddess and God, sometimes the Circle.

Over the years I've seen kites, mobiles, poems, songs, dances, clothes, cakes, models, pictures, bags, photo essays, woodcraft, metalcraft, pots, sculptures in children's clays, plaitings, baskets, casseroles, drinks, sweets, miniature gardens, pathworkings, stories, jewellery, incenses, candles ...... I always invite people to either use a craft they know, or risk exploring another they don't know. People often go through nerves. But it's been a great delight to all participating, not least myself, as the circle fills with life through shared creativity.

USING INCENSES

Incenses have been used for thousands of years to influence the atmosphere of important events; before modern hygiene incenses masked crowd sweat smells! Most people are familiar with Indian joss sticks which are very pleasant. Real incense burnt on little charcoal cakes gives a much more pure and powerful fragrance. It is a bit fiddly compared to joss sticks, but well worth it. Real incense leaves its own natural atmosphere behind for several days, perfuming curtains, clothes and hair as well.

The choice of incense to use is a very personal one. There are Egyptian incenses, Celtic incenses, Nordic incenses, Arthurian incenses, New Age incenses, Meditation incenses, Astrological and planetary incenses, lots of Goddess or God incenses, incenses for the five Elements of the Circle, Magician's incenses ... Many suppliers do a special service to make up an incense to your own wishes.

Like perfume makers, incense makers talk impressively about 'high notes' and 'base notes', and how they are blended. A good incense maker can pick out what's in an incense, because years of their art has so tuned their sense of smell. For most of us the important thing is how we respond intuitively to a smell; it is the sense closest to our instincts. You have to try out some and see how it feels. The names they are given often affect how we react to them a lot as well.

Incense is made up of herbs, tree resins, flowers and oils, often blended according to astrological correspondences. The result is like a rough crumbled cake, with hints of colour in its grains.

This raw incense will not burn by itself: you need a packet of charcoal blocks. These are fat little discs of black, chalky charcoal.

Charcoal is fine grade coal, so it burns very hot, once lit. You need a safe container, made of metal, thick pottery or stone. Don't use an ashtray because they are usually not strong enough to stand the heat, and will break apart. This can mean a burn on the table, shelf or cloth it was on, or the start of a fire.

Metal containers get very hot too, so put them on a tile or brick, unless they have legs.

The safest container is a bowl half filled with sand or earth.

LIGHTING CHARCOAL Open the silver foil of a packet, and take one brick out. If you can store the packet in an airtight jar. Have the container ready to hand.

Matches do light charcoal, but it's a great deal easier with a taper, or spare candle. Hold the brick in thumb and forefinger on one side, put the other side in the flame. Hold it there until sparks start spitting off it - they won't hurt you.

Keep holding the brick in the flame after the sparks start, until they start to move away from the edge of the disc towards your fingers holding it! The sparks move quite slowly, though. The part that is alight behind the sparks goes blacker.

Now put the brick down on the sand or earth, upright like a wheel, standing on the part that's sparking. This will draw the fire up through the rest.

If the sparks stop before their advancing line reaches the other side of the disc, put the flame to it again. This can easily be necessary if the packet of charcoal has been open for a week, or even a day or two in damp weather. The charcoal absorbs damp amazingly quickly.

Charcoal, while burning, will also absorb any odours in the room very thoroughly. It's much cheaper, more natural, and genuinely clean, than any air freshener on the market.

Once the brick has burnt through, the sparks stop. Knock it over flat, with its little hollow all ready to act as a cup for the incense. The other side is flat.

It's now very hot so don't touch it with your hands. Tweezers are useful, or a spoon, or pocket knife.

Now you can put a pinch of incense in the hollow brick, and enjoy delicate tendrils of smoke spiralling through your room. Don't smother it; it's better to feed it again later. It will be ready for more about 15 -20 minutes later, and it will burn better if you push the debris left from the last pinch away - with tweezers, spoon or knife.

One block will burn for about an hour, so you can add different incenses if you like.

DON'T THROW THE REMAINS IN A BIN when you've finished. They can often look entirely dead but have a lot of fire in them. Either leave it to burn out by itself; if you're going to bed, if there are small children or lively animals likely to jog it, put the container in the sink, or tip the ashes into the toilet.

Although the first try or two is fiddly, the process of setting incense up acts as a preparing meditation. It slows you down, and reminds you by association of what you are doing. Try incense before meditation, ritual, sex, special discussions, a party ..... Don't light it just before a meal. Smell and taste are very close together, and the powerful smell of the incense will overpower your taste sense, so you can't enjoy the food.

THE SIMPLEST INCENSE to use is plain frankincense. The majority of incenses use it as a base, and it smells beautiful. It's associated with positive, hopeful attitudes, with wisdom, and birth. You can buy it cheaply in larger amounts from any traditional herbalist and some health shops.

The balancing incense is myrrh, a drier smell, less pretty, but excellent for purification work, banishing, cleansing, honouring the dark. It is associated with endings, death, mystery, and renewal.

Here are two basic incense recipes, courtesy of Nature's Bounty, Tooting, London:-

RITUAL WORK INCENSE One part Frankincense, one part Myrrh, one part Lavender, two parts Sage.

MOON INCENSE One part Sandalwood, half a part Eucalyptus gum, a quarter part Myrrh.

For excellent classic recipes and advice I recommend Herman Slater's 'Magickal Formulary' originally USA published.

CANDLEMAKING

Few rituals happen without candles, and they're surprisingly easy to make. They do need a careful attitude to safety though, because hot paraffin wax starts a fire easily.

The first steps kind of candlemaking is to get a packet or two of plain, white household candles, melt them down, and create your own shape and colour. Doing it this way means you have both wax, and wicks, cheaply to hand, without having to find a special shop.

Hobby shops sell kits of wax granules, wick thread, and dyes. For equipment you will need a heating pot, and moulds. If your kitchen doesn't have a fire blanket, get one (it should have one anyway).

IT'S BEST TO MELT THE WAX in a double boiler; i.e. a pot inside a larger pot of boiling water, but an ordinary pot can be used at a pinch. It must have a heavy bottom, to distribute the heat gently, and be steady standing. It should be a bit higher than it's wide. Use an old one, as it'll be a pain to clean afterwards. Preferably use one with a wood or plastic handle; or bind metal handles with strips of fabric, tied tight. A couple of heavy oven gloves are worth having.

MOULDS are interestingly available around the home. Cardboard toilet roll centres are popular, with a good size amd shape. They're not reusable though, as you peel them off. They also give a slightly textured finish, which some people like and some don't. Look around and you'll find various containers of suitable shape and size; eg mugs? Remember that thin plastic containers like yoghurt pots distort as the hot wax runs in, which can be nice if you like odd shaped candles.

BEFORE STARTING GET ALL CHILDREN OR ANIMALS OUT of the kitchen. Make sure they can't run in suddenly. If you are jogged or startled you could hurt yourself or them with nasty burns. A splash of hot wax on the skin is very painful. Worse, you could start a fire.

CLEAR A WORKING SPACE on table or worktop. Setting wax goes cool quite rapidly and you don't want to be distracted at the creative moment by things in the way. Put the moulds and dyeing discs (see below) ready. Check where the fireblanket is. Put any bottles of cooking oil, aerosols and other hazards a good long way away from the stove.

PUT THE WAX TO MELT IN THE POT. If you're melting ordinary candles, put them upright so you can pull the wick strings out as they begin to melt.

PUT THE POT ON VERY LOW HEAT. DON'T LEAVE TO DO ANYTHING ELSE even if it gets boring waiting, and don't read, except maybe to check this. Paraffin wax is the same stuff as firelighters, so you don't want a spill or boilover on to the gas or electric burner. DON'T TURN THE HEAT UP even if you get impatient. If you get really fed up, just turn it off completely. Put the pot outside to cool and set again. Find something more fun to do.

IF MELTING CANDLES, pull the wicks as soon as you can and push the candles down into the pot to be safe.

YOU CAN TELL WHEN IT'S MELTED because the opaque wax becomes a transparent liquid. In effect, you have a pot of hot liquid paraffin. Careful now.

DYES come supplied by candle-makers suppliers in discs of wax soaked with concentrated colour. A little of one of these goes quite a long way. Alternatively, you could try experimenting with ordinary cloth dyes. (I don't know how well this works, or what the result smells like burning.)

A THIN WICK in a fat candle gives a glow light. The middle burns down leaving walls of wax, making a natural lantern. A thicker wick creates brighter light, burns down quicker, burning the wax evenly all round.

RAINBOW build up layers of different colour in a row of pots. If each layer is set before the next is poured, the colours are clearly separated. If the second layer is poured on a half melted layer the two edges merge prettily.

WATER candles are made by dunking a half melted candle in a bucket of water and twirling it, holding it by the wick. Wings of wax swirl out around the bottom.

SCENTED candles add essential oils to the molten wax before pouring. Use quite a lot of perfume in the mix, or the candle smells lovely cold, but the scent will be destroyed in the flame. You have to fairly saturate with scent.

THE WORST CASE, WHAT TO DO IF IT ALL GOES "WHOOMF".
This is unlikely, especially if you follow the safety instructions
above. It's really no more dangerous than cooking with oil. But if
it does, all is not lost. It happened to my husband and he says: "If
you're not prepared to consider what you would do in the worst
case, you shouldn't be playing with pots of hot oil over a flame.
The vital thing is not to panic. If you work out in advance what
you will do, you won't waste time flapping.
YOU HAVE A LITTLE TIME. If a pot of molten wax catches
alight, the flame is certainly big, but it will be quite a while
before anything else catches alight. The danger to you is the
smoke. So have a quick go at getting the fire out. If that doesn't
work, leave it and call the Fire Brigade."
FIRST TURN OFF THE HEAT - THE STOVE, or it's very difficult
to put the fire out; if you do, it will flare up again.
NEVER THROW WATER ON AN OIL FIRE the water vaporises,
burning oil clings to the drops; it explodes spectacularly. USE A
DRY POWDER FIRE EXTINGUISHER if you have one - let fly at
the base of the fire from as close as you can get. SMOTHER THE
AIR SUPPLY WITH THE FIRE BLANKET, or with any large
heavy cloths you have. Don't remove them until long after it goes
out, or you risk spontaneous reignition. IF YOU CAN'T PUT IT
OUT FAST, LEAVE IT FOR THE PROFESSIONALS Or you risk
being knocked out by the smoke, and badly burned, or even risk
your life itself.
In spite of all that, this is the worst case situation,
very unlikely to happen if you follow safety instructions above.
Like magic, this is dealing with power, so we must respect its ways.

WOODWORKING

Gathering a wand from a tree is a traditional magical task. You
can sometimes find newly dropped wood especially after storms.
Runes are a native craft of this Land; simple, straight lines
making letter like shapes, cut on small discs or staves of wood.

If you cut or break wood from a tree or bush, ASK them if you
may do so first, or you can expect little help from your wand, or
runes. No matter how you desire a branch, ask several times if you
may take it, and be very sure the answer is yes.

The old lore of wands is that trees live very long lives, with slow,
healing rhythm   from our point of view. They observe much
from their rooted places. And each hazel, for example, is part of a
group hazel personality, connected with all other hazels, what
they have seen and what they know. Many people know how
comforting a tree is to talk to in time of need, and how they can
give guidance if one waits patiently, and slows down to listen.

All this is the gift of the wand, providing it comes with consent.
Our part of the bargain is to provide moving about, - seeing the

sights. So take your wand about to pay your dues; better still explain a bit what you're visiting. This informs the group tree mind of that wand, which in turn becomes more able to help us.

Wands are used formally in rites to direct and focus energy; longer ones are also useful for walking staves, or as support for the injured, tired and elderly.

In the symbolic Great Rite where the chalice represents the female, some witches use a knife, or athame, to represent the male. The male is then dipped into the female. However, others feel the knife is an overly aggressive symbol of the male, and would prefer the wood of a wand.

A shamanic wand is left with its bark intact, plus any small knobs and whorls. Larger twigs branching off are cut away with a sharp blade; often leaving a V shaped fork at the top for a horned wand. Bare parts can be stained or dyed. Rather than varnish, which seals the wood completely into a dead shell, why not oil it with teak oil, or furniture oil, which dries into a varnished look, protects the wood, but lets it breathe? You can decorate your wand with plaited ribbons, wools, feathers, small stones etc.

A more high magic wand is stripped, scraped smooth, sanded with three grades of sanding paper, perhaps dyed, and varnished several times.

Either type can be scored with symbols, runes, astrological signs, or plain bands, with a scalpel. This has a slot in it for changing its narrow blades, like a stanley knife, and there can be a choice of blades. A sharp penknife will do the larger bits of your design. It can help to draw what you want on paper, and press it round the wand: shapes look different bent round a curve.

MAKING RUNES

For Runecasting cut flat circles of wood like slicing a sausage. The Runes themselves are supposed to be incised with a knife point.

To practice, or write a Runic talisman, slice a thin branch or twig along its length to make a flat surface; incise Runes close together with a sharp knife.

Choose wood according to need e.g oak for strength, willow for acceptance and healing, hazel for women.s work etc.

NOTE ON BUYING TOOLS:- Asking for tools in a DIY or handy shop used to be embarrassing and even hurtful, especially for women and novices. Men working in them used to ignore customers who were not obviously craftsmen or builders, and asked impossible questions without trying to be helpful at all.

Thankfully these were the bad old days, and competition to get customers has pushed these churlish clods out from behind their counters.

We have gone to considerable lengths to give you exact names of tools you need, so you can ask for them with confidence. The best shops are established ironmongers or tool suppliers where local people work who know their stuff, and are prepared to help you to get you back as a customer. Check the Yellow Pages; asking any handy or DIY types you know who they use and see which names come up several times.

The big discount houses with huge racks of stocks like Wickes and Do it all have clearly labelled shelves, and can be cheaper, but don't expect much from the assistants in help.

CLASSIC WOODWORKING GUIDELINES-

CHOOSE WOOD WITH CARE.

WORK WITH ITS GRAIN & SPIRIT

TAKE CARE OF YOUR TOOLS AND DON'T BLAME THEM

KEEP TOOLS SAFELY SHARP

FASTEN WOOD DOWN WITH CLAMPS AS YOU WORK IT

REMEMBER TOOLS ARE SHARP

"KEEP BOTH HANDS BEHIND THE CUTTING EDGE"

KEEP THE ELASTOPLAST & NEEDLE HANDY

CHOOSE WOOD WITH CARE Much of what you can buy is no good for crafting. The universally available white deal may be okay for knocking up a quick run of shelves, but it has a loose and wavy grain, is full of splits, knocks and shakes, and is incredibly frustrating for any sort of creative work.

Basic carving, to make a figurine, or sculptured shape, is very easy with balsa wood, so this might be a good starter. Unfortunately it's so soft it crumbles quickly.

The carver's wood of choice is lime. It works beautifully, takes a lovely finish, and is altogether a pleasure and a delight. Unfortunately, it is hard to come by, unless you are prepared to buy a chunk from a craft supplies shop, at great price. It might be worth investing in a little piece to begin with, on the basis that when you're learning a new skill, you don't want to be using a material which makes it more difficult.

There are various sources of good quality, well seasoned hardwood available, either cheap or free. 1) Fallen timber which has lain for a year or two is one. 2) Driftwood is another. 3) For the city witch, old furniture is a treasure trove. Pieces which are beyond repair as furniture can supply large chunks of the sort of wood you simply can't get today, in a variety of shapes. A flat piece from the back of a wardrobe can be transformed into a lovely picture carved in low relief. If you want to work in the round, a table leg can supply the raw material for a statue of the goddess, or the god. Always, there is the added delight that you are keeping the body of the tree-spirit in beloved use, and not causing any more trees to be cut down.

Old close-grained yellow pine is a nice wood. Ash has a grain so straight it could have been put in by a ruler. Some people swear by elm; personally, I think it is a wood which doesn't like people. Teak works nicely, and has a fine oiled finish.

110

Old mahogany (not the rubbish that goes by the name today) is a rich wood, full of the red heart of the sun. It is a little more difficult to work than some. If you don't treat it with respect, it is prone to splitting. But it can be worked up to a supremely beautiful finish. Did you know that a lot of mahogany was painted over, because it provided such a smooth surface as a base? If you come across old painted victorian furniture, there may be a treasure trove waiting to be revealed. King of the woods is the oak; strong, close grained, hard to work, but he gives lovely shapes without treachery, and lasts and lasts. Beware, old well-seasoned oak is as hard as iron. A lot of sweat will go into the finished item.

YOU HAVE TO COOPERATE
Some woodworkers delight in studying a lump of wood, watching and feeling the grain, allowing it to suggest the shape of an animal perhaps. Others already have an image in mind as they choose their wood. You have to cooperate with the grain of the wood. Once it was the body of a living being, and it still has a will of its own. Treat it with respect, and you can make anything. It can achieve an amazing variety of textures, from splintery-rough to silky-smooth. This is a very sensuous craft. With a little practice, you will find you can listen to the grain with your fingertips. But treat it without respect, and your lot will be splintered wood and cut fingers. Ignoring its nature means you'd be better working with plastic.

SAFETY WITH WOODWORKING is largely a matter of common sense. Secure the piece you are working on firmly, using a vice or clamps, so it doesn't skid about. Remember that many woodworking tools are edged, and as such potentially dangerous. They are perfectly safe, provided you treat them with respect.

ALWAYS CUT OR SLICE AWAY FROM YOUR OTHER HAND. As John's grandfather, who was a cabinetmaker, said, "Keep both hands behind the cutting edge". Stay alert as you work. It's very easy to forget, and be tempted by the convenience of holding the wood in an unsafe place. If the blade slips and jumps, you will stick it right into yourself.

IT IS SAID THAT A BAD WORKER BLAMES THEIR TOOLS. John's grandad commented tartly that only a bad worker let their tools get into the sort of state where they would let them down. He reckoned to spend five days a week working, and Saturday morning cleaning, sharpening, and oiling his tools.

REMEMBER THAT A VERY SHARP EDGE IS FAR SAFER than a blunt one. Accidents happen when the blade skids. A blunt blade takes extra pressure to drive it through the wood, which multiplies the risk that you may lose control of it. A properly sharp blade will slide through the wood with a feather touch, under careful control.

With all the care in the world, you will get a few small nicks, so keep the band-aids handy. Apart from anything else, it's a shame to spoil a nice job by leaking over it. Splinters are a common pest,

although in general, the better the wood you use, the fewer you
will get. Remove splinters by pressing one end, or poke out with a
needle sterilised in boiling water, or through a flame.

YOU CAN MAKE A START ON WOODCARVING with a good
quality penknife. You will need one with a strong blade, so that
you don't risk snapping it if you apply pressure. A scalpel can be
used for fine detail work. Blades come in all shapes and sizes.

If you get the bug, you will want a set of carver's gouges. These
look like deformed chisels, with the cutting edges in a variety of
cupped and skewed shapes, enabling you to acheive whatever
effects you like. The handles should be domed, broad and generous,
because a lot of the work is done with simple hand pressure, and
you don't want a handle which will dig into the palm of your hand
and raise painful blisters. If the work is not a pleasure, you are
unlikely to do it well. For cutting out larger pieces, you will also
need a wooden mallet to tap with. A beginner's set of decent
gouges costs about £20.

You can reduce the investment by trying the tool discount houses,
but beware of rubbish. It is a good principle to buy the best
quality tools you can afford. It is usually better to buy one nice
tool, than two poor ones. A good tool will be unlikely to injure
you by turning or breaking in your hands. It will also be a
pleasure to use, and after all, that's a large part of why we do it.
Finally, it's worth checking weekend auctions of antiques and
bric-a-brac. There are some very nice old craftsworkers' tools
around, at remarkably low prices.

A FIRST PROJECT is best done on a piece of fallen wood. Cut
away any soft or rotten bits. Now keep the piece of wood around
you, clearly visible, by your bed or chair, for several weeks.
Handle it a lot, smell it, taste it.

Eventually you can see what the shape and nature of the wood
suggests to you. By gently chipping away small bits, and sanding,
you can help what you see emerge. *Slowly.*

Working wood is immensely slow. Trees live about three times as
long as we do. Meditate on that as you stroke it and hold it
between cutting and sanding.

If you allow yourself to work wood when you are impatient or
irritable, it will protect itself, slip in your hands. You may cut
yourself.

After you've got the basic shape, you may leave a slightly rough
finish, or you may like to get a smooth feel and look by using
several grades of sandpaper. Rubbing down is a quiet, rhythmic
meditation, needing time. Start with coarse, and go on to finer
grade. Colron products have a good range of cleansers and oils for
finishing off, bringing out the hidden voice of the grain and the
depths of colour.

Of course, you can take this as far as you like, and invest in a full
set of chisels, a router and a lathe. Before you spend the money,
it's best to find out whether or not you like it, by trying

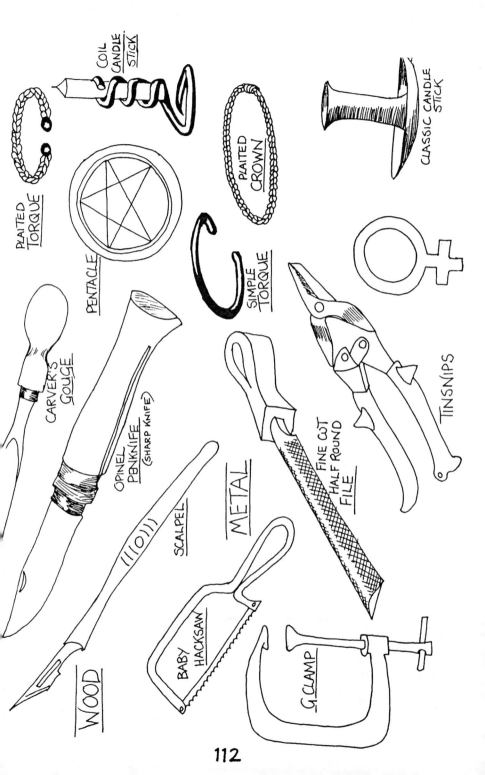

PLAITED TORQUE

COIL CANDLE STICK

PLAITED CROWN

CLASSIC CANDLE STICK

PENTACLE

SIMPLE TORQUE

CARVER'S GOUGE

OPINEL PENKNIFE (SHARP KNIFE)

TINSNIPS

SCALPEL

METAL

FINE CUT HALF ROUND FILE

WOOD

BABY HACKSAW

G CLAMP

112

something simple, and of course to learn how to use it all safely. But whether your work is a small wand, or a foliate Green Man, or fecund Lady, you cannot waste your time working a meditation with the World Tree.

COPPERWORKING

Copper was the very first metal technology, used and held sacred in early civilisations centred on the Goddess, when technology was a woman's profession as much as a man's. In later civilisations copper was held sacred to various goddesses; the famous one was Venus, originally from Cyprus where copper was mined, and from where it gets its name. The Celts on the continent mined copper, and made careful thanks to the Mother whose body they had to plunder to do it. Britain once had our own copper deposits in Cornwall, mined out long ago.

Copper is also fairly simple to work, and does not demand elaborate tools. It can achieve a wide variety of shapes, finishes nicely, and polishes up beautifully, with a lovely deep rosey glow. Although it is a fairly expensive metal to buy, there are a variety of sources from which it can be obtained free of charge.

A SIMPLE TORQUE

Supplies:- Length of power cable. Sharp knife, scissors. Baby hacksaw (borrow ?) Fine cut file, half round; emery paper, medium and fine. Duraglit, soft cloth.

1) Scrounge a length of power cable, not the light stuff used to wire houses, but wire about 3mm thick. Try the electricity board's workers when they're working on a job, and ask respectfully if they'll let you have an odd bit.

2) Pull/ stretch the plastic insulation away from the end with your fingers, to get the point of the knife in. Scissors might help to cut the edges into a fringe.

Scrape off plastic insulation with the sharp knife, leaving a length of bright copper wire. Remember to scrape the blade AWAY from your hand, never towards it; and that a sharp blade is safer - see safety under woodworking. This is the tiresome part of the job.

3) Bend the copper round your neck, with the ends at the front. The opening needs to be a 2" -3" gap. Mark the place you'll need to cut a piece off.

4) Bend your almost- torc open a bit to get it off. Now cut the extra bit off with a baby hacksaw. Copper is a soft metal, so it cuts easily. Ask around to borrow one if necessary; or beg a favour from a handy friend if this bit puts you off. Watch how they do it though, so you could manage it next time. It doesn't have to be a neat job.

5) Round the ends off with a file,then use first medium, then fine emery paper to rub it smooth.

6) Polish with Duraglit metal polish. It comes all ready soaked into fluffy stuff in a tin. You rub the metal with a lump of it, until the shine shows through the polish. Finally rub hard with a soft cloth to bring out the bright magic of the Lady's metal.

A COIL CANDLESTICK

Supplies: 2ft/ 60cm copper from power cable Fine cut file, half round; & emery paper. Example candle. Pencil, paper. Duraglit, soft cloth.

1) Get copper from power cable, prepare about 2ft/ 60cm. 2) Round off the ends with the file.

3) Draw round the candle's base with the pencil on paper, as a guide to the size you need your coil to be. Use a size of candle you're most likely to use often.

4) It's a good idea to give the copper a preparatory cleanup now with the Duraglit unless it's pretty shiny anyway. Once coiled into shape it'll be harder to do any strong rubbing.

5) Bend one end of the copper round in a small circle to fit the drawn circle on the paper. It will need patient coaxing, bigger and smaller to get it just right. Test it with the candle to see if it fits snugly. If not, keep fiddling with it. Patience is a virtue, sometimes.

6) Bend two more rings the same. The candle should slip down them but be firmly supported as well.

7) The rest of the copper is bent round in a bigger circle to make a base. Test it to make sure it doesn't lean to one side or the other with the candle in it.

8) Final polish with Duraglit.

A PENTACLE.

 Supplies:- Sheet copper 1mm thick, 3" - 9"" across.

Compasses, or round bowl, plate etc. Pencil. Rubber.

Tinsnips, or piercing saw. Fine cut file, half round.

Metal scriber, pointed. Steel ruler. Duraglit, soft cloth.

1) Get some sheet copper about 1mm thick, from a metal stockist (you'll find them in Yellow Pages). It's not cheap, although as you will only need a small bit, about 3 - 9", you may get an offcut left over from a larger job. Mark out a circle with compasses, or draw round a plate or jar, the size you want. Pencil lines mark smooth copper pretty well, and they also rub out.

2) Cut to this line, using either tinsnips or a piercing saw A pair of tinsnips cut metal rather like scissors cut paper. The "Aircraft" type are best. Snips leave one side of the cut fairly flat, but curl the other side, so put the waste bit on the curly side.. Experiment on a bit of scrap until you're used to it as a new tool. A piercing saw, for fine cutting is like a fretsaw, a very fine blade with lots of very small teeth.

Tidy up the cut edge with the file & emery paper. 3) Mark out the pentagram design in pencil, using the rubber. (The key to drawing a pentagram is to draw an equally balanced triangle in the circle first, pointed upward like a pyramid.) When you're happy with it, set it into the copper with a scriber and steel ruler (the scriber would cut an ordinary ruler). There are various kinds of special metal scribers; you need one that comes to a point. Again, practice on a scrap piece first.

4) Polish with Duraglit metal polish.

A TWISTED TORQUE. Supplies:- 3 lengths of copper power cable 3ft long; the lighter stuff for house wiring, 1mm thick, in flat grey plastic coating. Try skips; builders are often wasteful.

Clamp or vice. Baby hacksaw. Choice of drill if you like.

1) Strip the insulation as before. Take the 3 lengths of wire, clamp their ends together in a vice on a heavy table; pull them firmly until they are straight. 2) Twist or plait them, by hand, slowly. It is unlikely without great patience, to come out precisely even, but some of us would prefer it that way.

Alternatively, you can enjoy the assistance of a drill. Put their free ends in the chuck of a drill (the opening after you take the drill bit out). Clamp it up tight, pull firmly to keep the wires taut, and wind them together with the drill. For this trick to work, it has to be a drill you can control quite precisely; a traditional hand drill, or at the other extreme, one of those fancy electric drills with a variable speed control. (The simpler type of drill with one fast speed is only good for creating tangles, faster than you would believe.)

3) Take this plait and bend it around your neck to check the length; cut the ends off even with the baby hacksaw. Copper is a soft metal which cuts easily, but remember to secure the end firmly, using a clamp or a vice, close to the cut, so that the dragging action of the saw can't pull the wires apart. 4) Finish the ends. The simplest way is to use a wire binding, then file all smooth so there are no jagged ends to catch your skin. Cheap costume jewellery can be dismantled to yield all sorts of little treasures, such as metal balls to fit on the ends.. Small brass drawer handles can also be adapted with a little ingenuity. Cleaning with Duraglit can't reach all the crevices of the twists - a striking light/dark effect.

5) You can do a ninefold version in a heavy twist by twining 3 lengths of plait together. A plait needs Å its length extra to start with.

A PLAITED CROWN.

Supplies:- Enough copper wire to go 3 times round your head + a third again extra for safety - triple crown. OR Enough for 9 times plus a third - power of nine crown. Clamp or vice, Drill (optional), Baby hacksaw. Big hammer, or two. Extra flat copper for cutouts. Solder stuff (maybe).

1) Make a threefold plait, or the ninefold three-by-three twist, as for the torque.

2) Flatten it, to create a broad flat interlaced strip. Either squeeze it in a vice or clamp, hammer it. Hammer on to something hard and smooth. Some metalworking vices have a little anvil built in. Or, the head of a large hammer, or a firewood chopper, can be an improvised anvil. You can use the floor, or smooth stone. Beware of concrete: it's grit gets driven into the copper. You can protect the copper underneath with a polythene left over from packaging.

3) Try for size around your head; cut to length. Check this several times: you don't want to cut too short.

4) Lace the ends together; bind them with a thin piece of wire. Or solder the join , see under candlestick details.

5) Decorate it with stars, crescent moon, sunbursts, etc. cut from sheet copper and soldered on. Or twist leaves, flowers, ribbons etc into the plait design, as we did for our wedding crowns.

A CLASSIC CANDLESTICK.

Flat copper 6" across. Tinsnips. Pencil, rubber, example candle. Metal scriber. Small wooden bowl. Hammer + towel.

Ball pein hammer. 2Å" - 9" copper water pipe, sized to candle. Baby hacksaw. Fine cut file, emery paper.

Solder, soldering iron, tweezers, 'Flux' chemical cleanser.

3" plaited wire strip for handle if you like.

(Slightly more advanced project, real smithcraft.) 1) Make a disc about 6 ins across, as for the pentacle. For a tall candlestick, not less than 6". Mark a circle at centre the right size for the candle base, or a bit larger. Scribe it with any designs.

2) Make the edges curve upwards slightly in a dish shape, for elegance, and to catch wax drips. A small wooden bowl is ideal, for shaping, but not china or pottery. Press the copper over it, using the balls of your thumbs. Copper is a lovely metal to work; it is quite soft, so it can be bent and formed without tearing or breaking. In metalworker's jargon, it is a ductile metal. Use an ordinary hammer if you need to, but remember a steel hammer will cut marks into the copper, as it is a harder metal. To protect your copper, cover it with a towel. You can use a soft hammer, with a rubber, plastic, or even a copper head. Some come with all three kinds interchangeably.

A ball-pein hammer is one with a ball or dome shape on the back of the head, where some hammers have a claw for pulling out nails. It won't leave ugly marks, in fact the dome will give a nice rippled finish on the copper. 3) Take a small offcut of copper water pipe your candle fits into snugly (plumber supplies shop, DIY shop, or a skip).

Cut it to the length you want, with the baby hacksaw, to how high a candlestick you want, about 2Å" for the Wee Willie Winkie type, or 7 - 9" for a tall one.

4) Make each end spread elegantly outwards by belling them. Put the copper tube upright on a hard surface. Hold your ball-pein hammer with the dome into the open end. The dome, or ball, needs

to be a little bigger than the tube opening.

The flat head of the hammer, is now facing upwards. Tap it with another hammer (or a heavy spanner/ screwdriver/ something heavy) to push the opening of the tube wider open.

Smooth the ends with a file and emery paper.

5) Solder one end to the base with the soldering iron. Soldering has the reputation of being a black and arcane art. Actually, it's just a way of sticking metal together. But like any new skill, practice with a spare bit before tackling your project.

Clean the two faces of metal thoroughly. In soldering, cleanliness is not next to godliness; it is godliness. Any tiny speck of dirt will ruin the join. Take each piece in turn. Dip it in Flux, a chemical cleanser. The liquid is less messy than the paste. Heat the metal well with the iron, melt a little solder on it. Melted solder goes from matt silver-grey to brilliant silver. Properly melted solder runs like water; it'll spread easily to where it's needed. Keep touching the bit of solder with the tip of the iron until you get that bright silver liquid. It's very pretty.

(Partly melted solder forms a thick paste which will reluctantly allow you to push it into place with the tip of the iron. A join made like this is no earthly use.)

Bring the faces of metal together, heat both till the solder is melted. Run a little more solder into the join, (not too much, or the result will be messy, and you'll have to clean it up with fine emery paper). Allow to cool. A heavy, powerful iron (75 watts) is easier to use, enough power to heat the small working area quickly. The commonest failures are not heating the metal enough to melt the solder, and dirt. The iron is not a big safety risk: just don't pick it up by the wrong end. Hot solder stings and makes you swear but does no damage.

Copper absorbs and spreads heat fast. Finish the job quickly, before the heat spreads to the rest of it, and unsolders bits you have already done. A small iron heats the job up too slowly and gradually. This is a major cause of burned fingers and swearing - tweezers are a blessing. 6) For a handle, make plaited wire strip, for a nice circular handle which you solder on. By now you might be feeling confident, so you can take this further, adding decorative bands soldered around the stem, etc.

ROBES

Now some people like ordinary clothes, and some work naked. Some just want a robe for a special occasion; some would follow the High Magic way and always wear a specially kept robe to go into a special place.

Ritual robes are excellent for men, to wear, and to expand their skills by making. There are few occasions when men are permitted to enjoy the comfort, freedom and sensuality of not wrapping up legs and sex in tighter clothing. The loose nature of a robe is a delight only really to be discovered by wearing one. Ritual robes also allow men to wear certain colours, and have embroidery, or luxurious ornament like goldwork which are otherwise off limits to all except the more radical. A belt can ensure a masculine look.

A robe is very convenient if you're going to work sky clad. Wriggling out of modern zips and buttons and underwear is hardly graceful for most of us; so much more reassuring and ceremonial to have a Magical Bath, put on the robe, then let it fall away at the right moment.

Newcomers to the circle will find using a robe either a complete barrier which makes them feel silly; or a liberator into an expanded, more dignified, graceful self.

One of the best materials is China silk, available from any Asian fabric supplier in a beautiful range of many colours. It feels and behaves like silk, smooth, both warm or cool, machine washable, but it's cheap. Otherwise polyester cotton is the best alternative for a lightweight robe. It doesn't crease up with wearing and is easily washable. Cotton lawn is especially soft and light.

Light robes like these can be worn over ordinary clothes, providing what's underneath isn't too thick and bulky. Or you can just have underwear underneath. A really luxurious option is to have an ankle length lightweight robe with long sleeves, under a slightly shorter one with shorter sleeves in heavier material.

For a heavier robe, velvet is gorgeous of course - any old curtains you can use? A wool mixture is also lovely, though not cheap. Material for curtains or chair covers, found in specialist shops or department stores, is often satiny, or has an embroidered texture which is rich looking (but usually too scratchy to wear next to skin). There are also many types of linen look fabrics which are good for natural earthy robes.

1) Measure from the side of your neck to the floor; get twice this length, with another metre for long, fitted sleeves or any other extras.)

2) When buying material get thread in a matching colour and type - cotton or synthetic as stated on the label. Buy pins, the ones with coloured heads are the easiest. Scissors must be sharp, one large, one small.

3) You will have to fasten edges of fabric together by a) hand sewing (you need a mixed pack of needles) b) machine sewing or c) iron on sticky tape. Hand sewing and machine sewing use different threads. Tailors chalk might help.

The inexperienced could beg someone else to machine it for you! But make sure you stitch a little of it yourself.

4) Fold material halfway down the length. Lay it completely FLAT on the (clean) floor. Pin it along each of the long edges, pins facing same way, about 3cm, 2" apart. Leave a foot open each side at the top for arm holes.

5) Fold it lengthways so you have a long thin shape, four sheets thick, armholes together. Put a pin top corner opposite the arm holes. Put another about 9" down the fold. Open it all out again flat, pins at centre line.

Put a pin about 6" away from the centre pin, along the top fold, and another 6" away on the other side. Men with large necks allow 7", slender women 5".. Put a couple of extra pins in along the top on each side so there are 7 in a line. Put pins in a straight diagonal, joining this bar along the top to the pin 9" below down the centre fold. You get a triangle shape.

Check all pins are only through top layer of material.

Poke scissors through the material in the centre of the triangle and cut it out a little inside the lines of pins. Then take out the pins. You have a neck hole.

6) Now handstitch, or machine, or iron on tape to join long edges as seams. Handstitch:- Thread a larger needle with a length of thread shorter than your arm. Cut, don't break or bite it. Tie a knot at the free end. Draw a straight line between pins with the chalk as guide. Stitch from the head end of pins. Pull them out as you go. Before thread runs out/ gets tight to sew, end it with several firm stitches on top of each other. Rethread needle.

OR Machine:- Get help to thread machine - keep helper available with suitable bribery.. Practice on spare material going slowly enough on treadle or wheel to control a straightish line of stitches. Tips - leave a good foot of both threads hanging at the start; this stops the machine unthreading. Start the machine at the line of pins with the heads pointing at you, not the points. Put the edge of the material on the inside (right), the bulk of it on the outside (left).

OR Iron on tape:- instructions on packet.

7) Edge the neck with 'facings', or 'binding'.

Facings are extra strips of material you cut out round the shape of the neck:- One piece along the top, and one down each side - make them a bit longer than the neck lengths. Turn the robe so the seam stitching is inside. Lay one facing strip along the top, pin it, and make a seam (not with iron on tape). Do the ones along the diagonals, leaving plenty of extra at the corners where they meet.

Now make a little seam by pinching together two of the ends of these facing strips where they join so the edges stand up together, and the rest of the two facings lie flat along the main fabric. Do 3 of these.

Turn the whole robe inside out again so you can work on the inside. Lift the single joined facing strip bit by bit over into the inside of the robe so it lies flat. Pin it down bit by bit, until the seam is folded back on itself.

Now turn the edges under, pin, and sew along the edge of the fold (hem).

OR Binding tape can be easier. Buy a wide one. You pin it along the inside of the neck, starting the end of tape at the back. Make the cut edge of the material run along the middle of the tape, with more clear above it than below. Stitch along the bottom edge.

Now work on the outside. Fold the binding over the cut edge. You should be able to cover the line of stitching from the inside with the tape. Pin it down and stitch it.

Elegant versions of binding are satin or velvet ribbon. You can also get decorative tape. Choose wide ones, 1" or more.

8) The bottom hem may need to be cut/ trimmed a bit. It's very

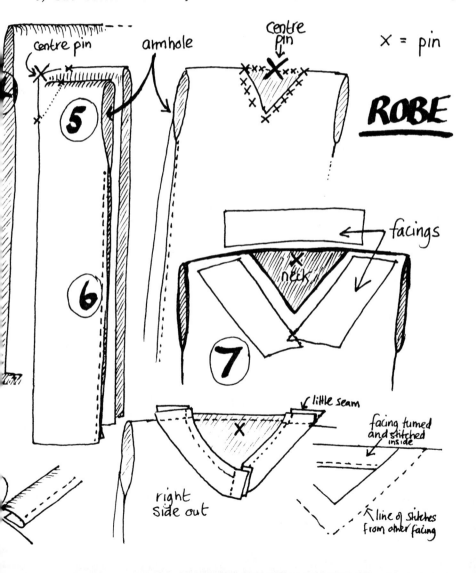

difficult to do this on yourself because when you bend down to check the material moves down with you. A rough measurement is to make all of it the same, against a measure from the side of your neck (place the higher nos. of the tape up here) down to your trouser cuff/ edge, or your ankle. Allow 3" extra for the hem. (Floor length designs are not best unless you're practiced - one trips on them.)

When using the single measurment way women with solid breasts need to allow about 2 - 3" more at the front, large bottoms ditto - this may balance up. Men with big tummies same as solid breasted women.

If a friend can help, you stand on a chair, and your helper cuts and pins. Trim tiny bits at a time - you can't put it back.

Fold cut edge along the inside and pin it. Fold this edge again, taking out the first pins; pin it again. Stitch it.

9) For extra long sleeves, put the robe on, measure from edge of sleeve to your wrist, along the top, add a bit extra for safety. Cut a rectangle this long.

The width is the length of the edge of the armhole opening + 2" extra. Make one of the armhole length sides a selvedge - the existing edge of the fabric as you buy it, then you don't need to hem it. Mark the width side with chalk or pin.

Measure round your fist. This is the size the sleeve needs to be at one end to go over your hand.

Fold the sleeve in half, pin it along the longer edge. Put pin at centre fold at the hand end.

Measure half your fist measurement + 1" along from this pin. Now draw a diagonal from this to the other corner along the long edge. Stitch this seam.

With the robe inside out, put the new sleeve in the armhole. The edges of the armhole lie together to make a seam; the sleeve points inward into the robe. Check this by pinning round the armhole seam first, then turning the robe right way out. When it's right, redo the pinning so the long seam along the sleeve meets the long seam along the robe. You may have to tuck or fold it to fit; do this under the arm out of sight. Stitch the seam.

10) If not completely fed up by now, you can decorate your robe with gold, silver, patterned braid or tape. This looks great stitched along edges, or down the centre. You can also get ready made patches to sew on, stars, butterflies etc. Or make your own from felt.

A heavy belt in plaited work is an excellent finish, or a plainer one with a worked ornamental buckle. Ribbons plaited make fine cords, and are sacred to the Triple Goddess. To plait a cord belt or hairband, you need half again the length of ribbon you want a plait to be.

Wear soft boots; sandals; plain slipper shoes; heavy or light socks; bare feet with a robe.

SELF

Your first and foremost tool for all magic is yourself. You may sometimes have no other tools available. Even if you do you also need to use your own resources.

The first task of life, and your greatest sacred duty is to take care of yourself. Creation gave you a body, mind, heart and will to work with and this time round you only get one set, so take care of them. The Goddess is a fine craftswoman; don't insult her work by neglecting its maintenance.

Philosophies which ask you to put others first sound good; but they carry a hidden assumption that if you do, others will take care of you. Much of the time they won't. They haven't read the same book, signed the altruism pledge yet, or they're just preoccupied with ordinary struggles right now. Some just really don't care.

People will usually come up trumps in real life and death crisis; as a race we survive by cooperating. Very often people will be gentle and caring if you ask for what you want. If you don't, telepathy is erratic, so results are patchy. In the end the day to day business of your comfort, health and happiness is down to you.

It's as if we each have our own garden. We cultivate plants in it. We can make paths, grow sweet grasses to sit on. We might be ambitious and put in an arch, arbour or greenhouse. Some of us want roses, some prefer veg. But what we get is what we grow. A neighbour might come and help out a bit, especially if we're extra tired. Experienced gardeners will give advice - sometimes unwanted. We can borrow a wheelbarrow, or barter for good fertiliser. But these are extras which will usually carry obligation to return the favour.

If we each take care of our own gardens and help each other out a bit sometimes when we can, we're a lot less likely to get guilty about being naturally selfish, resentful when others don't repay us, and despairing when we're left with empty patches after trying so hard to be nice.

This self reliant code can seem hard, especially when life is agonising. When deeply damaged, we all want mum to appear and kiss it better. There's a strong feeling of wanting to go back to being a child, of wanting to burrow, don't ask me to do anything yet, and perhaps of really deserving help for once. The Circle can be the appropriate place to be that hurt child, and to bravely bring out without shame the tears and silly, crazy things that well up. They are not silly or crazy at all. There is an immense dignity at the core of all grief and pain.

There are healers, friends, help agencies around to give some kisses. But adult hurts last a lot longer than a bumped head, and other people can't cuddle us continually. At some point we have to make our own healing. Maybe you can't do it all at once. But little steps really do climb a long way, so you can tackle one small bit at a time.

The point about saying it's down to you is not at all that it's your fault what happened. You're not to blame, and your suffering is not punishment. But you are at the centre of your own storm. You have far more need to deal with this than anyone else, so the best person to be in charge of your difficulty is you. No one else can possibly feel as involved or determined about it as you, because it's not them stuck in it. Pain is a great motivator.

Going through struggle needs time, effort and priority. So don't try and pretend everything is OK all the time. By all means put on a brave fake sometimes; it'll help your self respect to know you can. But also allow lots of times to be what your really are - an initiate in struggle.

In ancient societies such initiates wore different clothes, white, sackcloth, simplified gear. They gave up everyday responsibilities full time or part time, lived as beggars or on charity, or on savings or relatives. They wore certain symbols, an arm band, a hair style, a ring, which told others 'Don't expect me to be normal. I am not able to be fully adult at the moment, I may behave strangely.'

We do not have much of that in our society. But you can make some of it for yourself. The biggest thing is to demand others leave you alone, and give you special consideration as much as you need either. The more you demand and take help the faster you'll get through this. If you're a parent or carry a lot of responsibility it can be especially hard to make demands for your needs. Do so in small ways as much as you can. And prepare a shortlist of emergency helpers, retreat places in case you get very badly frayed. You owe it to those responsibilties of yours.

Protect yourself. EARTH: Cherish your body. Think about especially nice food (don't diet while life is bad). Music. A new T shirt in a pretty colour you like. Parks and gardens and peaceful places to visit. Don't wear all black (devotees of it can wear a tiny touch of something else underneath).

WATER: Cherish your feelings. Avoid people who don't make you feel better - really. Use as much choice as you possibly can about it. Make your sensitivities your guide. There'll be time later when you're stronger to be easygoing, considerate and generous. But if you waste your resources when you're fragile on others' feelings you'll take a long time to heal. Try to find experiences that soothe you. Let yourself have mopes, and crying fits, and tantrums - they're nature's cleansers.

FIRE: Cherish your will. Put your foot down and say NO to what you don't want. Ask for what you do want. Listen while you're in this special state to what you really want. A coffee now? or in 5 minutes time? To talk on the phone or go away and lie down? By listening to these small matters you will hear the voice of self more clearly, and then the deep Self will come through too. Often your distress is because you are not listening to what you really really want. It may sound a bit naughty, a bit crazy. But trust it. You wouldn't be in such a state if it weren't important for this need to come to light. At times of suffering we are very close to our deepest being.

AIR: Cherish your mind. Don't listen to depressing news on TV, in newspapers, or from people you meet. You need your attention for your own struggle; when you're strong maybe you can do something for the struggles of the world instead of just letting them weigh you down when you're weakened yourself.

CHERISH YOUR SPIRIT: Accept yourself, fight the self hater. Love yourself.

Take what you need wherever you can find it. BLESSED BE ...

The Self Blessing Rite is a traditional part of Craft
training. As part of my initiation I was expected to create my own style of it, including my own wording. To demonstrate your love for the Goddess, the God, the old ways, and the healthy, practical, down to earth spirituality of Paganism, this is an excellent first ritual.

Do it lightly (with just hand washing to prepare, and without the full ritual procedure) when coming home from a busy day's work, or after an unsettling personal encounter. Do it for seven nights before sleeping as a soothing, gentle reminder of who you are when there's a lot on.

It essentially blesses each key part of myself saying 'Blessed be my head' etc. I felt that if I am part of the divine Body anyway then I am already blessed. I just need to remind myself. So I say

'Blessed is ...'

PREPARE with a Magical Bath (next section) if you feel the need, or if life is very fraught. If you decide on the Bath, then lay the Circle all ready before running the water.

You need no special extras for this. But if you like, include an essential oil or perfume. With this you can anoint each place you touch in blessing.

With a pretty bowl, some hot water*, and a chosen essential oil or perfume to fragrance it you can ceremonially bathe your choice of hands, face and feet before doing the Blessing itself at the centre of the ritual. Small towel.

* Hot water: to have some available after prep stages - can be kept hot in a thermos; - or by putting a half full electric kettle within reach of the Circle if plug sockets permit. If you do it this way you need a jug of cold water too to cool the boiling water down.

- or put boiling water in heavy ceramic pot, with lid, or cover with folded towel. A saucepan will do if you wrap it round with a whole newspaper, sellotaped, because metals lose heat quickly.

AFTER PURIFYING, CASTING THE CIRCLE & ENERGY WORK

Sit at the Centre, or at one of the Elements which speaks to your feelings.

Touch or anoint each of these 7 points. Do it slowly and reverently, stopping to reflect and feel into each one. Say -

1 'Blessed are my feet which walk me upon the Earth.'

2 'Blessed is my sex which spins sacred energy.'

3 'Blessed is my stomach that feeds my power.

4 'Blessed is my heart that gives and embraces my world.'

5 'Blessed is my throat which speaks my words & listens too'

6 'Blessed is my mind which can imagine, think, and plan'

7 'Blessed is my crown which opens to the spirit/ God/dess.'

Sit in peace; enjoy your blessedness.

TAKE COMMUNION, OPEN THE CIRCLE.

You might like to do a sky clad (naked) Self Blessing. But don't do your very first ritual so unless you're already very comfortable with your own nakedness. An excellent self loving rite is to do a Self Blessing in front of a mirror, clothed or unclothed.

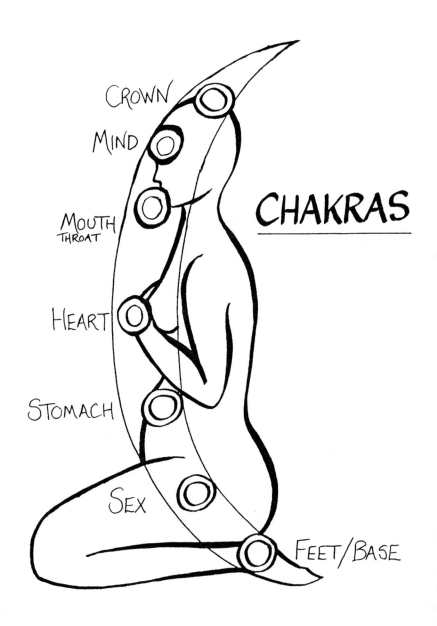

CROWN

MIND

MOUTH
THROAT

CHAKRAS

HEART

STOMACH

SEX

FEET/BASE

These 7 points are of course the 7 chakras. Some people do work with more than the classic 7 chakras, and anyway if certain parts of you feel like key centres to you, apart from these, then do include them in your Blessing.

Chakra is an Indian, Sanskrit word, meaning wheel or power centre. The chakras are the vital organs of your self and roughly correspond to the major physical systems of your body.

On touching chakras:- Touch gently but definitely, with love, stroking if you feel that is right.

CROWN Awareness consciousness life. - on top of your head, where your hair grows naturally out of a central point.

HEAD Thinking imagining planning deciding analysing taking information and sorting it. - between your eyebrows, and a bit above the eyes in the centre of the forehead. Rubbing it gently is very soothing. Try stroking it downwards to the nose repeatedly - it puts babies to sleep too.

THROAT Communication speaking listening; self expression bridge between self and outside. - is big, and takes in throat, mouth, and ears. It is your communication system, a magical bridge between inside and outside.

HEART Sensitivity sympathy affection caring beauty nurturing others protectiveness grief. - mid way beteen nipples. It is a tiny delicate place, requiring very gentle touch. If you are distressed it may feel sore; if it surprises you at how delicate and disinclined to contact it feels, you're ignoring your needs or stress level too much.

STOMACH Self willpower fighting success anger self-nourishment pleasure hope energy. - just above the navel at the waist. If you tend to give way to others, and have trouble standing up for yourself, give this one extra attention.

SEX Creativity cycles erotic pleasure making babies generating ideas depression orgasm birth. - may make you shy or slightly awkward, but try to touch yourself camly, with respect. In a group blessing, a polite way is to touch the base of the stomach.

BASE Security limits clearing out patience endurance fear death unconscious. . - feet or anus. Stroking feet is very soothing of course and rids a lot of tension. Relaxing the ring of muscles round the anus is also deeply helpful to relaxation.

Magical Bath

Water is one of nature's most powerful healers. Not only does a bath cleanse the outer surface and relax the muscles, the water bathes us in negatiive ions, which are proven mood changers for the better. And warm wet floating evokes deep memories of the womb with its safety and nourishment.

IF YOU PREFER SHOWERS, or only ever stay in a bath five or ten minutes it's worth considering a long bath for the medicinal reasons above. It's possible you don't permit yourself to enjoy the prolonged pleasure of warm, lazy waters because you tend to deny yourself deep private time for inner peace. If you have another way of lying alone completely relaxed, in dreaming idle pleasure, for an hour at least, once or twice a week, then I'll buy it - you just don't like baths - this is not for you.

If you're not used to long baths, then try teaching yourself in easy stages. If you're used to fifteen minutes, make it twenty five. If you're used to that, make it forty. The aim is at least a hour.

To keep the bath hot and soothing, run more hot water into it every 15 minutes or so. If it gets full, and the hot water is not that hot to start with, run some out so the heat is not so diluted by a deep, cooled bath.

Yes, you do get 'pruney' and it's a harmless ripple in your skin which disappears within ten to fifteen minutes of getting out.

CANDLELIGHT is beautiful, soft, kind, and mysterious. It also helps transform a shabby bathroom into a pleasant one, and a pretty one into sheer luxury.

Low lighting also stimulates melatonin in the pituitary gland; this is the essential hormone for dreaming, trance and magic.

White household candles make the same soft light as any others. You might enjoy choosing coloured ones, or special ones. Small nightlights sold at any household shop are delicate and pretty.

NOW SELECT ACCORDING TO YOUR DESIRE:-

FRAGRANCES are a great help to your state of mind, as smell is the oldest and most instinctive sense which reaches deep down within. Radox and other similar bath preparations are lovely, or you might like to try the original oil essences all perfumes are made from. Essential oils are sold in health shops. When putting an essential oil in the bath, take care to put only three drops or so - they're strong, and you can easily overdo it and spoil the bath. It takes a few minutes for the smell to emerge, so don't add more until four or five minutes after adding the first few drops.

Scents like pine or lavender are relaxing and also gently invigorating. Juniper is a strong tonic. Jasmine or 'Egyptian' are sensual, rich treats.

A beautiful magical recipe is a few drops each of juniper, cedar and sandalwood (courtesy of Dion Fortune).

HERBS can also make a lovely bath. Make a strong tea with a whole handful of your chosen herb in a teapot; pour the liquid into the bath. Sage is a traditional purifier. Some people put the herbs in a piece of thin cotton or muslin, tie it with string like a purse or bag, and hang it under the tap while running the water.

MAKE THE BATHROOM WARM, if you can, in the cold months. It'S worth putting a heater in there while the bath is running at least, so all the heat from the water doesn't flow off into the air.

DON'T LEAVE AN ELECTRIC HEATER in there while you're in the bath unless the bathroom is large and it stands well over the other side: electricity + water + your body all in contact means you're dead.

SALT is the other great cleanser, as in the classic Purification, so you can put a handful of salt. It's excellent for your skin health.

YOU MAY LIKE SILENCE, - OR YOU MAY LIKE MUSIC.

Put the cassette player just outside the door, or play music in the next room. Never use headphones in the bath - see electrical risk above.

CHILLED white wine? Red wine? Fruit juice? Norfolk Punch? Aqua Libra? Coffee? Tea? Crisps? Biscuits? Fruit? Yoghurt? Ice cream? Cake? Cheese and crackers? A selection on a tray is rather enjoyable.

A novel? A magazine article? A picture? A mobile? A plant?

A TOWEL ON A RADIATOR or by the heater or fire to get warm, maybe? A clean soft T shirt to get into afterwards is gentle to the skin. Or a nightie, or soft shirt, or dressing gown, or robe.

AFTER THE BATH a little time to lie naked in a warm place, by a heater, or in bed, wrapped in a soft blanket or large towel, allows the peace to linger and stay with you.

STROKING ALMOND OIL (the quality massage choice) or your chosen moisturiser over your legs, arms, shoulders, breast/s, tummy, bottom, face and hands is a fine closing.

IF YOU FEEL LIKE MAKING LOVE to yourself, this is a lovely

John, following his wife's teaching.

ompletion too. Linger over it, honouring your own inner magic.
'OU WILL SLEEP DEEPLY and profoundly, especially if you
ime your bath after 9pm. This is also the best plan to work with
ur melatonin (low light) hormone peak at 11pm.
:HECKLIST
'lean bath.   Heating both in bathroom and place for later.
:ssential oil, herbs, Radox or other fragrance.   Salt.
:andles or nightlights, matches.   Wine, fruit juice etc.
'hoice food. Music. Book, magazine, picture, plant to look at.
oft towel, T shirt, robe etc. Almond oil, moisturiser.
he Magical Bath makes a beautiful healing, or luxury gift, for
omeone else.

Guardians of protection

We all have times when we feel unprotected, and could do with a sense of a shield or barrier against what is hurting us. I am sometimes asked about 'psychic attack' and have worked with it a number of times.

First of all, whatever hostility or nastiness is directed at you, it will only reach into you and touch you if your state of mind and health lets it. Travel on a train and bus, and you can't help being near any number of people who've got colds. You'll only get one if you've never met that particular bug before and you're in a low state generally. A healthy, happy person can throw off attacks fairly easily, whether they're mental or physical. If someone hurls a spiteful comment at you that just isn't true, in fact it's the opposite of you (e.g. that you're really bossy when in fact you're quiet and tend to sit at the back) you'll know it's silly if you're feeling OK. But if you're low, you'll be shaken by it, and have a hard time pushing past it to who you know you really are.

I once treated an apparently acute case of psychic attack. The poor young man had vivid visions of magicians working foul magic at him; following them he had vicious migraines, frequently vomited, and suffered horrible fits of shaking terror. It affected his sleep, he lost his job, and became even more shaky with lost confidence. There was no medical basis for his devastating symptoms.

I asked him why these magicians attacked him. He did not know. Had he met them ever? No. Did he know where they were? Yes, he knew the street where the magic was done.

I suggested that it was odd that such a powerful group of people were so concerned to attack him, when he was quiet, ordinary, rather solitary, and had done no great harm. Even if they were doing experiments, a group of workers could take on someone who offered them more challenge, surely? He agreed, patiently.

How did he feel about these wicked people? Oh, he felt sorry for them. They were such undeveloped souls. Surely, I asked, he must have some ordinary human resentment about what they had done to him - like wrecked his life. No, no, he said anxiously, not at all.

Finally he admitted in a whisper that he did not want to talk like this because it might make them angry.

I explained that as a witch I could draw a circle around him so that he was enclosed in a safe bubble. They could not hear what he said now. Within minutes he was angry, and not long after was raging, red faced and thunderous, in his own defence. Rapidly his rage shifted to someone early in his background, and the rest of the healing followed on easily.

In all the cases of attack I worked on, only one ever turned out to be anything like an attack. All the rest were experienced by people who had been taught to think that anger is dangerous and bad to such an extent that they had learned not to feel it. Their rage solidified inside them into damaging illness, and aggressive visions. The visions could not be of themselves of course, that would be terrifying. It was better to be terrified of others. It was as if the visions were saying 'There is anger here' but the person could not permit themselves to see any more than that.

A journalist once asked me if I'd use magical methods to react if someone angered me. It puzzled me, and I answered that I'd not need to. I'd hit them, or take them to court, or retaliate using ordinary means like forceful argument and warning. As a witch I'm accustomed to thinking of myself as a strong person, able to take care of myself.

Unfortunately the article in the newspaper carried a headline Witch hits you or sues you if you anger her. That's the media for you.

There are plenty of methods in the magical tradition for creating a thick, solid wall of protection around you. The only thing this approach overlooks is what is shut in with you - you yourself. You are inside this container, full of your natural equipment of fears, aggression, sadness and so on, probably quite a lot of that if you're in a fraught situation. And a closed container is a pressure cooker to boil up what it contains. Ugh.

So when casting pretty circles of white light, make sure you do lots of purification INSIDE the circle as well as before you cast it.

Rite of Protection & Cleansing

The protections I offer here are very simple folk magic. The two can be done as spells without working a full ritual. But if you feel you'd rather not do a full circle because you're very tired, don't forget the circle itself will heal and strengthen you if you can possibly make the effort. Try to do a circle, and just accept doing it quietly and even a little skimped.

YOU NEED one mirror, or four. Small ones will do fine; if you don't have any, try to borrow; or they're cheaply bought in a hardware shop, chemist or Woolworths. YOU ALSO NEED one large onion, or three, or seven, depending on how many nights you need to do a working. This in turn depends on how seriously battered you feel. YOU NEED a kitchen knife for cutting onion.

PUT the mirror in the Fire quarter, or one in each quarter. If you know or can feel which direction on the map the threat lies in, then you only need one mirror. If it comes from several, or you're not sure/ don't know, use four. PUT the onion/s on the Earth altar.

PURIFY, CAST THE CIRCLE. AFTER RAISING ENERGY (just a bit if you're not feeling vigorous - try a walking circle) then

WORKING 1) Go to Earth. Cut the onion, or the first onion, into four quarters. Put one at each of the circle's quarters.

2) Next take up the mirror. Hold it over your chest (heart chakra) and slowly turn around until you come back to the same place. Whatever is directed at you will be reflected back by the mirror. Hold the source of your trouble in your mind as you do it, so this mirror shield will work mainly on this.

If you're unsure of the direction, then do it with all four mirrors, one at a time.

3) Go to each of the quarter Guardians of Air, Fire, Water and Earth in turn. Ask them to help in their own way.

TAKE COMMUNION, OPEN THE CIRCLE

AFTERWARDS, 1) put the mirror by your bed, facing in the direction of the threat. (If this worries you, consider that you are not throwing anything out independently. The mirror only reflects back what is given it. So you are not doing any more than ensuring natural karmic consequences that will happen anyway are working to protect you.) You can put four mirrors at the four corners of your bed, facing outwards.

2) Put the four quarters of onion in the four corners of your bedroom overnight (not necessarily matching the four directions of the circle). They will soak up your accumulated fear and tension as you sleep.

The following day they must be gathered up without touching them with your skin. Use cloth or paper. They must be offered to one of the elements to be cleansed. Cast them into running water, burn them, or bury them well down in the earth.

For a particularly trying problem, you may like to do the onion cleansing overnight for three or seven nights. Only the first night needs a full ritual. The mirror/s can just stay in place.

The power of desire

Making your desire happen is a core part of the Western magical tradition. You may want health, sex, love, money or status; these are the basic desires common to us all, although one or two of them may seem a lot less important than others. Then there are more desires more individual to each person.

PAGANISM IS A KINDLY FAITH. Our desires are accepted as a natural part of our lives. Like Buddhists, we understand that we are creatures of desire. At any one moment you and I have powerful desires, whether to gain something we need, or to get rid of a discomfort or worry. At those pleasant times when we feel content, with no urge to change a satisfying situation, we still hold desire: the desire to continue it, or to make it happen again.

Unlike Buddhists, our approach is not to teach ourselves to detach from desire, but to accept what we want, get it as far as is humanly possible, and only then to accept what we cannot have. We are a passionate people, given to ambition, independence, creativity and making dreams come true.

An old associate of mine used to say he found the common Christian attitude of denying life's joys not only silly, but downright rude to the one offering us gifts. It's as if, he explained, as if the Lady is giving a mighty garden party. The tables are piled with food, the music is playing, people are dancing, singing or deep in conversation. Here and there young lovers have retired into the bushes. Some intellectual types are measuring the angle of the sun's shadow by the sundial. The children are running in and out, full of fun. Some people are sitting alone, or with a sympathetic friend, a bit tearful or down, sorting it out so they can come back into the fun. The sun is shining, the birds are singing.

Then there are these peculiar people who hang back and say 'Oh no, I won't have anything to eat thank you' and 'No I don't dance' and 'That's not allowed.' They're really being remarkably rude to our hostess.

WHY did a faith that told people to expect suffering, to wait for rewards till after death, not to expect pleasure and to reject it when it did happen - why did this become so important? The only situation where such attitudes would be helpful would be one of bad times, long passages of suffering, where there seemed no other sensible course than to see life itself as a form of suffering.

In fact the medieval centuries when Christianity came to power were overpoweringly awful. There were wars and violence across

Europe; plagues killed off huge numbers of people, wiping out whole villages, with people dying in horrible pain and filth. Other diseases also struck down many (the Church had destroyed much of our medical knowledge so little could be done to help). Women died young from frequent childbirth encouraged by Christian beliefs; the babies died too.

People reacted sometimes nobly and caringly, often not. Surrounded by ugliness and violence, people were stripped down to a very basic survival self which was driven to desperate, crazy, cruel behaviour. The sick were deserted and left to die unaided; cannibalism, forced sex, all kinds of violence, thievery and murder happened. Our native priestly tradition which might have helped and guided us through had been almost destroyed by the Romans.

In desperation the new priests taught a harsh doctrine of eternal punishment attached to a simple code of don'ts. It was commonly thought that humanity had been dumped by our god in disgust; our deep guilt meant only strenuous purity could win him back and bring better times. Accepting life was just suffering was actually less painful than living with disappointed hopes. Pleasure was best avoided as it raised one's expectations, which would only be brought down again by reality.

In hard times it can be easier to just plod through like a robot, feeling as little as possible. In such a massive life hating those who bring forth new life, women, were hated for creating suffering, and sex was logically the tempting gateway to creating suffering too. Earlier faiths that loved and celebrated life, sex, birth, women, were detested as a mockery of the current misery.

Perhaps such a tragic philosophy was inevitable. Perhaps a Pagan priesthood could have done better, but who knows? What we can see now though is that, however much we criticise our own society,there are whole continents not ravaged by war, most of the worst diseases of history are now under control, millions have enough to eat and do not crouch in ruins in fear of daily violence. Most of our babies live and grow up, without facing starvation or crippling labour.

We are still inclined to look on the gloomy side, and emphasise our faults and mistakes. We've had centuries of the harsh fathergod standing over us and we can't forget that overnight. But it is time to to be brave enough to take the risk of hoping, and to join with all the others who are working to make a healthy, happy world. (see Ecomagic)

To work for others' happiness and not my own is not sensible. Even if only to maintain myself as an efficient service agent, I have to take care of myself.

Actually, I have often and often found that by following what I most want and need I am most magically fitting in with others' needs too. The cliche about being the one to ask questions gets everyone else's questions answered too is quite true. I find that when I feel very tired and have to face the uncomfortable feeling that I need to let others in a group down, it usually means those others are ready and waiting to be more actively involved. And frequently two people can assume they're putting up with something they both don't like for the other person's sake, because nothing is said about it.

THE BASIS OF DESIRE MAGIC is that desire is crude. It's rooted in passion, a passionate hunger. If you don't feel an intense passionate desire for something you're unlikely to create it. A wishy washy 'it'd be really nice if ...' doesn't attract the attention of a busy universe.

ONE OF THE MOST EFFECTIVE RITUALS I did to get what I wanted was when I stormed into my temple and shouted 'If you don't put the pay up, you cow, I'm just not doing this ruddy job any longer.'

My finances improved steadily and definitely since then. My passion was strong, my doubts and hesitations about what I deserved in life were all burnt away. Perhaps it helped that I did it in a place I was used to making my circles.

But I think what really worked it was the sheer massive spontaneity of it. I was extremely angry - too angry to go through ritual stages. I just insisted that the Goddess (cow aspect) listen.

The really essential thing is to have an undivided will. This is actually unusual. We naturally exist as it were as a parliament of selves - and they quarrel. 'I want X' says one. 'No, no' quavers another, 'that's too dangerous.' Or one voice wants it and the others think it's boring.

LISTEN TO YOUR DIFFERENT SELVES. Help them talk it over. Let the scared child talk; and the ambitious organiser; and the wild animal .... However silly or naughty they sound you won't get them to agree until they get their point expressed and heard.

If you let the less admirable or less convenient parts of yourself have a say, and try to sympathise with their point of view, you have a good chance of winning them over. Once they stop fighting your active self part, you can get going.

GETTING WHAT YOU WANT is like going into a vast cosmic supermarket. You can buy anything you want; provided you are willing to pay the price tag. They're fairly clearly marked. For example, if you want a great deal of money, you'll have to be ruthless, do a lot of hard and probably boring work, give up social life and friends almost completely and accept being disliked. Getting a comfortable amount usually means teaching yourself you're entitled to it.

If you want the love of a particular person who isn't terribly interested in you, you can usually get them if you put in about three years determined loneliness and cunning. You will miss out on a lot of other self development, become dreary, lose friends, maybe damage your health. This may be worth it.

Set your WILL like steel and you can have it.

But look carefully at what you have to pay, and decide if you want to. For some people love is worth moving to the other side of the world. Money can be worth steady years of patience.

MAKING IT CLEAR When working desire magic it is important to make it very clear what you want. When I hurled my complaint at heaven about money, I knew exactly how much I wanted; not riches, but enough so I don't have to panic when the electricity bill arrives. I got it. When I worked patiently to get a life partner I made a thorough list over a year or two of what I wanted - and what I didn't. (Have you noticed how we are trained to put months or years of effort into training for and getting the right job - but put a tenth of the same effort into getting love?) Even so, I knew him for two years before I suddenly realised he checked ticks all down the list!

This brings out how again, it is the inner landscape which determines the outer reality. For I had been hurt badly in the past, and thought I was ready to love again long before I was. That's why I did not recognise my love for two long years.

If you want love, and haven't got it, you're afraid of it. Most of us are afraid of love - it's a huge risk, letting someone have real power in one's heart. Admit it, whatever is the shape of the fear, and you can begin to heal it.

WORKING ON THE INNER WORLD is surprisingly powerful. I once worked with a woman who very much wanted a former lover to return to her. We sorted out what had gone wrong between them and she gently but definitely changed her attitudes and feelings in that area. Then we did a circle, asking the Goddess to give her a renewal if that was best for her.

That night the person concerned phoned her from Australia, after a three year gap.

NOTICE that we did not only do a circle. We did some very practical counselling on how her attitudes had helped to drive them apart. Some people think you can do money magic and cash notes will come through the letter box. It's something you can make happen as a one off, but the laws of magic don't like it to be relied on. We are put into earth form to learn the ways of Earth. So make the marriage happen, and work both powers together,

WHO KNOWS BEST? The other thing that is very important is that we did not demand that X happened without saying 'if that is best for her.' I have heard this called the cop out clause. It can certainly look like that. One way to look at it is that however strong and powerful I am I don't quite match up to the total wisdom of the All. And how many times have I not got what I wanted at the time, and found later that lack led me in a fine direction?

It's like the difference between passive and receptive. To face an obstacle and just wilt, saying 'I can't' is passive. Having a go, several different ways, then after getting frustrated, sitting down and asking 'Now what's this about? Is there something I've overlooked? What do you want to show me here?' is receptive.

So blasting my Will out, but then saying, 'over to you Lady' is not weak, but wise.

AS A RITE OF DESIRE, try writing what you want on the bottom of macaroons and eating them - making that idea part of your body. Or write it on tiny bits of paper, and stuff them into cake.

Also do a meditation to prepare, then vividly and thoroughly imagine yourself as you would be once this thing has actually happened. Not on the way, or trying, but when it's all done, and your situation is complete.

If you can't imagine it, there's fear blocking it.

If you can, but you find it doesn't feel good, you have a divided mind about it. Work on what you secretly don't like - or even change your goal to be closer to what you really honestly want.

If you can, and it feels good all the way through, keep doing it, and do sensible outer things to get it too.

Oh, yes, one last thing. When people work away for a while, then say in awful despair 'it's never going to happen' it's about to.

Birthday

PREPARATION You need a birthday cake, and the right number of candles for the person's age; a taper, or pretty box of matches.

For an adult, the number of candles may be too many to fit on the cake. Put the cake on a tray, covered with silver foil with the extra candles round the base of the cake; or put one candle on the cake, and put all the other candles in a pattern on the foil covered tray. They can be small cake candles, or larger ones.

The Cake, or Cake on its tray, is put at the Centre, if space permits.

PURIFICATION

After the ordinary purification, a ritual washing of the birthday person may be nice. This could be a slow and careful washing of their hands in scented water. It could also include their feet. Alternatively a riotous dunking in a ritual bath may appeal to some.

Or the birthday person may like to have a long luxurious version of the Magical Bath. This would be especially appropriate for anyone celebrating alone. The Bath would be more enjoyable after doing a Salt Water Purification.

CASTING THE CIRCLE

1) After invoking the four Elements, everyone settles down for the Invocation of the Years. If no guests are physically present, the birthday person may like to call for the presence of anyone they wish from past, present or future time, to attend in spirit.

2) The birthday person takes up the taper or matches, and lights one candle. They speak of the circumstances of their birth and first year.

They light a second and third candle speaking of anything they wish from these early years.

As they light each new candle they refer to something about that year in their life, in any way they wish. (for older people with more years to honour, this can be a fascinating journey whether done alone or with guests.)

3) With only the centre candle on the Cake left unlit, the birthday person does a quiet meditation in silence, listening to their own mame singing through the tunnels of time. Guests can help, by gently stroking arms and legs, softly singing the name of the birthday person over and over.

4) The centre candle on the Cake is reserved for the birthday itself. Light this in silence.

RAISING ENERGY

How about 'Happy Birthday To Me/ You' sung repeatedly until the peak of energy is felt? Or any other song or chant.

WORKING

The giving of gifts. For anyone at an isolated time of life, this is an important time to gift yourself; if the budget permits, three times over.

COMMUNION

The birthday person blows out the candles on the cake and as is customary, cuts it. (If the cake is surrounded by an outer ring or rings of candles, it may be safer to lift it out first.) The pieces of cake are passed round, and each eats. Then the chalice is consecrated and passed, speeches can be made by guests if so desired, and the feast follows.

OPENING OF THE CIRCLE.

IN THE CIRCLE YOU CAN'T DO IT WRONG

WHY A GODDESS?

When I first taught my Circlework courses, like any other teacher, I had a Plan, a written guide I prepared for myself to make sure I could take people step by step through the necessary list of subjects and skills. Such a Plan is helpful in putting some basic items near the beginning, like the idea of the Circle, or the four Elements, so that later these can be mentioned and used, and built on, knowing that everyone understands. Some topics however are 'floaters' that is, it doesn't really matter when they crop up, as long as they do. My early Plan listed these, and I'd earnestly tick them off as they emerged from a group's spontaneous discussions. (I like following the way each group wants to go because it lets each group be different and keeps me interested as I teach it again for the 35th time.) Towards the end of a course I review what's emerged in this way, and then try and make sure anything left out gets covered before the end.

I soon found there were two topics which came up every time, without fail, and I never had to 'mop them up' towards the end. So I dropped them from my 'floater' list and trusted the appetite of the group to demand them. They are GODDESS & GOD and THE ETHICS OF POWER, and of course they are not entirely separate subjects.

The fact that I never have to introduce the Goddess and God shows plainly what a burning issue female and male power is, how hurt we are about it, and how eager and determined we are to heal it. There are lists and lists of books about it; magazines thrive on it; it's a major theme of alternative workshops and courses; therapy and counselling works away at it; few areas of life are free of the questions asked about it and the changes that are happening in our lives about it.

So much fuss In fact there's so much fuss about feminine and masculine nowadays that quite a lot of people are sick to death of it. Feminism itself has become a dirty word that sells yet another stereotype to tell us what to do. Some people feel strongly that we should beware of getting dangerously separated off from understanding the other sex's point of view.

Some people's beliefs centre on a divine force which has no sex, or they want to nourish a sense of being first of all a person, who can act and feel in ways that were once called masculine or feminine but without being limited by that. Exploring the great principles of the Feminine and the Masculine can look too much like bringing back most of the old stereotypes in a prettied up package.

Just is This is important stuff. In terms of our spiritual beliefs, most of us who follow the way of the Goddess know, or feel, that somewhere way back when before it all began, or somewhere deep below everything on the most basic, primal, simple level, there is a core to all that is, which just is. Thinking about the essential power that holds life, the universe and everything together, we have to accept in the end that we can't understand it, describe it, imagine it, at all.

In tranced vision, out of our minds somehow, in personal exaltation, we may glimpse it for a wondrous moment. Returning to the state of mind that can remember and think, what remains with us is an image - a circle, a dot, an explosion, a whiteness, a darkness, a radiance, a web, a movement, a sense of peace, love, action, wisdom, timelessness, wholeness. But even these are pieces of what we know from our own individual experience; perhaps important pieces, profound places inside us, but still only pictures to represent something much larger than we are.

We cannot connect with such immensity more than occasionally, for a brief moment.

Scientists discovered atoms. Then they broke atoms up into smaller pieces. They dug deep into basic forces of gravity, entropy, anti- matter. Sooner or later, whatever they have spread under us to make a floor, has opened up into another cellar. Another level of mind boggling whatchemacallit arrives with its own challenges and gifts. Finding the alphabet of the universe seems to be an endless quest, with each stage teaching us different things.

In the end, though, it is not a place we need to visit often. The cosmic origin of all things may be something that needs a hello very occasionally, just to make sure I don't lose the big picture. But it doesn't do a lot to help me make a living, mend a broken heart or broken toy, and all the other tasks that make up a real, everyday existence. When I want to connect or relate to the deep levels of the spirit for strength, guidance or celebration, I generally find I can do it much more easily by way of an image which is individual, and personal.

143

A free thing What that image is has to be a totally individual free thing. For what occurs deep in each of our hearts and souls must have respect and privacy.

Many authorities in our lives such as government departments, police, educators, priests, doctors, and employers may try to invade us, dominate our inner lives, and tell us what to think and believe. Even the counsellors, teachers, parents and trusted friends we turn to for help, may push their own beliefs at us as we also tend to push ours a bit at them.

But in the end what works best for me is what fits me as I really am. So whatever you put on the altar in your temple, in the outer world or the inner one, put what serves you best. When you are struggling with crisis, it doesn't matter if what someone else has given you is heap big magic, or the most transcendent beautiful wisdom of the ages - if it doesn't crack it for you, it's junk for you. Maybe your shabby teddy bear is what you need, so look carefully and honestly at your beliefs to see if they're really yours.

I have heard that some alternative groups in America work rites around Tolkien's world or some other fantasy writer. Oh groan and feel superior, to those crazy Americans, and their instant, plastic habits, is yes the first response. But if it works, don't walk away. Maybe Mickey Mouse has something to tell you, if you let him sit among your candles, incense and flowers for a while.

Idols We are dependent on idols.

Some religions are horrified at this, such as Judaism or Islam. The contempt for the 'graven image' comes in part from a fathergod's reaction to the universal Goddess habit to make sacred images of the female through 30,000 years of our history. Those 'graven images' usually had breasts. The horror can come from a faith that does not celebrate the body, and cannot accept divine reality as an enormous, sacred Body of which we are part.

Some strict minded, ascetic teachings do not like idols because they want to lift the peasant from her worship of the little painted wooden doll, to a knowledge of higher things. Others are more tolerant, as in the many forms of Hinduism, Buddhism and some Christianities where people may choose a way to worship facing an idol, a book, or an empty space. These understand that asking someone to wrench themselves from old established, ancestral, comforting methods is hardly kind. And who is to know what the worker really feels who bows and kisses the image? In the heart, is it really the doll which is important? or is it the knowledge of the doll taken away and carried about within through the days?

How free of mana beliefs are we who think we know that the object is no more than a link, a focus for our inner working? Perfectly sensible, intelligent people are distressed if asked to remove their wedding ring before hospital surgery, because they can feel the love of their partnership more easily if the ring is in its place on their finger. I used to be a bit bewildered by people wanting me to sign copies of my books, or to shake my hand, or kiss it - until I realised that of course I feel just the same thing if I meet a writer or teacher I admire (I'm shyer about it, that's all).

Finally, how much do we know about how our concentrated focus of attention on an object for a period of time affects it? Some people appear to have a sensitivity which can feel a charge like electricity in such objects. And I have often noticed that if I have been working for several hours on some office papers, or sewing fabric, or Tarot cards, my cats will immediately go and lie on them when I stop working. Cats are sensitive to magnetic fields, and I respect their wisdom in general.

If the teachings of my faith tell me that body and spirit are one, then perhaps my little terracotta Goddess is not 'just a pottery figure,' because of her shaping, and her significance to me over the years.

And if everything is sacred, because all is part of the divine whole, then whatever I put in the place of veneration is of course sacred. It's just my individual pattern that needs its appropriate surroundings and tools to work well.

When I was first here as a person, there was a very early period of my life when I did not know about female or male. I am speaking of being a tiny baby. Strictly speaking, perhaps I did know femaleness since I was born from it, and then held and cared for by it. But since men caring for newborn children is still very rare, our first experiences can't tell us 'female and male: two things.' It can only tell us about cuddles, and food, and basic discomfort.

There is a first stage, a few months, when we don't know who is doing the caring and holding. We don't even know that there's a ME separate from all the rest - a state like a daydreaming drift, or being mildly drunk, perhaps. Just an awareness of WARM, HUNGRY, SOFT, WET and so on.

After that, by the end of the first year, comes the knowledge of ME. Now I'm standing up, surveying the world, and I know there are separate people in it and one of them is me.

Very shortly after that, I know there are two sorts. Certainly as I begin to talk, frequently in my second year or so, I show I know it. And by three the knowledge of female and male is deeply established, with extensive detail on what each sex is like and what each group is useful for. I know that mummies and babies go together, and that they may or may not have daddies attached. Unless I have been prevented I will have picked up some awareness of sexuality, and of its place in life.

Psychological research tells us that without really being aware of it, we talk to and hold girl and boy babies differently. Carefully observed, people change their approach if told they've made a mistake about a baby's gender (it's an easy mistake to make). Roughly, we tend to hold girls closer, and more gently, and we talk to them more, and in softer voices, tending to cooing. Boys are held away from the body more, there's less conversation, and much more tumbling about, with a jolly voice telling him he's a clever little chap. This has all been observed on video film, and tested by things like people being told they're playing with a girl, when in fact it's a boy.

Children brought up as the 'wrong sex' because of medical problems, are so strongly affected by all this that it's extremely difficult and risky to change them back to the 'right sex' after three years old.

All this goes to show how very deep and basic our view of a two sex reality is. I learn that I exist in a world of other beings, and then immediately I start learning about these two powerful types. The first question we generally ask about a small creature is 'Is it a girl or a boy?' And although we can talk in a general way without referring to male and female, it becomes difficult to use language for very long without mentioning it. In some languages it's impossible to make a sentence without female or male in it.

In a meditation, pathworking or myth drama I can focus on a wolf, a flower, a tree, a star, or the waters, rather than a human personality. But unless I consciously make an effort not to, I'll - usually - begin to experience these as more one sex than the other.

Such is the grip that gender has on the shape of our minds. Therefore most people relate to the divine quite a lot of the time as female, as male, or both in relationship.

If you are one of the interesting minority of people who just do not relate powerfully to Goddess and God, but prefer to think in terms of a Force, or Power, or something like that, then the next section may be of detached interest, or it may amuse or irritate you. It may be best to skip it.

THE LONG LONG TIME OF GODDESS

Most of human existence has been guided and centred on the female principle, for 30,000 years and more. When we lived in caves our deity was definitely female; the skilful art of our ancestors shows the female form as sacred everywhere.

Old Europe In the first civilisations, the Goddess is well in charge. Seven thousand years ago there were highly civilised cultures in Europe as well as the Middle East, with large towns or cities of seven to ten thousand people, living in comfortable houses and streets, with Goddess temples in each part of town. These societies come before Crete, Greece, Rome, and Egypt, even before Babylon and Sumer. Their remains were often thought to belong to these later civilisations, until better dating methods showed the huge mistakes which had been made.

These societies, Vinca, Gumelnitsa, Starcevo, flourished in Eastern and Central Europe up to 4,000 BCE. In Turkey the great cities of Catal Huyuk and Hacilar flourished from 9,000 to 5,000 BCE. Temples show various major Goddess traditions; different cults within a complex of religion,

There's Mother Bird with a bountiful nature, who loves to feed us. She holds within her inner body the mystic Egg.

Harvest Mother leans against the great grain bins, resting her massive belly. She is full of promise and reassurance, heavy, solid, and strong.

Birthmaker shows us her sacred cleft in open power; or holds her child close for us to love too. She can be the Elk Queen, or the fierce Clan Mother Bear.

There's the stiff white Lady of Death, with her staring Eyes, with her own kind of birth.

And Snakey Woman's body is marked with spirals and water waves, whose powers are danger, risk and renewal.

About 5,000 BCE the God appears. He holds his pride and joy out in both hands for us to admire with a touching trust that we will enjoy him, as our foremothers surely did. He sits, head in hands, a mature figure, quietly thoughtful on his place in the scheme of things, and on the great realities of life. Like this he is sometimes described as 'sorrowful', seen as an earlier version of the sacrificial god who came later in history.

It is likely that another cult existed of the Horned God of the hunt, developing from the hunter shamans of earlier times. The lack of surviving images of him may be because he was venerated outside the towns, when hunters were in the forest. Hunting doesn't usually provide a large part of the total diet of a community, but it is an important part of men's contribution to society. It provides survival food in the hard winter months; its essential heavy protein tends to stimulate feasting and celebrations, which strengthen us in both mind and body.

One of the truly remarkable things about this period of history, these societies, is that there seems to be no sign of war. The cities have no defensive walls; the graves hold no armour or warlike weapons. Civilisations were not demolished by conflict, and lasted about a thousand years or more each, building wealth and art and trade, generation on generation. The graves of clearly important males hold craft tools, or beautifully made things showing their skill and how very much it was respected. Other important male graves hold foreign goods; they may have been esteemed because they were successful traders. Goods from other cities far away show that trade was impressively well developed.

Women are buried with plenty of indications of priestess roles; their jewellery and regalia is religious in design, and model shrines show miniature women seated in council. The temples were the administration centres of community life; they often had kilns, ovens, large looms, toolmaking and other technological resources in ground floor workshops with the meeting room above on the first floor. Genetic testing shows clan groups centred on the womens family; in some places such as Catal Huyuk male burials are actually a bit smaller or less elaborate.

We are in the first stages of discovery of a whole new history of Europe. The first scholarly work has been done and the evidence can be discussed but not denied. Matrifocal society (women centred) was a reality for thousands of years, with a clearly

developed balance between the sexes we can envy from afar. Human beings are not essentially warlike. The sexes do not have to live in conflict.

Marija Gimbutas, the pioneer archaeologist who has unearthed this knowledge, died early this year (1994). As eminent death usually does, this will stimulate interest in her work, and that of many others who have done associated work. The recent explosive reunification of Europe has made available a mass of Eastern European research not before known in the West, and this will all now bring a rapid increase in the spread of our awareness of Old Europe.

The destroyers
Around 4,000BCE horse riding clans developed further East, on the Russian plains, and their speed meant they could make a quick getaway after raids, nor could they be chased. Their aggression developed rapidly, and they smashed the settled towns of Europe, the Middle East and the Mediterranean coast. A cult of a harsh sun god appeared, a father who competed for power with the Great Goddess herself.

By 2,500 BCE a kind of Dark Age reigned with warlords triumphant; and violence was supreme. The empires arose to combat the isolation and discomforts of raging disorder, and a warrior based society was established, either to protect periods of peace, or to plunder it.

The familiar empires of Sumer, Babylon, Egypt, Greece and Rome still had their goddesses. But they clearly spell out for us in their myths how the gods eventually took over.

Inanna
In Sumer, we have the earliest written story, the Descent of the Goddess, the first messiah. She went down into the Underworld, hung three days on the World Tree, and rose again to life. This and other biblical material, such as the story of the Flood, which came from Sumer and Babylon, were learnt by captive Jews, and transmitted in a distorted form into the Judaeo-Christian religion.

The Goddess of Sumer was Inanna, Lady of Civilisation. Before making her mystic Descent, she is described as a young maiden goddess, source of wisdom and technology, who invites men to apply for the position of her consort. Having chosen Dumuzi the shepherd as her love, she celebrates and honours him in the first recorded love song. It is a call of open passion which honours her body and his in a totally frank and joyful way.

'*At the king's lap stood the rising cedar ...*'

'*My honey-man , my honey-man sweetens me always.*
My lord the honey man of the gods,
He is the one my womb loves best.'

'*Bridegroom, dear to my heart,*
Goodly is your beauty, honeysweet,
Lion, dear to my heart,
Goodly is your beauty, honeysweet.'

'*Lion, let me caress you,*
My precious caress is sweeter than honey.'

'*He watered my womb.*
He laid his hands upon my holy vulva,
He smoothed my black boat with cream,
He quickened my narrow boat with milk,.'

'*Now I will caress my high priest on the bed,*
I will caress the faithful shepherd Dumuzi,
I will caress his loins, the shepherd of the land,
I will decree a sweet fate for him.'

Sadly, all this goes to his head, he gets uppity later, and she decrees a harsher fate for him. Her great Descent is made down to face her twin self, the dark Goddess Eriskegal, death itself, as Inanna is life. Eriskegal only releases her from death on condition that Inanna sends another to take her place.

On returning to the world of light, Inanna finds that far from mourning her absence, Dumuzi is ruling, from her throne, holding a festival. She therefore repays his betrayal by sending him down to her sister as the required sacrifice. Their cycle of love and separation becomes a seasonal set of festivals, with teachings of birth, love, loss and rebirth. This can be found in all the Mediterranean cultures.

Isis   Isis of Egypt similarly adores and celebrates her consort Osiris. He is killed and torn in pieces. Isis searches for the pieces of his body, mourning his loss. In the Egyptian mode this is her Descent, for she becomes an ordinary, sad woman, while she searches, and the earth cannot grow things without her. She actually puts Osiris together again and brings him back to life, showing that the Goddess who, creates life is still there at this time in history. Her religion was a great focus for healing work.

The Queen of Heaven
The patriarchy of ancient Israel is not quite as strong as it appears. It is quite possible that Solomon's temple was in honour of the Goddess. The Song of Songs celebrates the same sacred marriage as Inanna and Dumuzi, in a slightly disguised fashion. There is a famous quote where the prophet Jeremiah is challenged by the Israelite women: 'We have no intention of listening to this word you have spoken to us in Yahweh's name but intend to go on ... offering incense to the Queen of Heaven and pouring libations in her honour as we used to do ... The Shekinah, or wisdom tradition of Judaism, preserves the Jewish Goddess in an abstract poetic form right up to the present day.

Demeter
of Greece, however, shows how the patriarchy had definitely got the upper hand by the time of Greek prominence. Demeter loses her daughter Kore, and like Isis, is devastated. But Kore has been taken and raped by a god - raped. Demeter searches, mourning, as Isis does. She refuses to allow her earth power to renew and continue the cycle of fertility so nothing grows, like Isis again. But Demeter can only sulk, and appeal to the king of the gods for justice to get her daughter back.

Here is the balance clearly gone to the masculine side. The power of the female is still present, but only through witholding her gifts, sulking, and by wangling connections with powerful males.

Rome, the most recent of the ancient empires, brought Isis, among other religions, to Europe. In fact Isianity was so powerful and widespread in the late Roman empire that historians question why Christianity became the dominant religion in the end, and not Isianity. One answer at least lies in the political usefulness of a religion which asked its followers to be patient and wait for rewards after death, not to expect too much, and to be obedient. The mystery teachings of Isis, still taught in the Western Mystery tradition and by the Fellowship of Isis, are very different. They emphasis a healthy pride and self respect, intelligence, maturity, salvation through one's own efforts, and insist on happiness on earth.

Violence
Three hundred years after the Christian cult got going, it became influential and was adopted as the State religion of the Empire. Its form was similar to hundreds of other sacrificial

god traditions from the Middle East, like Osiris, and back to the beautiful, arrogant Dumuzi of Sumer. However, outside Judaic society, already badly cut off from the Goddess, people were stubborn about their devotion to the Lady. Violent methods were introduced to persuade them, with the burning of the great Temple of Diana in Ephesus,with an attendant massacre of Goddess people serving as a major example (380 AD).

Mary

Significantly, it was shortly after this that a Church Council of Ephesus raised Mary to her Madonna position. The mother of Jesus was almost unknown before, but quickly took on some of the much loved character of Isis: blue cloak, red robe, divine mother and child, mourner and comforter. Goddess peoples were somewhat reassured and conversion increased.

Mary is a fascinating religious problem. On one hand she provides an essential helpline of compassion through centuries of a harsh, violent religion. She ensured that the idea of female spirituality did not completely disappear, especially through her Black Madonna images. Yet she is used to teach us that the actual powers of femaleness are shameful.

Mary is not worshipped as a female, but in spite of it. Complicated theology insists that though pregnant, she is not sexual at all, strikingly unlike Inanna; and that she is helpless around her beloved's suffering and death, unlike Isis herself. The most profound female act, giving birth, is in Mary's myth always kept politely invisible, an embarrassing necessity in a masculine religion. She is completely unlike the earlier goddesses who calmly display their sacred birth gates for us to love and honour.

V Gordon Childe argued that a goddess religion such as those I described before, does not at all mean that ordinary women had power and freedom at the time. He gives Christian Mary as the main example of how a sacred female can coexist with or actually contribute to a poor society for women.

However, this does not hold. Mary is never seen on the central altar of her cathedrals. Although crowned and radiant, she bows her head, all her images and hymns direct us to put her male family first. Her female sex is gracefully hidden beneath flowing robes.

Brigit

Celtic art and religion, in this country, preserved the sacred female longer than any other culture. In Christian churches no less, there are half hidden carvings of Sheila Na Gig, who does show us her divine vagina. She even holds the lips back with her hands to open her gateway of life and death for us (9th century CE).

St Brigit, as the most popular Celtic saint, rather like Mary, preserved the religion of her goddess self - Bride, Brigit, or Brighde. Once as widespread in the north of Europe as Isis was in the south, Brigit had her most powerful centre in Kildare in Ireland. Her temple fire was tended by nine priestesses, who sensibly became nuns under the new order. In the 13th century the bishop of Dublin attempted to squash them, and ordered the eternal flame put out as too Pagan. It was extinguished, and promptly relit on his death! and survived up to the 15th century (Cromwell's Reformation). Her local customs survived even longer, in Western Britain and Eire, through into this century, and are now being honoured once more by modern Pagans.

Many, many more goddesses peopled these cultures and others throughout the world, far more than a quick outline here can suggest. One of Isis' titles is 'Lady of the Ten Thousand Names.' Occult teaching tells us that

'ALL GODDESSES ARE ONE GODDESS,
  ALL GODS ARE ONE GOD.'

The Goddess today
We have only recently as a society begun to welcome the Goddess back. Growing up in post war Europe meant growing up in a Goddessless place. Since the late '70s much has been reclaimed, building on the work of extraordinary pioneers such as Dion Fortune of the Golden Dawn, who was, like me, a priestess and a psychologist, but who lived during the first half of this century. Another great lady who opened the way was Doreen Valiente who worked and struggled with Gerald Gardner in the founding of the modern revived Craft. Her brave, wise, and friendly books guided many a lonely soul into harbour from the '50s to today.

More followed, with Marian Green (Quest) here in England, Olivia Durdin Robertson (Fellowship of Isis) from Eire, Zsuzanna Budapest and Starhawk from the USA during the '70s.

A group of feminist women (Nozama, Mary, Jean Freer, Magenta, Asphodel & others) set up the Matriarchy Research & Reclaim Network (UK) around women's spiritual interests. By the '80s the feminist   challenge stimulated a far greater Goddess awareness both in Pagan groups, and in ordinary society. Ideas like ecology (the Earth Mother) and the New Age (archetypes/ yin.yang) have drawn on Goddess power and extended its influence. The personal growth movement also embraces the Goddess by way of Jung's anima theory, and feminist therapy. In 1984 I set up my own temple as one part of a whole new generation of priestesses and teachers.

The recent courageous move by the Church of England to accept women's priesthood is a powerful sign of the great Return. I am glad for those women whose sincere vocation   can now better serve other devout people of their faith, and provide an inspiration more widely still.

I am sometimes asked why I did not put my own vocation into the Church. I answer that I have sat in the inner sanctuary for a whole generation, watching all those women over there knocking on the door asking to be let in. What an exhausting, and to me, unnecessary fuss. It is by no means over; the institution is still run by men, by masculine standards, celebrating a masculine guru and his god. All the other 'major' religions are similar. There is still a huge difference between a woman priest, and a priestess, although there is common ground.

Why? The big question over all is always asked 'Why?'

'Why did the Goddess go away? Why have women and men had to live under such horrible tyrannies?' Research and study uncovers more and more, as does intuition. Marija Gimbutas talks of the invention of horse riding seven thousand years ago. Many writers think that humanity either did not know the connection between sex and birth, or did not think it important. Fertility, and life itself, was therefore a female mystery.

Elizabeth Fisher describes the invention of agriculture by women, then how cattle herding made the paternity question clear through cows' short pregnancy. Other stock such as goats and sheep already kept in towns would be female, for their milk and young, but a visiting billy from outside would go unremarked. However the presence or absence of a large bull would be a different matter, and soon showed the link. It also, she thinks, introduced the idea of one male or a few males being top males, with access to all the females, while other males were neutered slaves. Bull cults do show up in many societies in transition from matrifocal style to patriarchy.

155

It is possible that the sheer success of the peaceful agricultural civilisations started some population pressure. Better food supplies and cooperative societies meant more and more people. Eventually competition had to occur, and an increase in aggression.

Diane Reisler thinks that the matrifocal peoples practiced selective breeding by exiling males who were too aggressive. These males plus a few women then formed exiled tribes, who then became the destroyer raiders.

Demetra George now takes us a step further. If we learn the mysteries of the Goddess through cycles, and renew ourselves through cycles, perhaps she herself does too. Many Goddess cultures have renewal festivals when the Goddess figure is washed in river or sea to renew her power, then dressed in new made richly worked robes. This occurs once a year, at the dark point of the cycle.

Perhaps the Goddess' law of endless cycle, through dark and light, action and replenishment, is made from her own nature: she also must withdraw for a time to renew herself. If so, that time is now done, and she is awaking among us, right now.

Marija Gimbutas 'Goddesses & Gods of Old Europe'
                 'The Civilisation of the Goddess'
Elisabeth Fisher 'Woman's Creation'
Diane Reisler 'The Chalice & the Blade'
Demetra George 'Mysteries of the Dark Moon'

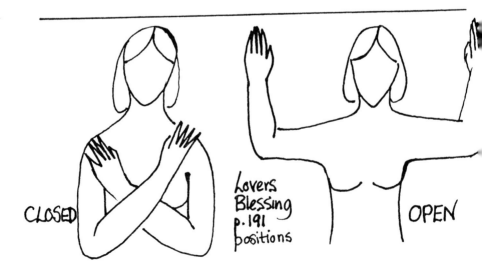

CLOSED

Lovers Blessing p.191 positions

OPEN

The Triple Goddess

MAIDEN - intelligent - curious - quick - impatient
spirit of the wild - Lady of the Beasts - huntress
self centred - self contained - independent
playful - sexual - affectionate - artistic
aggressive - forceful - warrior - initiator
gentle - caring - nurse - midwife - sister

As the virgin in us, she belongs only to herself. As the huntress she is persistent and willing to learn the necessary skills to reach her goals. She is at one with her animal instincts, yet delights in her intelligent brain for understanding her world.

As midwife she serves thecircle of sisterhood, to bring forth new life, new self, the child of flesh or spirit. Her lovers are male or female,   her   sexuality   direct   and   innocent.

MOTHER - protective - responsible - connected
providing - responsive - patient - healer
Earth Mother - Spirit of the Harvest
judge - arbitrator - governor - fixer
angry - avenger - vulnerable - tender
deeply sexual - committed - enfolding

As the maker of bodies and the feeder of them she is the centre of the race. She is the focus of a household, the guardian of the hearth. Her skilful communication holds networks together, and her sense of justice arising from caring for the young and needy makes her a natural judge.

To serve the deep needs of childbearing she goes into her sacrificial descent which brings her into the ultimate power of the vulnerable, of blood and animal being. From this her sexuality opens out into a great trust, in longer, larger cycles,as like much else she does,it is expanded by commitment. Her fierce protection of her charge makes her the formidable avenger.

CRONE - experienced - sensible - survival
crazy - ecstatic - unpredictable
erotic - artistic - peaceful - sweet
savage - painful - compassionate
comical - sad - mourning - hating
free - whole - dead - real

As the one who holds the other modes within her she is multi dimensional, impossible to describe ! She can be the wise guardian, the protector, the healer, the teacher. She can lead if she feels the need, but it would be unwise to cling to her unnecessarily. For she flings off all burdens if she pleases and takes young lovers, travels, studies, or gets splendidly drunk. She lives close to mortality, her own and others, and knows the lessons of pain and loss. She is magic, dark moon, madness.

If honoured and given her due, she guides and consoles us, enriching us with her wisdom. If denied and insulted the subterranean force of her resentment unleashes the primal forces of destruction.

The Three Fates, who spin, weave and cut the thread of life.
The Three Sisters, Three in One, One in Three.

For modern, long lived women, the Maiden shapes our lives until 28 years old or 30; perhaps this is our true coming of age.

The Mother moves in us mainly from then until the mid 50s, when most of us have menopaused.

Some of us complete the freedom and self exploration of the Maiden by 30. Some do not, and revisit it in our 40s to finish it. For some this happens because they take on the Mother early. Some of us are thrust into the Crone's lap early on.

A TEACHER IS A GUIDE NOT A BOSS

me

How can I tell you what it meant to me?

I lived in a world of polite lies, of harsh lies. They hurt me and squashed me. I felt small, childish, unable to grow up. Even this was all my fault. Everywhere I looked in increasing desperation there was always something rotten underneath, saying I was not really here, not important, not the centre.

I lived fiercely unhappy with it. I went to the groups which helped excitingly at first. But then they too cut bits off me, and said I wasn't to have them.

I didn't even have a name for it. I was alone with it, with people who were unkind; or people who were kind, but indulgent of my overdue growing up. I didn't want to grow up then, not if it meant giving up being a person.

Trees and cats and sex understood what I wanted.

Until at last I just said it, amazed at my dangerous madness

I am making a temple here. I am a priestess.

Like a child learning to say a word for the first time I put my tongue around the shape and heard it in my skull *GODDESS*.

Oh yes of course the word had been in the dictionary all the time but I hadn't heard it because it hadn't been said properly.

I screamed for a while. Then I laughed. Then I learnt to sing, I who had been told I couldn't, because I was tone deaf.

All those scrappy experiences, the mess, moved in a great heaving heap, and settled into the patchwork of what I needed to be this job that gave me no job description.

Things made patterns.

I followed the mysteries, became a sacred detective, hunted clues. I taught other women knowing only a few sentences more than they did. They taught me the few sentences more they knew.

I met men again, amazed at the difference.

I found my place at the centre. I surrendered to the mighty wave.

I am proud and strong; I am tiny. I have found love.

I am the voice of the future.

3 Rites of Woman

These are three separate rites for the three aspects, or ages of woman. They are meant to be worked separately; they need at least a month between them to allow their power to soak through you.

You may decide to do only one of them, as the one you most need or like. Or you may like to put them all together in one rite, once you have done each separately. In this case, revisiting each in turn during the same circle will be a very powerful working; please don't treat them superficially by lumping them together straightaway.

Rite of the Maiden

PREPARATION
You may like to wear white, or do this sky clad. Your hair is best loose, without pins, bands or any constraint. If you would like to time it carefully, try doing it at the new moon, or when you have just menstruated.

The Centre Candle is solid, sturdy & white; leave it unlit. Put matches beside it.

PURIFICATION Have a purification bath with salt and sage before the Salt Water purification. Don't use any 'pretty' fragrances; stick to pine or herbal smells.

CASTING THE CIRCLE Air is your young self, curious and intelligent. Fire is your selfish, fierce self, warrior or amazon mode. Water is your motherly self. Earth is your elder self. The Centre binds them all (leave the Centre candle still unlit).

RAISING ENERGY Work up to spinning, or physical movement. Focus the sphere.

WORKING Sit comfortably facing towards the Centre candle. If you have a fire in the room, real or gas, face that.

1) Meditation: Relax carefully. Use a slow drumbeat if you can.

* You are walking into a high mountain forest as dusk falls.

Tall trees surround you.

A pack is heavy on your back. All is quiet.

You walk on for some time, until your muscles are hot and tired. You find a clearing, and build a fire. You eat.

160

* As you sit dreaming into the flames, a wolf howl rises into the starlit sky. Then another.

You tense, in the ancestral fear of our kind, and move closer to your guardian fire.

* In the darkness, yellow eyes gleam between the dark shapes of the trees. You watch the shadowy bodies slipping through the trunks around you.

* One comes forward to the edge of the firelight. She is snarling, with wet red mouth, cruel fangs; the nipples on her belly drag low on the ground. She shakes with tension, and so do you.

Know the held power in her savage hairy body; know her hunger as you see her ribs sticking out. Her saliva drips on the ground.

* Throw her a piece of your food. She bounds away, but comes back, snatches and gobbles. She crouches, watching, with her yellow eyes.

You throw food again, she comes a little closer to feed, with a wary eye on the fire.

Gradually through the night you continue to feed her, dozing in between.

* Dawn comes, with pale light and the song of birds. You wake, with the solid, warm body of the wolf along your back.

When you get up, she waits, her head on her paws. You move slowly, not to startle her.

When you continue your journey, she walks beside you, padding softly at your side. When you come out of the mountains she will stay with you as you go down into the city. She will lope invisibly at your side; but when you need her to defend you, she will turn all her ferocity on any who offend you.

You have befriended your anger.

2) Light the white Centre candle.

3) Stand up, and walk the edge of your circle. Walk fast, walk slow. Keep moving, on and on. You may dance, or leap, or just skip a bit. You might crawl on all fours. You might roar, howl, hiss or moan. Call the animal nature within you to speak. You are the guardian of your circle. None may touch you here.

COMMUNION When the animal needs to drink, do so.

OPEN THE CIRCLE.

Rite of the Mother

PREPARATION

Make a beautiful sacred bed in the centre of the circle, the head to the east, foot to the west. Drape it with your best bedlinen, decorated with ribbons, lace, pieces of fine fabric. Colours could be any that feel good to you. Strew it with flowers and herbs.

Prepare and dress as for a bridal, with delicate attention to hair, face, hands, feet. Pagan brides wear red, which is also the colour of the Mother. You may like to wear a crown, of ribbon, or twined flowers or leaves. Don't wear knickers, trousers or leggings.

Time the rite for around your ovulation (midway between two menstrual peaks) or at the full moon.

The Centre Candle is a short, red candle in a solid steady holder; leave it unlit. It needs to be on a small tray, with matches.

PURIFICATION Put into the bowl the fears and pain of mothering; your own mother; of labour, birth and being a mother.

CASTING As for the previous rite:- Air, wise child. Fire, amazon self. Water, the mother. Earth, the elder, as aspects of yourself.

RAISING ENERGY Walk or move slowly round the bed you have made. Kneel at the side of it. Stroke it.

Say *'Great Mother, your bed is made. You are welcome here'*

Say it three times.

Wait in silence for her to come. Don't worry if nothing obvious happens to indicate her presence, for she is with you always anyway.

Lie gently down upon the bed. She is with you, holding you safe. Focus the sphere.

WORKING

Lie on your back. Make sure the Centre candle is close enough to reach, plus matches.

Draw up your legs. Part them, and let your knees relax and fall apart.

1) Meditation: Relax carefully: you are being held lovingly.

* The dark starred sky above you is her protective breast curving above you. The deep earth below is her belly supporting you.

* The cells of your body each hold the patterns of your DNA, your genetic link with your ancestors. Those millions of women who have lain on this female bed like you now, live on in you.

* The circle of women surrounds you with delicate but deep power. Once a woman giving birth was surrounded by women who drummed, and sang for her, and stroked her body to ease her working. Our time is returning, in your generation.

* When we birth, we flood with female hormones. Drunk, out of our minds, our everyday minds, we become primitive, immensely powerful, greater than ourselves and less than. It is not the everyday self who does it.

* All men are our children. We are the mothers whose sacred task it is to guide and teach our children.

* In the ovaries of our female body, lie the eggs of our daughters. They too will come to the bed of initiation, and the motherline will go on.

End of meditation.

2) Sit up, pull skirts etc up above your knees out of the way. Put the tray between your legs; and light the red centre candle.

3) Put both hands gently between your legs, holding them flat over your sex, touching her and honouring her.

This is the gate of life. Look at the flame, or lie back again, as you wish.

Know the swell of your power deep in your pelvis. You can give birth to your need, or to your desire.

When you feel it coming, open your hands to free the gate.

COMMUNION

OPEN THE CIRCLE.

Shan, Marijka & Cath: We sang her name, stroked her, and held her. Women's magic is so simple, so old, so effective.

Rite of the Crone

Do not do this rite unless you have done at least two other circles before, whether the Maiden and Mother rites, or others.

PREPARATION

You need a mirror, of any size, one that can be propped up or stands in its own frame, and large enough to see your whole face easily would be best. It will help if you have a practice about where to settle and place the mirror at the start of the working.

You could wear black, or work skyclad. If skyclad you might like to have a dark cloak, robe or rug to fold round you for the meditation.

Plaited hair honours the Triple Goddess, and the Crone holds within all three, so consider whether you would like to have plaited hair. Alternatively a plaited headband, belt etc?

The Centre candle is black, and is left unlit.

You need a black or dark blindfold, something soft.

PURIFICATION A Purification bath with salt, but also using country flower fragrances - rose, lavender, lilac etc.

Salt Water Purification.

CASTING THE CIRCLE As for the previous rite:- Air, wise child. Fire, amazon self. Water, the mother. Earth, the elder, as aspects of yourself. Honour Earth with some silence.

RAISING ENERGY Best done in silence, and built very slowly.

Focus the sphere.

WORKING

1) Sit in front of the mirror, propped against the Earth altar. Take the black unlit Centre candle and put it on your left. Or with a free standing mirror, place it to the right of Centre, you sit and face North. Take the blindfold.

2) Meditation: Relax carefully. Put on the blindfold.
   *Call the Crone. Build her presence bit by bit.
   She is big, with dark robes, smelling of sweet herbs.
   You are standing at her knee, like a child.
   She towers above you into the night sky.
   You can put your hands trustingly into her lap.
   She smiles down at you. She is old, and beautiful.
   *Tell her she is lovely, that you love her.
   Tell her you know pain, and its teachings.
   She puts her arm around you.
   She says she knows you have come to love & understand her
   ways. That is why you must leave her now.

*She points. Follow her dark arm, and the pointing finger.
   A young girl is playing over there.
   As you go to her she begins to cry.
   *Remember crying as a child. Remember feeling desolate,
   afraid, hurt, and helpless.
   Comfort her, cuddle her, say silly soothing things.
   Tell her you will always look after her now.
   When she trusts you, and nestles close, rest together.
      (If she does not do so, tell her you will come again.)
3) Return from the meditation gently.
   Take off the blindfold.
   Light the Centre Candle.
   Enjoy the light, then look in the mirror.
   Examine your own face, until a change occurs.
   Whatever you see reflects your inner self.
COMMUNION
OPEN THE CIRCLE.

MENSTRUATION

'WHENEVER YE HAVE NEED OF ANYTHING,
ONCE IN THE MONTH' From the Charge of the Goddess.

There is ancient magical teaching about the dark, veiled Goddess. She may not be seen except at certain special times. She is seen clearly in times of pain, and at death. Initiates of Isis speak of the sacred unveiling; the dance of the seven veils reveals a mystery; the veil of the inner temple is referred to with awe by magicians; the Hindus tell us of Maya, who is the veil of illusionary reality.

Once a month, all younger women tear their inner veil away. The mantle of life is shed, the chamber cleared so that a renewed magic may occur.

In ancient societies, fertility was closer to survival than it is for us, and the way of the Goddess was honoured openly everywhere. Women's cycles were understood to be extremely powerful. We have inherited taboos from all that:- women are forbidden to cook food, carry water, associate with men for several days. In my youth women were still expected not to swim, or to do active sports, and never to speak openly of our flowing blood, especially not in men's presence.

It all looks negative, a state of shame. But what if we look at taboos or forbidden things as no more than indicators of something powerful going on? If women are not supposed to cook or carry loads at this time, doesn't this protect us from heavy work? If we are supposed to stay away from men, doesn't this ensure men will stay away from us, and their various demands with them? If there is a special menstrual hut where women go wouldn't this be a kind of sanctuary? a women's club?

Many menstrual customs include bathing to ritually purify. This can carry with it a disgusting idea that a woman is dirty. But ritual purification is not about washing off ordinary dirt. It's about getting rid of what we do not want. So menstruation is a time of shedding, a renewal, and a new start. I actually feel sorry for men in not having this 'new year' every month, although our hormone influence on them is so powerful that they do experience a reflection of the menstruation of a woman they live with, mother or lover.

Ordinary blood signals danger, injury, death.

Menstrual blood signals life, health, and safety.

The oldest calendars in cave times were kept by women to mark their monthly cycles. The first civilised calendars were all moon calendars in honour of female life giving power.

Most of us modern women have been taught about menstruation as a biological necessity around having children. But this is only half the story - the half even the most immature men can understand and accept. The other half has become a lost teaching.

Occult sources speak of two rivers, the white and the red. One of the great Tarot cards has a lady mixing two streams together. This can be interpreted as mixing male and female, semen and blood, and a whole cult of sacred menstrual sex resulted as a part of Tantra.

It is also a purely feminine teaching. A woman has always got a white river cleansing her; delicate juices flow from her tiny Bartholin glands on each side of her vagina gate. She is eternally cleansed, a self purifier. At the time of the month when a fertile woman ovulates, the stream shows definitely white. At other times it may go white instead of clear to warn her that her inner place is unhappy or sickly. Some women even use the regular signal of the white flow to help them practise birth control.

Balancing this is the red flow of menstrual blood.

Now this could be just a pretty picture of the two coloured rivers, but it's more. For a start, many sex surveys have a lot of women telling us they have different kinds of sexuality at the different times of the month. Many of us (but not all) like sex to be more clitoral, or more selfishly for us, around menstruation; and we become more vaginal and more considerate around ovulation. The pattern often means sharper, intense reactions at menstruation, with gentler, more solid reactions at ovulation. And as scientists have puzzled at it, if sex is all about conception, why do we have a sex drive all month round? Again many women find sex just before menstruating a great help and relief because it stimulates the muscles into a more even rythmn of cramps, which is more comfortable.

The selfish appetite of the red flow is a clue. The reputation of menstrual women is another. Hags. Bitches. Screaming maniacs. PMT Weeping floods. Touchy. Unreasonable.

Manhaters. Sex avoiders. Impossibly sexual. Just impossible.

Well, it's all true. But why? Why do otherwise pleasant, well mannered women who are otherwise affectionate to their families, well adapted to their place in life, suddenly erupt into all this rage and pain?

It looks as though we swing between extremes. Wouldn't it be nice of we could be a bit less crazy at one end, even if we became a bit more disruptive at the other? Could it be that all that well behaved stuff is a bit unreal?

I call menstruation the truthteller. It is not only a flesh veil which is torn away, or the mystery veil of the Goddess. It is the veil of pretence.

At this time, whatever you dislike in your life will express its cramping hold. Your resentment and irritation at all the times you have been nice when it wasn't really what you felt, will come out claws first. And any stress or struggle currently around you will move through your body.

A menstruating woman is a sensitive woman. Many of us in the magical ways think that we are more psychic, more open to dream guidance, better at divination at this time. Providing we have the retreat we need, we can touch the inner places inside ourselves easier when we bleed. For now the inner walls are naked and delicate.

Our selfish needs surface unstoppably at our red, angry time. We may try, horrified, to suppress these feelings, but they will out. If we suppress them less at other times, this one can be much more comfortable. When the dark mirror arrives we can look and see where we overlooked our own sacred needs before. And the more we nourish ourselves in our dark retreat, the more we will emerge with smiles and love to radiate out during the bright time.

On manhating. It's entirely sensible. This is not a kindly society towards women. Too many men are badly brought up, overgrown toddler monsters with dangerous powers in their hands. It is only reasonable for any self respecting woman to be wary, to test and test again. If your feelings scream hatred, honour that. It means you have been insulted or damaged. Get help from other women. Do not force yourself to be nicer to men than you genuinely feel like - except to manage everyday survival. Every time you force yourself to be nice you hurt yourself, and you encourage them to continue to be monstrous. Better a time with no men, or very little contact, while you rage and grieve towards your healing, than live a monstrous lie.

To honour menstruation more fully you can consider these possibilities.

KEEP A MENSTRUAL CALENDAR to record your mood changes and learn your own cycle. After several months comparing the months will tell you a lot. For best results only look at this month's record as you do it, or else the record for another month can influence how you perceive what's happening now. I did it by coding my days +3 to -3.

WEAR RED Perhaps a red scarf, a belt, knickers (!) T shirt, a petticoat. Red is the colour of life, freedom and love.

TRY SPONGES Menstrual sponges are incredibly comfortable and very kind to the vagina, and have been used by women for thousands of years. A damp sponge is much softer to push in on the swollen days than a hard tampon.

A friend of mine who uses them went to her gynaecologist. When she mentioned she had to take out her sponge he got very excited and asked her if she'd mind if his students came to look at her 'so they can see what an untraumatised vagina looks like.' Untraumatised means unscratched, unhurt, in this case compared to tampons.

Sponges are great if you don't mind putting your fingers up yourself to put them in or take them out, and the sight of blood when rinsing the sponge under the tap isn't too much for you. Otherwise it's not for you.

Buy a real sea sponge from the chemist. A big bath sponge can be cut up, or they might have little ones. When dry it needs to be about the size of your palm. It shrinks as you wet it, so don't worry about its large size. Wring it out, squish it up between finger and thumb, and push up and back. It needs rinsing out as often as a tampon needs changing, perhaps a little oftener.

When getting it out, you can find it awkward the first few times because it warms up and feels like you! so getting hold of the right bit and tugging can take two or three tries. But if you tug at a bit of you instead it won't hurt, your fingers will just slip off.

The really big advantage is not having to carry supplies about with you.

FREE MENSTRUATING Having a quiet day with nothing challenging is very important anyway. If you can arrange time without going out, try leaving all pads, tampons or sponges out of the picture entirely. During the first, tender day this is especially lovely, but even a few hours is refreshing. Wear easily washable leggings, but skirts are better - they fold up under you when you sit. If the flow is heavy, put a towel on the seat or on the bed.

A wash with cold water is also pleasant, and holds off the flow for an hour or so if you want sex.

Honouring the blood like this, instead of fighting it, and hating it, will help ease the pain that expresses our fear.

Red Circle Rite*

PREPARATION Why not ask your friend or lover to prepare your list of what's necessary? If this doesn't appeal, or is not possible, be your own friend and put things together in advance of your inner, vulnerable time.

An excellent place to do this rite is in bed. Otherwise, make a nest in the circle with plenty of cushions, blanket, duvet, hot water bottle.

A bottle of almond oil, body cream or moisturiser.

Red water paint, water pot and brush/ or thick red felt tip (water based).

Red candle for the Centre.

Hot drink, or whatever especially pleases you for Communion.

PURIFICATION A Magical Bath, perhaps a simple salt one by candlelight would be excellent. Allow yourself to bleed freely without obstruction in the bath if you can. Salt water bowl as usual sitting in your nest.

CASTING THE CIRCLE as you like. You may like an all female circle, Air as Maiden, Fire as Self, Water as Mother, Earth as Wisewoman or Crone. Stay nested and have candles near enough to light if you like.

RAISING ENERGY Gently as you like if you're tender. Perhaps just by rubbing oil or cream gently in circles round and round your tummy and your lower back.

WORKING 1) If you didn't stroke your tummy with oil do it now. 2) Watch the flame of a candle for a while then let yourself snuggle, and drift into the dark cave within. Remember all the other women who share this with you. Let whatever comes be welcome, including angry, harsh feelings, or sadness.

* FOR NON MENSTRUAL WOMEN THIS CAN BE A RITE OF THE DARK MOON.

3) Paint or draw a spiral on your tummy with the paint or felt tip. This is the symbol of renewal, going back 30,000 years to our cavemothers.

4) If you can, touch your blood. Look at it. Touch it to your brow chakra for inner wisdom. Snuggle and drift to the dark mirror again.

COMMUNION Drink deep, to balance the flowing out. Eat delicacies to feed your specialness.

OPEN THE CIRCLE - but don't get up for a while.

MOON MAGIC

Moon month mental mind menstruation measure

Moonlight moonshine moonflower moonlit moony

Moonlight flit moonshiner moonstone moonstruck

New moon Full moon Waning moon Dark moon

Honeymoon Harvest moon Blue moon Hunter's moon

By moonlight everything looks different. Ordinary things cast strange shadows. Things are not what they seem.

The Waters of the planet flow and ebb in answer to the mistress of the heavens. 90% of our bodies is Water.

Women shed red waters to the same cycle as the Moon.

The relation of the moon and the sun at a woman's birth determine when she will be fertile during her maturity.

There is no organic life on the Moon and yet the cycles of the Moon rule the growing of all plants on Earth.

The calendar has been blurred but the 13 moons lie just under its surface, the origin of measuring time.

Marked bone/ ivory has been found showing menstrual moon calendars dating back to 30,000 years ago, cave clan times.

Seven days is a moon quarter, a sennight. Fourteen days is a half moon, a fortnight.

The moon appears as crescent or full moon constantly changing, yet the reality does not change.

The crescent on the right hand is young Maiden moon.

The full complete moon is mature Mother moon.

The crescent on the left hand is sinister Crone moon.

Isis Selene Diana Hekate Morgaine Arianrhod Hathor
Yolkai Estsan Ishtar Lilith Tiamat Al-Lat Selene
Moira Norns Shekinah Fata Morgana Bina

She changes everything she touches
And everything she touches changes.

In some societies the moon is a man.

In one of these his name was Sin.

Machines with men have walked on the moon.

No one has touched the moon we see in the night sky.

Invoke by the full moon. Banish by the waning moon.

Invoke energy, or banish fatigue.

Plant by the waxing moon, weed on the wane.

Lady of Changes. Mistress of Initiation. Huntress.

She who gives lovers to the lonely.

Sweet Maiden. Mother of Night. Old Wise Woman.

This is perhaps not the first moon we have had. Our previous companion eventually came too close and crashed to Earth before the age of Atlantis.

Standing stones which are still live, are conductors for a spiral current of magnetic energy sensed by dowsing. These spirals change direction with the moon phases.

The moon is the Veil of the Goddess, the appearances around us, behind which lie the forces of life and death.

The moon is a magic mirror.

For more moon lore look to 'Moon Magic' by Dion Fortune, a detailed account by a 20th century priestess and pioneer of modern Paganism; and 'Moon Madness' by Paul Katzeff a recent book with two sections, one on myth, legend and custom past and present, the other on scientific research findings.

Moon rite

PREPARATION Check the moon phase: you need a waxing or full moon. A waxing moon curves on the right like the letter D. A waning moon curves on the left, like the letter C. If you can't see the moon to check because of cloud and you've lost track, a good diary has moon phases marked in it.

Put two similar glasses to stand in moonlight of the waxing moon, after sunset. Fill one with water, slosh the water into the other, then pour it back into the first. Stand them on a windowsill, or in a quiet outside place. The more it looks like the moon rays are striking through the water the better it will feel to you.If where you put them permits, then meditate on the moonlight and water in the glass for a short while.

Leave the water to soak moonlight for at least one hour. Don't do this the night before, as the day's sun in between will overlay the moon's effect. And a dark cover isn't enough to prevent that; it takes lead to shut out sunlight.

Put the glasses of moonwater at the Centre of the Circle.

You may like to wear white and silver.

PURIFICATION It might be nice to purify in a silver bowl, or a shiny one. Silver has special magical links with the moon.

CASTING THE CIRCLE Speak to the four quarters of the Moon: the first crescent (Air), the full face (Fire), the waning crescent (Water), and the dark, hidden moon (Earth).

RAISING ENERGY Make sound and movement to honour cyclic power, rising and falling, on and on. Focus the energy with the sphere as the moon itself. If you particularly like the vortex, it could go up to the moon.

WORKING 1) Take up the two glasses. Stand facing the Centre.

Pour the water from one glass into the other. Pour it back.

Keep doing it over and over, until you can't do it any more, or until you reach a peak feeling of peace, power, beauty or insight.

2) Sit. Even out the water in each glass. Drink the first, and ask for your desire. Drink the second and make an offering.

3) Meditate as you will; draw, write, sing, dance, be sexual.

COMMUNION Moon cakes?

OPENING THE CIRCLE

MANHOOD

It's been rough for men in society lately, especially for any that have tried to not just follow the conventional model of a man, but to find a new way. It means not getting the rewards the existing system gives men who continually compete with each other and squash women. It also means very unfairly that you may not be understood even in alternative circles. The braver, and more pioneering you are about your maleness, the more you may feel very isolated at times. You will find sometimes that you are actually less likely to impress women - who can (quite infuriatingly) be remarkably old fashioned when it pleases them, about how much money, status, and achievement a man's got. Other men are difficult to reach, for male communication is centred a lot on practical tasks, or expressing competition; these don't bring you closer in understanding each other as fellow fighters in this most magical transformation.

You are fully entitled to times of severe annoyance, frustration; wanting to give up the whole fuss as a bad job; wanting to retreat into your shell, be a hermit; or just get back to the simpler way of just being an ordinary bloke for god's sake. For god's sake?

I think you must do these things, when you need to. For honestly, my beloved brother, if you force yourself to be a lie, if you behave like a good boy with me and other women, that's too much like all the obedient, submit and be glad awfulness laid on us women through history. Try too hard to be the perfect man, try too much to pay the blood price for other men's crimes, and sooner or later your natural resentment will boil up and you'll just do something nasty anyway.

Men tell me Some men have told me in confidence, in counselling, or in sheltered group discussion, how the fear of their own aggression lurking within, haunts them. Those with harsh or violent fathers especially know this. Those who lacked very much fathering feel it often too, for mother may not have felt kindly towards the sex that did not help her when she most needed it. Many men have known the red tide rise up within them, and know how perilously close they came, or could come, to being the violent monster. Some already know how it happened to them, they did it, and live with the memory, somehow.

The truth

When I was told that I carried a boy in my belly, I was terrified. For now I was condemned to find out the truth: are males by nature monstrous? or is it society that makes them so? I discovered that it was one thing to be a friend to the male, to engage in loving struggle with him as my consort, to teach ideas about Goddess and God. It's another, bigger thing to find that twenty years of my life stretched ahead, devoted just possibly to rearing an enemy of my sex.

I was lucky in the support I got through those scary hours as I came to terms with it. And I am telling you this, because I can finish the story with a happy ending. My little son is vigorous, boisterous, very male, and quite able to control and contain his power. His gentleness delights me, and of course in common with all parents, his raging energy exhausts me. We have found that he did need help and guidance to understand how his strength could hurt us, other babies, or the cats. But he was well able to learn self discipline if shown both gently and sharply, and all of it repeatedly, for a critical few months.

My therapy training had taught me that dangerous aggression erupts only when anger and resentment has been bottled up for a long time. Mass murderers are always described by those who 'knew' them before as mild, quiet men, who never lost their tempers. My healing work is therefore often about teaching people how to safely express the angry part of the self. Some people don't even know they have one until reassured that it's not wicked, but a natural forcefulness for protection - noisy, disruptive, but not damaging. It's also the root of self confidence.

To apply the same teaching to my son, we encouraged him to show us when he was angry. He was never, never prevented from shouting or crying; the famous face down on the floor in a restaurant classic incident was quietly left to blow over (with an great effort I admit). He is asked if he is cross, and taught that he can smack us on the legs if he is.

Hardly any of the famous toddler tantrums occurred; his tempers rise to a brief peak, then subside into settling the matter. He is renowned for his peaceful, happy, gentle character.

Once upon a time

Now, there was once a time in history, when there was no war. Not a primitive time, but a time of cities, with seven to ten thousand people in them. There were no defensive walls round them, and town planning laid out orderly

streets and neighbourhoods. Houses were two or three stories high, well built, with solid stone foundations, plastered walls, and internal stoves.

These civilisations, for there were several, not just one, because they were not broken and destroyed by wars, lasted for about a thousand years each. Their remains, in Central and Eastern Europe, were at first thought to be early Greek and Roman colonies. Better dating methods have uncovered a whole age of Old Europe we did not know, from 10,000 to 4,000bce.

Women were clearly central to these societies, as priestesses, administrators, clan mothers. Men's graves are completely free of war weapons or armour. But the eminent, highly regarded men with more elaborate graves hold craftsmen's tools, or finely crafted things, showing how honoured the craftsman technologist was. Some graves hold beautiful, foreign items, indicating perhaps a special respect for men as traders, for the trade routes of this time were well developed.

Anthropologists and psychologists are increasingly showing us that cooperation is far more basic for human beings than is hostile aggression. Isolated tribes exist who do not kill or attack others. The frantic levels of aggressive competition come out when people are forced into tough conditions too long and too hard. Then it's difficult to give them up.

Sin The teaching of original sin has much to answer for. If I am basically bad, and so are you, I don't have much to lose by being cruel to you - it's only my nature after all and you probably deserve it anyway. And I better get you, you bad creature, before you get me.

If you, and other beings, are like me, in search of happiness, independence, sex and safety, and we are all sacred children, it looks rather different. I may have to be wary, and have fighting skills ready, in case your needs conflict seriously with mine. But at least the place of peace is not just naive dreaming, best kept for the hereafter.

Please,

my beloved brother, claim your deep, beautiful, wild maleness; claim your full nature with all the heroic strength in you, and the tenderness of the protector that flows from it. By all means respect us women where we merit it; listen to us carefully before you interrupt, for our wisdom has been too long ignored. When we are foolish and do not invite respect, either pass by on the other side quietly leaving us to mature as we must, or tell us what you think. Keep faith, when you can, that your restraint is gentleness, your wildness is your male birthright, that you too are guided and sacred in your own way. Those who do not understand your new maleness (that is really very old) are not all there are. And while not all women are prepared to handle the savagery and splendour of your true, male self yet, some are. Others, when challenged, grow stronger - after all, we are supposed to be becoming strong women these days, aren't we?

Finally, do not despair of other men. You are gradually coming closer to each other, as we women did in the '70s. It's hard, and can be scary. Your competitive training needn't be too much of a problem if you accept it and let it have its say, - without letting it say it all. My observation from the outside is that you men seem to communicate best when you're alongside each other, sharing a task, rather than in face to face gossip as we do. There may be silences, and a lot of brief, practical comments about tools, or some debate about ideas. The personal stuff leaks through in glimpses, just a bit here and there, eventually. Maybe it emerges out of mutual respect, exchange of help, and the pleasure of a job getting done.

Maybe male friendship has a different pattern; very sticky and slow to start, especially while the dances of status, and then the reserve, play themselves out. Perhaps it's the more solid when forged. We women by contrast, make easy connections through our pleasant courtesies, our shared childcare, our quick cuddles and fuss. Much of this does not last, as the same problems of inequality and distrust that you have only emerge later.

As the economy destroys the old man = wallet type of male, fathering is becoming more the image of maturity. A local bloke in our pub told his mates 'None of you lot know what being a real man is about - you've never changed a nappy!' Interestingly, no one argued with him. As fathers, men can talk to each other about soft things, and the tiny, warm body awakens their lost skills of cuddles and total sensitivity. The protective Lord arises, and all that fierce strength surrounds the one who needs it most.

Here is my offering for you, then, in honour of the maleness I love in my husband my son, and other special men who have taken a part in my education as a woman and priestess.

Rite of the Male

PREPARATION A prepared speech as described below.

A gift to the Goddess. Use any creative craft you already have, or explore a new one, but it's important this gift is made with your own hands.

An ear of wheat.

PURIFICATION as you wish.

CASTING THE CIRCLE

You may like to invoke gods at the quarters. There are the Celtic, Nordic, Saxon, Egyptian, Sumerian or Graeco-Roman forms to choose from. Or if you are intrigued by my description of Old Europe there are our native shamanic modes. Air is the Boy, the innocent Baby on her lap. Fire is a beautiful image of the god holding out his pride and joy in both hands to be admired. Water is the thoughtful, mature male, sitting with his head on his hand (Rodin's Thinker). Earth is the Horned One, animal himself, and hunter too.

RAISING ENERGY as you wish. There are chants in my Songbook which celebrate the male.

WORKING

1) THE BOASTING SPEECH OF THE HERO

This was an extremely ancient custom, extremely male. You need to prepare about three main items to boast about; anything you personally consider your strength and nobility as a male. 'I am he who struggled with X and ...' 'I am he who won X skill...'

If this is a shock demand, you may need some time to mull it over, and grow greater self respect. Consider that I am asking you to genuinely value yourself as a male.

Make your speech to the Goddess, or to her and the God. Do it thoroughly, at length, repeating the your proud boasts several times. Work up your pride. Stride about in your circle. Show us and them your natural vigour in your voice and moving. Keep going till the energy naturally falls into quietness.

2) THE GIFT & THE VOW

Go to the Lady and offer her your prepared gift. Tell her how you came to make it, its inspiration, the effort to gain confidence and carry it through to completion. And anything else, for she understands all.

Now make a vow to her service. It must include your undertaking to use your strength to be a protector of children, animals, hurt & vulnerable folk, or the Earth herself. Don't take on the whole lot - you're only one person and your energy is most successful if focused on one or two targets.

3) SHAPECHANGER

shapechanger   walker between the worlds   dreamer singer

shapechanger transformer craftworker honeymaker

shapechanger   lord of sweetness lord of storm

* * * He lies softly sleeping between my legs, waiting, restfully, without a care. He is perfect, quiet, lovely in his workmanship. He trembles, quivers & rises gently like a bird. Delicate as a bird's wing he takes to the air, silken feathers shining in the dawn. Dancing up & down, my little bird delights in his freedom.

* * * He rises, ah he rises, full of pride in his power. He rises, craving with desire. Sweetened with honey, glistening, he stands in majesty. Thick, solid & tall, fed from deep roots of power, he is grown truly wonderful. Rampant stallion, fierce bull, kingly stag, your beauty is the raw miracle of my best moment, the wild grace of my sacred flame.

* * * He swims, moving silent and slow in the darkness. His large silvered body gleams through the shadows. My stamina comes through slowing, knowing my way step by step up the rushing river to the source, onward slowly & carefully, touching every crevice as I go. The wisdom of the salmon guides me. The laughter of the dolphin calls me, until skill & surrender bring me home at last.

* * * The very sun itself has exploded. Its crashing radiance has blinded me. All I can see is dark shapes in the stillness. It is all gone now, the thunder and the power that once was. I lie helpless, enfolded in mystery. I have given myself, I have sacrificed to the old ones. I am the sacred servant of time.

TAKE UP THE WHEAT & EXAMINE IT.

* * * From this my seed will grow once more a mighty tree. For though my time of glory is brief, I hold the mystery of instant creation in me, the spraying seed comes each time new made from me. In each season of my power I come again. I send my roots deep in the earth to the very underworld itself. My trunk is encircled with living bark. My branches cover the sky, touching heaven. In my quietness, all these powers are at one & my own.

COMMUNION

OPENING THE CIRCLE

The Hero

He is vigorous, beautiful in his strength.
He is quick, intelligent, curious, endllessly searching.
He is restless, uncertain, easily frustrated.
He weeps and laughs easily, and is quick to anger.
He watches, content to learn and observe.
He is shy, unsure, passionate, awkward, affectionate.
He is wild, sexual, chaotic, intensely proud.
His task is to find his strength, achieve, win his renown.
And to learn the skills of the lover.

The Guardian

He is contained in his strength, with hard won discipline.
He is thoughtful, wrestling with the peak of his powers.
His achievements, his vigorous body and acquired skills
are now ready for the call to serve and protect.
Within him the fierce savagery is leashed, but
remains close to the everyday, provoked rapidly by cruelty,
or any threat to those for whom he cares.
His hands, knowing how to grip, crush and destroy
are endlessly delicate in touching a child or a lover's body.
He struggles through dedication, patient, loyal.
He knows fear, anxiety, loss, and hurt
yet he rises ever again from these times of shadow.

The Fool

This one is all things and none. He is wise, peaceful.
He seems to want to play with the children's toys.
He moves swiftly into power and skill when he wishes,
but is unlikely to stay there consistently.
Sometimes his face sharpens, and the beast fleers out,
still blazing within the banked fires.
He does not need to prove anything for that was done
long ago. He potters, enjoying himself immensely.

SEX MAGIC

Sex is magic. Anyone who has experienced good sex knows this without being told.

I mean it absolutely seriously when I say that sex is magic. Think of the sheer power that lovers throw off around them in ordinary circumstances; and then of the raw energy they generate around them as they make love. Think of how making love on your own shifts you into another reality, so that the book you were reading, the meal you were looking forward to, the very sight of the room around you, all dissolve into an intense, dreamlike moment of power.

Unfortunately, we have grown up in a society hostile to sex. Liberation movements have undone some of the damage, and begun to create a better sexual climate. But too many people still live in ignorance and nervous fear. Faces and bodies everywhere show the stiffness and misery anti-sex attitudes produce.

Our trained sex roles supposedly ensure we know what to do. In reality, feminine behaviour forbids any effort to make anything happen except indirectly by presenting an inviting appearance and atmosphere. Massive expectations fall on the masculine half, who must know how to courteously seduce, deducing the wishes of the partner from stifled signals. This is in spite of receiving no training for this skill except very inaccurate information in men's magazines and gossip. In actual performance, this sexpert masculine must still intuit what will work for both, with no clear instruction, while maintaining a discipline of lengthy erection. Meanwhile, the feminine must discover new, virginal delights in the experience, regardless of what is actually done. For any lack in response is this poor feminine's own fault, in spite of having very little say in what happens.

Finally, both collapse, exhausted with the struggle. Hopefully they look at each other. 'Did I do well?' If the answer is felt as yes, the relief is as much about a job done properly as anything else. This kind of fake sex is not very magical.

Whole sex expands the whole organism into a larger than life state, returning back to normal, but with renewed energy. Sex is creative energy, birth energy, free energy.

Sex is dangerous to dictators, employers, anyone who tries to exert authority. It can en-courage a timid person to skive off work and stay in bed with a beloved. It can inspire the downtrodden to imagine a better life and rebel against limits imposed by others. It can make someone so satisfied and happy they lose the need to fight because they are ordered.

Sex transforms people. Aggressive, jumpy people calm down. Withdrawn people open out. Conventional people strike out of their usual patterns. A plain face glows and looks beautiful. Sex is an alchemist, a changer, a healer..

Sex threatens any religion that tells you you need a priest in your life. Create an orgasm, and you know a timeless, intensely happy, whole, bright, beautiful, totally individual, yet totally universal momemt of being. What else is enlightenment? How about an experience of heaven where you are at the centre of the cosmos, the only person that matters, filled with intense waves of bliss, yet blended with all other life in an unlimited expansion of awareness, and the whole is rooted in pure pleasure?

You have a hotline to heaven between your legs. It's called the sacred serpent, the kundalini, the mystic spiral, the serpent power. Serpent images express the wavelike movement of this sexual earth energy. Tantric texts speak of the magic serpent coiled 'at the base of the spine' rippling upward and outward into ecstasy. Tantric yogis and yoginis (male and feminine titles) seriously explore sex energy to reach insight, bliss, and renewed energy. You do not need a partner. Sex by yourself is just as beautiful and effective - sometimes more so. However, with your chosen lover, ritual circlework sex can open up richer and deeper possibilities. For sex with someone else not Pagan, link it to a special occasion, like a birthday, anniversary, or Valentine's day. Explain this as a sexual meditation if you like, but do explain it.

In the Circle
Prepare the place lovingly, providing plenty of warmth, cushions and pretty things.

PURIFICATION begins with a special perfumed bath, as relaxing and luxurious as you like. Then the personal Purification is done as usual, with Salt and Water. Go gently and slowly, expressing any discomfort or anxiety about this sex, from previous experiences of sex, or whatever you imagine might happen. Allow all distractions to have their say and fall away.

CASTING THE CIRCLE: invoke each Element in sexual terms. Choose colours for the candles that are special to you. Purple is the colour for profound female sexuality, and goes well in the West. I will return to the importance of female energy. Provide favourite food, and wine, mead, beer or another special drink or intoxicant. Use loose robes or dressing gowns to begin with.

Ask AIR perhaps for the bright clear awareness to fully experience everything. The sex organ often forgotten is the brain, which affects us by how we think about what we're doing. Ask for the playfulness of a child to tell you what to do.

Ask FIRE for stamina, for confidence, for the heat of passion, for clitoris or penis to swell with power. As you speak, touch your spinner of energy. Standing beside your lover ask that you be free to ask her or him for what you want.

Ask WATER for depth, for sensitivity to nuances. Stroke the skin of breast(s) gently, say softly how you want to create loveliness and pleasure. Ask, if you like, for any meaning from within to come to you; say you are ready to hear the inner guide. Ask that the intensity of your feelings not frighten you, or old inhibitions hold you back.

Ask EARTH for a beautiful orgasm, as long as that is right for your body right now. If you don't orgasm, ask that you reach a feeling of true pleasure and beauty. Ask for a willingness to let go, to go with what happens, to surrender to the needs of this experience. Meditate a little on receptivity. Touch caressingly the vagina or the penis.

At the CENTRE, disrobe. Say carefully that you accept whatever happens, even if that means sex does not happen. This is very important, because otherwise the stress of expecting special sex can mean spoiled sex.

Use the traditional words at the Centre.

For RAISING ENERGY, sit on comfy cushions. Massage legs and arms briskly. Alone, massage as much as you can reach. With your lover, massage anything except the sexy bits!

Light a particular incense you have chosen; Fire, Beltaine, or a God/ dess of love.

Now lie back on the cushions. Breathe deeply and slowly for a while, then go through the body relaxing each part as you go. Take it slowly, and really make sure of each step of thorough relaxation.

Imagine a cocoon of coloured gossamer around your body; see what its main colours are. Give some time to this as your auric or pure energy body is essential to sexual or ritual creation.

Then sit comfortably up with your legs bent (not lotus though). Begin leisurely caresses. Attend thoroughly to legs, arms, toes, shoulders, as well as the more obviously sexy parts. With a lover, sit facing each other.

Unhurriedly, let the energy come. Have some music, or attractive pictures, or other amusement available to entertain if there are patches of low erotic feeling.

In the Circle especially, even more than elsewhere, a female body is the Goddess, a male body is the God. So honour them as such, with the greatest pleasure and love you know.

Let your feelings build to whatever height they will. The first time you try ritual sex you may not reach great sexual peaks, as a new situation may feel odd. However the soft, candlelit atmosphere in the magical Circle will definitely provide a pleasurable experience you'll remember.

If you want to direct your sexual power magically to a purpose, fix the imagined purpose clearly in your mind when you complete your relaxation. Then return to the image at intervals as you build up erotic feelings. Then finally, if you transfer into orgasm dimension, think of it one last time, as sharply and clearly as you can. Then let it explode, opening out to fill the cosmos on the waves of your orgasm.

Let the quietness afterwards unfold. If any image or particular feeling rode on the orgasm let it stay with you; this is how a message comes from within.

If you do not orgasm, or just do a male 'sneeze' instead of the full spiral, the images can still come, and you can still cast your will.

COMMUNION is your love feast. Enjoy it. And if after a while, strengthened by food and drink, another swell of energy wants to develop, then Communion can be a sexual celebration of the joys we are given, so let another sexual rite take place if that suits you.

Thank each Element for whatever their special power gave you.

Most people in our society are unused to the Paganism of older societies where sex went beyond solitary or couple sex. Sexual rites at Festivals once meant a good deal of sex with strangers, with divinely conceived children as the result. To bring such customs back is not at all easy as our feelings are far more trained in conventional style than is apparent to us. Experiments in freer modes of sex generally cause considerable hurt once the first excitement wears off; possessive feelings, and insecurity do not just disappear because we'd like them to. It is frequently men who pioneer these experiments, only to find at the crunch that they are less able to bear it than they thought.

Auras

The cocoon of energy around your body is what many call the aura. Your aura is as personal to you as your eyes or your fingerprint, only more. It carries a complete pattern, in its colours and weave, of your personality. When you move closer together with someone physically you overlap your auras a little. During sex, you not only overlap auras, you unite them. As you separate afterwards, something of the other aura stays in yours, and something of yours stays in theirs.

Clearly this explains why we take some care in choosing our lovers. Even a very promiscuous person usually thinks about a bit more than just the prospect of a sturdy body; if not, people begin to find that frequent sex without careful choice makes a person sickly. All that mixture of auric baggage they've taken on is indigestible. The resistance to infection is lowered, and mild to severe depression occurs.

However this doesn't mean that a genuine, desire for someone as a lover is harmful. It is only if we ignore our true feelings; making sex a habit when we don't really want it that ill health develops.

Couples who regularly share a bed and make love are therefore frequently mingling their auras. This actually means they are mixing personalities on a fine level.

When we're strongly attracted to someone a certain something indicates the difference between liking someone and feeling attracted to them. There is a kind of excitement kindled between us and certain people, which may or may not be expressed in sex. With others, although we feel drawn, and enjoy the other personality, the spark is not there. The second feeling may be as strong or stronger than the first, certainly in the long run. But it is definitely different. One is primarily erotic. The other is primarily friend-ly.

Just to confuse matters, you may have a friend response to someone of the opposite sex, and an erotic one to someone of your own. This does not necessarily mean you're homosexual (unless you make a habit of it). After all it takes more than one blade of grass to grow a meadow.

What it means is to do with the magical dimension of erotic relationship. Friend relationships are based mostly on similarities, common tastes and attitudes. This makes them best at mutual support and loyalty. Erotic relationships are based on an intense spark of difference. If you reflect on the people you have felt most attracted to in the past you will see what it was in them that was different to you, that originally entranced you.

We are intrigued by the different, and it is the excitement of the unknown that provokes sexual response to begin with.

Love is ... In Athens, once, a dinner party discussion developed about Love. Different ways of praising Love arose, calling Love wondrous, beautiful, strong and so on. Finally Socrates spoke up, an ugly elderly man, whose philosophy was well respected. 'Love ' he said, 'is none of those things. For Love always wants those things. And why would one want beauty or strength if one had it already? Therefore Love is essentially a feeling of lacking something.'

The quality that draws us is unknown because we lack it. The bright vivacious person who has trouble being peacefully quiet will be drawn to a quiet person, seeing them as intriguing and profound. The practical person who lacks creativity will be fascinated by the maker of beauty. And the buzzing creative spirit will go for the secure, practical type.

You may say that you and your lover are both creative, or both practical. Then it is not that particular polarity that drew you together. In that you are 'friendly.' Something else sparked your erotic response to each other.

The reason why sex is magic really is that it performs a magical task. By mixing your auras you open up to transferring the qualities you need from the other, and to giving what s/he needs too. Unfortunately this key part of Pagan magic was suppressed under the 'sex only for children' perversion. Sex makes magical children; new made people who are whole- d.

What too often happens because this Pagan magic is not known, is that the couple just continue to delight in the qualities they lack as they discover them in the other person. After a honeymoon period of this delight they find to their bewilderment that the same qualities that once delighted, now infuriate. The admirable maturity now seems stuffy. The glamorous style is now pretentious and boring. The practical, organised type becomes a nag. The sweet childlike creature is a silly neurotic. The forceful decisive one is an insensitive bully.

Or you find that they're not at all what you thought, that was just your first impression, so it wears off. In this scenario the decisive force cracks to reveal a weakling or the childlike creature is really tough as old boots. But it lasts longer and has more effect the other way.

Now if each had followed through consciously on the mingling of the auras, and tried to acquire the fascinating qualities of the other, the result would be truly creative and magical. If you were attracted to practicality, learn it. Then you'll not be exasperated by the other's fussing because you'll see the point of it, - and they won't need to fuss so much either. If you were attracted to independence make it yours. Then you'll not be threatened and irritated by unpredictability. Your partner will be less likely to be weighed down by your attachment as well.

Even flirtations and crushes have a very important role as teachers. They allow us to see from more of a distance what we're drawn to, and so realise what we need to balance up. Then we can also try out our attempts to express the new quality, without risking real involvement.

The mystery of deep love is that it calls out desire for powerful lacks we do not know are there. It is harder to see what the pattern is, the more involved we are. Often it is only at the very beginning we can see clearly. Much, much later, the exasperation signals where we failed to see.

If we do manage to see it and learn it, a great and wondrous change takes place, the deepest alchemy of sexual love. Where there were once two parts who each lacked what the other had, there are now two wholes. These sometimes decide to part, their task for each other done. Or, if there is now so much in common and the shared past means enough, the two wholes will continue on together. Now there may be less of the acute frantic sexuality of their first few years, but more a profundity and creative understanding as loving friends.

One of the strangest magics of relationships are ghost lovers. Often a powerful alchemical connection drew people together, but its exchange was not completed and the relationship ended suddenly. Either a long period of recovery is necessary, while the tasks of acquiring the lacking qualities are finished off before another relationship can occur. Or a 'new' relationship chosen quickly will replay in uncanny accuracy the underlying pattern of the previous one. Both ways the ghost operates as powerfully as if the original relationship is still going on; you could say the original relationship is still going on.

The alchemical exchange also explains, to those it puzzles, the nature of homosexual relationships. Whether in a body of the same or opposite gender, a person can carry the qualities we lack. There is another teaching of the magical tradition which was very hidden until recently. The troubadours of Aquitaine sang of it and practiced it as Courtly Love. The Tarot gives us signs of it in Strength, and other cards. Masters & Johnson, and other modern researchers have rediscovered it.

Women have much greater independent sexual capacity than men. Not only can a woman begin to build another orgasm almost immediately if she wishes, but her actual experience is more intense and more profound. Her body is sexually designed more powerfully. And her capacity can last more reliably to a later stage in her life.

No wonder a religion that preached male superiority also forbade sex except under strict control. No wonder women were seen as more evil, more dangerous. How significant that women who dislike patriarchal sex are labelled 'frigid' ie not men's fault. Valerie Solanas in SCUM points out that patriarchal men's genius is persuasion. They have persuaded the first sex they are the second, and puffed the second sex up to pretend, uncomfortably, they are the first.

But although men are less heavily gifted on their own, they have a magical potential that rights the balance. Tantric yogis are taught to use the greater power of the woman to reach greater depth themmselves. They hang the room with purple to enrich female sexual vibrations. They use female attuned perfumes. They learn the capacities of female bodies carefully and what male bodies can do to attune to them. They take note of their female lover's tastes and preferences. Then they offer her their service, all their gentleness and vigour. Traditionally the woman sits above the yogi, and he either lies,or sits with bent legs, beneath her.

Attuning as sensitively as he can to her feelings the yogi makes love to her, or allows her to creatively use his body. She guides him to her wishes and he responds. She is his living goddess on earth. He is the god to her. She welcomes him and directs him, to be delicate or rough, slow or fast. He becomes so focused on her that his orgasm becomes irrelevant; he is sublimely lost in her. As she builds her labyrinth on his work she carries him with her. And so he too can spiral as long and as profoundly as she.

But he can only do so if he puts her experience first. It is a magical paradox that by putting himself second, he can reach greater experience than by putting himself first. (But it won't work if his wish is only to prove what a good lover he is!)

Neither can a woman giving sex as a reward, or faking her reactions, work the ecstasy of tantra.. She must truly welcome him, and actively show him how to help her create magic for them both. When she does not wish it, she must not force herself even the tiniest bit, or her insulted sacred gates will close in on her power.

Of course, I am not suggesting that every occasion for making love be tantric in this style. Sometimes one lover is the focus, sometimes the other. But the most profound sex comes this way, and finds a noble place in the ritual Circle.

LOVERS BLESSING

The Drawing Down of the Moon is a very old ritual; some think it is being shown on a fresco of devastated Pompeii. The Wicca have adopted it as one of their special rites, as part of their fine work to uphold the sacred role of the priestess through the middle years of our century.

In its usual version, the male honours the female by offering ceremonial kisses from her feet up to her crown, with suitably adoring speeches at each stop, and after, invoking and acknowledging her as the Great Mother. I've always had difficulty taking it seriously that my knees are particularly mystical or symbolic. The kisses feel much more workable to me as openers or salutes to the seven chakras so that's how I do it, leaving my knees to strictly private moments with my husband.

The other great difficulty I had in understanding the recent teaching about Drawing Down the Moon, is that the rite as usually described doesn't involve the Moon hardly at all, and doesn't draw anything down; rather it draws the attention upwards from the feet to the head. I suspect this is because until recently work in serpent/ kundalini/ sex magic from Eastern sources started at the base of the spine and worked upwards to a superior place at the top of the head. This fits with a sky pointing religion which relies on caste, inequality and dominance.

Also there are obvious similarities between the rising penis and an upward soaring flow of energy.

By contrast, the frequent experience of women is to feel diminished by an upward pattern which emphasises height. Over 15 years of women's meditations I have found that we are far more strengthened by downward images, which value depth, and reach down into the power source within our pelvic bowl. The ancient myth of the Descent of the Goddess tells us of the Lady going down through the seven gates, giving up her powers as she goes, only to find the greatest power of all when she has given up all at the end. Giving birth is like that, a profound surrender of control to receive the greatest treasure.

This Drawing Down the Moon includes traditional Moon magic, and does indeed draw down: my partner priest begins by kissing my crown, and moves downwards. This has two practical advantages. We start with fairly gentle kissing at a socially acceptable level, the head, so that by the time he gets down to those interestingly intimate zones we are both well attuned to the ceremonial and don't wobble into the personal at this point. Strict ritualists will tick me off and say I shouldn't be bothered by that kind of self consciousness in a serious rite; all I can say is that I work in the circle as a whole person, not a superwoman, although there are moments of superwoman transcendence of course.

The other advantage is that we end up with me upright, with him down there at my feet, doing the adoring. Wonderful! Much more likely to put me into a state of majesty, female authority, and sacred womanhood, than having the top of my head kissed and then looking up at him - or looking at his chest or chin, which is fairly common, heights between the sexes being what they are.

To create an honouring between lovers I offer you my variation of the Drawing Down of the Moon, done as an exchange.

For lovers of the same sex, the only adjustment needed is to choose who is taking the first honouring and who the second. You may feel very clear as to who feels more feminine at present, or usually as a matter of course. Obviously you will use the words Goddess and God in the rite in the way that suits you.

It may be good to do a Lovers Blessing twice, a month apart, at the same time of the moon cycle, with reversed roles.

This is very definitely not a beginners rite; at least one of you needs several months familiarity with Circlework before you try it. The more experienced one needs to be familiar with working skyclad in the circle, and the other either not much bothered by it, or has done it also.

Lovers Blessing/
Drawing down the Moon

PREPARATION

This rite needs the Moon to be on the increase; its crescent must curve on the right, like the letter D. (The crescent curving on the left is a Crone moon, letter C, for banishing work.) For this rite the closer to full moon the better. It doesn't matter if you can't see the moon behind a cloud layer; the rays are still bathing us. But of course it is more satisfying to actually see what is going on.

Put two similar glasses on a windowsill or outside in a quiet, safe place. Fill one with water. Leave them to soak with moonlight for at least one hour. Put them on the Water altar/ corner, in your circle.

If you are inviting someone to share a Blessing with you who has not entered the Circle before, they deserve careful explanation, and a sight of this chapter, or maybe the whole book. Only proceed together when BOTH of you feel completely comfortable about it, or else you will create a fake rite where one or both on a deeper level is pretending - not good enough for real sex magic.

You can enjoy making a feast for the two of you. Have cushions, and blankets or duvet ready beside the altar to make a cuddle nest with. Make the room extra warm; turn the heating up, or put on an extra fire. You will be most comfortable in robes, or very large loose clothing like big T shirts, easy to pull off.

Make sure you feel comfy taking up the 'Osiris' pose, which I call "closed." Also check the "open" position for the priestess (Snake priestess.) You may like to practice the sevenfold kiss, and the changes of arm position. (see page 155)

Decide on the wording to complete each stage of the Blessings (check Self Blessing chapter and the chakra Purification in the Purification chapter.)

PURIFICATION

1) You may like to share a Magical Bath, giving each other a sloshy shower with a bowl or saucepan. Anoint each others bodies with scented oil or moisturiser if you like.

2) Dressed in robes or loose things, separate, and do a Self Blessing meditation each.

3) Do a Salt Water Purification together.

CASTING THE CIRCLE

You may like to be conventional and the woman invoke Water and Earth, the man invoke Air and Fire. Or it may depend on who feels close to each Element.

RAISING ENERGY

Do not touch each other, in order to emphasise the coming together later. I suggest sitting on opposite sides of the Circle for chanting, and then individual spinning. Robes/ T shirts can come off as part of moving, or can come off more slowly, after the energy has been focused.

To focus the energy, you could consider one of you spinning the sphere, and one sending the vortex. But use only what you're used to here; this is not a good time to experiment with a new technique. You are doing a new rite, a powerful one, which involves two people's sensitive feelings. Best rely on what you know best.

WORKING 1)The priestess stands in front of the Earth altar.

The priest stands in front of her.   When she is ready, and wishes him to begin she takes up the closed position.

He kisses the crown of her head. *'BLESSED IS THY CROWN ...'*

He kisses her forehead.   *'BLESSED IS THY MIND ...'*

He kisses her mouth.   *'BLESSED IS THY MOUTH ...'*

   (Here she moves her arms into the Open position)

He kisses between her breasts/ or on each nipple

'BLESSED IS THY HEART /THY BREASTS ...'

He kisses her navel/ just above the waist

'BLESSED IS THY STOMACH ...'

He kisses her sex triangle *'BLESSED IS THY SEX ...'*

He kisses her feet, separately *'BLESSED ARE THY FEET ...'*

He kneels, looking up at her.

He says *'THOU ART THE GODDESS.*

THOU ART THE GODDESS ON EARTH.

THOU ART THE GODDESS ON EARTH TO ME.'

2) He now goes to the Water altar, fetches the two glasses, one full and one empty, gives them to the priestess.

She takes one in each hand, pours the full one into the empty one, and back again repeatedly until she feels a sense of balance and peace.

Each stays like this, perhaps with closed eyes, for a little while. If the priestess wishes to do anything at all as well, she does so, handing the glasses to her priest if she needs freedom of movement. She may speak, sing, say the Charge of the Goddess, embrace him, weep, dance ....

When she feels she has really and fully had enough sacred time for her divine self, she again crosses her arms on her breast hands flat towards shoulders (closed position).

3) Transition: The priest stands up, arms in closed position. The priestess unfolds her arms, checks where the glasses are, and kneels, still with her back to the Earth altar.

4) The priestess now gives the sevenfold Blessing to her priest, but starting at his feet first, going up to his head. After she kisses his sex, he unfolds his arms, leaves them at his sides. He may have to bend his head for the last two.

You end up standing facing each other. She reaches forward with both hands, takes his hands in hers. Joined like that she says

THOU ART THE GOD.

THOU ART THE GOD ON EARTH.

THOU ART THE GOD ON EARTH TO ME.'

5) She now takes the glasses and gives them to him so that he can pour one into the other repeatedly until he comes to a sense of peaceful balance.

He now says or does anything, according to his own spirit, as she did before (she takes the glasses from him if necessary). When he has fully completed his time, if he has moved away he returns to stand before her, and takes her hands again.

6) Now the Lovers embrace, and do as they will.

You may wish to drink the moonwater now, if you feel like making love. However, including the full act of love at this point should not be pushed; if there is even a little hesitancy or unsureness, it would be a better blessing to keep this for another rite when trust has deepened even more.

COMMUNION Even up the moonwater in the two glasses and each drink it. Eat, and feast.

OPENING THE CIRCLE If you have been making love, the legs may still be shaky, so you don't have to stand up to say thank you and farewell.

SEPARATION

When living through broken or finished love, there is an important place for mourning and step by step returning to a new beginning. Endings cannot just be declared; there must be time to absorb the idea, act on it, recover from it, and let it go.

Like a death, which this is one form of, separation is easier to recover from if there is a period of preparation; either talk of it over a few months, or lots of nastiness that suggests the serious possibility of breaking up even if it is not actually spoken. What is much harder to get over, and so takes longer, is a sudden break, happening unexpectedly.

It is also harder, much harder, to be the person rejected. The one who makes the break has chosen their time, when they are more or less ready. The other has it thrust upon them at a time not of their choosing; it dumps a horrible state of helplessness which takes time to overcome and heal. The guilt of dealing out the hurt of rejection does not take as long.

People often react to a breakup with a flurry of sex. We need some simple reassurance that we are alive, sexual, capable of linking, of doing it. It is unwise to continue this for more than a temporary time, as it blocks out the necessary sadness, and looking inward that healing needs.

There is frequently a nasty stale feeling after breaking it. I have survived it, and helped many others through the same sense of being old, finished, diminished; that's it, I will never love and be happy again. The fact that we can feel flooded with this aged, finished feeling just as painfully and hopelessly at 20, 25 or 30 as at 50, 60, or 70 shows that it is a state of mind and body, not an effect of the passing years. The spirit is saying it needs a retreat, your resources are not yet up to risk and passion.

Accept the tiredness, rest, honour the retreat time you need to heal, and you too will emerge once more, renewed and ready for another cycle, at 70 or at 20.

Those who flash off into a new relating look enviable, as do those who swan about with one companion after another. Try not to envy them too much; those who deny the dark time its needs will pay more in the long run. Plunging into another go too soon means you have not understood the lessons of the breaking, and have not had time to build that knowledge into a new and different you who will not make the same mistakes. It takes at least half the time you were together, to recover, for any relating up to five years.

Living alone without a partner is cheerfully described in magazines, many people thrive on it, and getting the hang of independent freedom is a magnificent achievement of true maturity. But it is definitely a difficult craft. A pleasant flat mate is a great help; not always easy to get though. Do not dismiss yourself as a hopeless ninny if you dissolve into tears of loneliness, even if this happens often. If the emptiness gets to you, struggle through it step by step, knowing that this is natural - we are a herd species, and most of us are not hermits. Lots of us put a brave face on it, which makes it look as though not enjoying solitude is a shameful weakness. It isn't, so accept your very human nature and do small things to comfort yourself as best you can.

That said, even the frailest flower of a spirit can grow tough roots eventually. The very same person who feels despairing and bleak about being alone, can thoroughly enjoy the excitement and creative possibilties of being free and in charge of one's destiny - sometimes all on the same day. Both are equally true.

Finally, do not give up. Hearts bruise agonisingly, but they do heal. Don't try to forgive, for forgiveness is a grace that falls from heaven in its own time after you allowyour anger and pain to have their time with you.

Men and women are both changing, becoming stronger and more loving. Love exists. You can have it too. It's not just a crazy, soppy dream; it's a solid reality.

So mourn as long as you need, then come out of the cave, and insist on another chance.

YOU ARE YOUR OWN WISEST GUIDE

Rite of separation

This ritual of separation is for whenever it feels right to you.

PREPARATION

Check carefully when you feel ready for this. Several people who asked me for a separation rite thought about it after I described it, then told me that thinking about doing it made them very clear that they were not actually ready to let go yet.

You may like to put mementoes of your ex on the Earth altar.

Photocopying or writing out the four meditations on four cards might help you do them clearly and comfortably. Put them at the quarter candles.

Having a witness can be very powerful so you might decide to ask a sensitive friend to quietly be there, and go round the quarters with you.

PURIFICATION A magical bath would help, with lots of salt, after an ordinary purification.

CASTING THE CIRCLE Ask each Element to help you do this in their special way.

RAISING ENERGY Do this through more than one peak. Ask a spiritual guide or friend, Goddess, God or any other inspiration to accompany you.

WORKING 1) Face the Earth Altar. Imagine your ex is standing on the other side of your altar, facing you. Take your time, build the feel of her/his presence there.

Now bring to mind the things physical between you; the joining of the bodies, the everyday material connections etc. Stay with this as long as you wish. Finally, say

THIS CAME INTO BEING. IT HAS HAD ITS SEASON

IT IS TIME FOR IT TO GO.

2) Move round to face Water. Imagine your ex is standing on the other side of a gulf. Deep down at the bottom of this ravine, water is rushing along, icy cold and beautiful.

Bring to mind the love that has flowed between you, the sweetness, the passion, the giving and taking, the bad and the good woven together. Stay with this very thoroughly, even if it makes you cry.

When you come without forcing it, to peace, say the words

THIS CAME INTO BEING   IT HAS HAD ITS SEASON
IT IS TIME FOR IT TO GO

3) Move to Fire. Imagine your ex is standing on the opposite side of a roaring bonfire to you. It is dark now, and your ex is no more than a solid but shadowed silhouette.

Bring to mind the final pain of the ending. Voice whatever anger you feel, whatever bitterness.

Look now at the overall shape of your sharing. Try if possible to see at least one great gift it has given you, together with the price you have paid. Say

THIS CAME INTO BEING.   IT HAS HAD ITS SEASON.

IT IS TIME FOR IT TO GO.

4) Move to air. Imagine you are standing on a high place, a rooftop, or a hill. It is early morning, the air is fresh and sweet. Look down on to the place where your ex lives, far away in the distance. Watch her or him going about their daily business. For as long as you wish, watch. Say

THIS CAME INTO BEING.

IT HAS HAD ITS SEASON.

IT IS TIME FOR IT TO GO.

5) Go to the Centre. Say the words one more time.

COMMUNION

OPENING THE CIRCLE

If you begin this rite and find it's too much for you, you really don't want to complete it, don't. This will be difficult for you, but holds a hidden gift of measuring where you are in recovery, or purpose.

At the point where you decide to stop, go to the Centre. 1)Pull an imaginary handful of stuff from behind you, cup your hands in front of you. 2) Offer it to the Centre as your honest and real state of self. Ask for help if you feel the need of it.

3) Let your hands fall back to your sides, accepting the love and wisdom of the great web that holds you.

Take Communion and open the circle.

You can repeat this ritual up to three times for the same person to deepen and finish off its effects; not counting any attempts which are not completed.

HOUSEWARMING

Housewarming is a delightful tradition which has survived well into modern times. This isn't surprising as research has shown that moving home is surprisingly stressful. It's actually about equal with divorce, bereavement and losing a permanent job, in its upheaval effect on us.

Long long ago, when we lived in caves, finding a new cave meant checking it was safe - not still in use by large dangerous animals. Then it had to be considered for size, shape, heating, distance from water etc. Finally, goods were installed, and a ceremony held to get everyone used to the idea that this was now a home, a new reality.

Later in history, there were customs burying special items in the building as it was built. A piece of burning wood from the hearth fire of the old house was symbolically carried over in a pot to make a new one in the new hearth. Does this make a new fire? or continue the old one? one of those mysteries.

Neighbours, friends, relatives came at an agreed time to help move everything in, fix anything that needed repairs, and get things at least roughly arranged: in return the new householder gave them food and space for a party. Good wishes and toasts are enjoyed, and the first days in the new home filled with the cheerful feel of busyness and celebration.

GUESTS Try to give your chosen guests at least a month's warning. You will get the most out of your housewarming if the people that are important to you are there - those that live in your spiritual house as it were. Given only a week or two's warning people will too often have other things important to them already arranged, and you're less likely to have them with you for yours.

Write them a note explaining that you are following old customs in having a bit of ceremony at eg 7pm and to let you know if they will be there for it or whether they'd prefer to come later at 8.30 for the party only. If you're only inviting up to 5 people then you could explain this by phone. But having a written card invite helps people understand that something important that involves planning and their definite commitment to attend is going on. Add a few words saying that while drinking is an important contribution to the proceedings later on, there must be none till the last step of the ceremony itself.

DOING IT BY YOURSELF WITHOUT GUESTS can be a beautiful experience.

So can doing it in a one room home.

THE TIME TO DO IT is the first day in the home, within three days, or within seven. It can be done within the first month too, but done later than that some changes need to be made to make it a celebration of having moved in, rather than to get moved in.

A rite to celebrate the yearly anniversary could be lovely, but not as a burden to make you feel harassed. You may feel you'd like to keep the thread going through the years of a regular honouring of your contract with the place. If the date falls at a busy or bad health time, a quick half hour or so given to recalling the original ritual, will keep the continuity thread going till another year when you hope to have more time and energy.

WHAT THE NEIGHBOURS THINK You might like to give them a courtesy warning of something going on, as you would about having a party anyway. Mention that you like folk customs, and one bit of this one involves a bit of banging about, or singing, but not late in the evening. Reference to your family traditions and customs is usually easily understood - and we're all distantly related somehow, so that covers whichever customs you want to include really.

Housewarming Rite (SUMMARY)

PREPARATION Invite guests 1 month in advance.

Move house! Arrange enough space for minimum 9ft circle.

Extra kit: broom, dustpan & brush, pots & pans.

Small bowl of special water as well as purification bowl, OR cleaning materials, OR both.

PURIFICATION Salt water bowl in laid out circle.

CASTING THE CIRCLE Ask all 5 Elements to bless the house.

Honouring the house:-

Leave the newly cast circle, making a gateway gesture.

1) Simplest style:- Make a silent and courteous progress round the home, stroking parts of the house with the hands.

OR 2) Carry special water sprinkling it as a gift.

OR 3) Carry fresh salt water (not the purification bowl), incense and candle around the house to all parts. Sprinkle salt water to represent earth and water, waft incense smoke, present flame.

OR 4) take cleaning materials round, touching them
to places that need work.

RAISING ENERGY Return to the circle, through the gateway.

Cleansing the Gateways:- Collect broom, dustpan & brush, pots and pans.

Make a second progress through the home with banging pots and pans, clapping and shouting *'Out! Out!'* to cast out previous influences and mark the new arrival. Noisy fun.

Return to circle through the gateway, closing it, then do the chanting and focusing.

See below 'Rekindling the Hearthfire'

WORKING: Dreaming the new reality. Sit in circle.

Houseperson explains. Make about 3 or 4 circles, one for each room or key place in the home. Each person imagines the new houseperson doing something nice and enjoyable in each place.

COMMUNION Toasts are drunk to the new household.

OPENING THE CIRCLE

If you have a custom from your own background, or you come across one that will weave into the whole and give you a gift you need for your rite, then put it in.

You can design the best ritual for you and your home by taking on as much as you can manage comfortably, choosing the right bits that feel good for you. A ritual done with guests especially, is better kept simple. The more challenging things are best done alone, or with one or two familiar friends sharing the experiment.

If you choose the simplest Honouring, for example, just making a gentle, silent walk round your new home, you are still sincerely honouring your place. And done slowly and reverently alone, or with your chosen companions, this will hold power just as much as grappling with carrying round a lot of gear.

In the notes below, I have also included kindling the hearthfire. This fits well when the raising energy is finishing as part of its final focus. It's beautiful and powerful. But be wise in assessing your ritual experience and practical skill. Fire is not something to mess with except calmly and surely. If you're not a very practical type normally this needs a helper who is. If you know you're going to be shaky with nerves because of the upheaval of moving, or because of hosting a group event, then be bravely sensible and leave it alone. You could perhaps do it separately, alone or with one helper, sometime in the next few days as a special rite on its own, when you feel calmed and centred by the bigger ritual.

Notes

PREPARATION Lay out the Circle in the room you're most likely to use for Circles; or put it in the largest room, or the one least clogged with heaps of boxes and furniture !

HONOURING THE PLACE: Once again a very simple honouring is well understood by the spirit of the house, as much as a more complicated one.

In a one room home:- move carefully and slowly round each 'station' in the room: the bed, the table, the sink/ washbasin, the seating - each of these is like a mini room with its own cluster of activities around it.

You can offer a gift to the house by sprinkling special water as you go. You may like to offer a chosen incense as well. I am suggesting water here because water is cleansing, and carries love and nourishment with it, but of course whatever you add to this, or feel you'd rather replace it with, will be lovely.

If you're working alone and you're choosing to carry round the Elements or the cleaners, you might find it easier to make 2 journeys.

If you have guests, you can ask them before Purifying to take various things round when you all leave the Circle. One can carry the water, one the incense, the candle, and the boxes or baskets of things for you. You do most of the key gestures with them.

Taking cleaners and tools round with you is demonstrating your real willingness to serve and protect the home with cleaning and repairs. You can stop and gently touch your tools to the appropriate parts of the house structure as you go: for example touch woodwork or a floor with a cleaning cloth and bottle of cleaner. Perhaps even rub a little piece of wood or lino clean in a few places. Touch a cracked or broken surface with a pot of filler, or dab a tiny bit on. Stroke a screwdriver or another tool over a place that needs repairs.

When all the home, including outside parts, has been honoured, come to the prepared Circle. Put the things you are carrying away in their accustomed places, or (broom, pots etc) round the edge of the circle.

CLEANSING THE GATEWAYS

Now that you have honoured the place, you have the right to banish its previous influences, especially any harmful ones. This is great fun, and excellent preparation for any partymaking later.

Get your broom, pots and pans, incense, salt water.

Working alone, take a broom for ceremonial sweeping, and a pot with a lid for banging round first. Then put incense and water in a dish or tray for easy carrying about.

With guests, you can include your dustpan and brush, a drum or two, bells, and the incense and salt water can be carried by separate people.

Prepare with a little breathing, some chanting, clapping etc.

Visit each GATEWAY of the home, outside and inside.

- Gateways are all doors, windows, and the places where electricity, gas, water or telephone connections come into your home. Sprinkle each gateway with salt water, puff incense around it, present the candle. This purifies with the 4 elements. Working alone try not to rush because there's a lot to cover here.

The fun bit is the clapping, shouting, vigorous brushing with broom and brush, drum banging, bell ringing etc which is absolutely essential to mark the new beginning and banish any unwanted atmospheres lurking stubbornly around.

Don't forget the garden if there is one (definitely warn neighbours about folk customs).

Come back into the circle through the gateway in it you made when you left it, and put things away.

Rekindling the Hearthfire

— ancient rite: fits well at the end of energy raising when the chanting focuses. But it can also be a separate rite entirely.

If you are lucky and your old and new homes both have fireplaces you can carry out this ancient rite pretty much as it was done in the past. If you don't have a traditional hearth you can adapt it to modern life without much fuss.

Carrying a flaming brand from one house to another sounds dramatic and inspiring. It is, but there are practical difficulties to attend to. Taking anything burning outside puts it under the influence of breezes, and it might blow out. If your move means very much of a journey then keeping the flame going matters, as does fire safety in a car or train.

The container to carry the fire is very important. It must be metal, or thick pottery. It must be large enough to allow air to get round the fiery object carried. It needs to be a third full of earth or sand so the heat doesn't make the bottom hot enough to hurt you or anything it's put down on. It needs a handle or strap for carrying.

The simplest solution is to carry the fire in a small charcoal block. If you use incense anyway you might have a container that's already suitable. If you're not familiar with charcoal blocks check the Crafts chapter about it.

The rekindling of fire is traditionally the work of the woman of the house.

DREAMING THE NEW REALITY

Having done active outer work to greet and honour the house, and cleanse its gateways of the past, it is time to go into the inner places and look to the future.

Sit in a circle. The householder can explain if everyone has not read notes beforehand or knows anyway.

You need to settle beforehand about three or four key points in the home. For example, the bed, the cooking area, the table, or

the bedroom, the kitchen, the sitting room, and the garden.

Take the first one, and each person round the circle clockwise or deosil, speaks of seeing the new householder doing domething enjoyable in that place.

Then take the next and do the same dreaming circle. As the images build up the powerful new reality surrounds the person just moved in to help them feel at home.

DO WHAT I TELL YOU ONLY ONLY ONLY
IF YOU WANT TO

John, Shan, Tal, Cath, Manjka, Ian ....

205

FESTIVALS OF THE YEAR

The seasons of the year are less crucial to our modern lives, with imported food, heated houses and indoor work. But our bodies and emotions still go through their important changes which we are foolish to ignore, for they can greatly enrich our lives if we honour their primal wisdom.

There are eight festivals, one about every six weeks. This gives us about 5 - 6 weeks of workaday life, then a break for a holiday or celebration, an entirely pleasant and very healthy rythmn. They are really two sets of four. The most basic ones are the four major points of the sun's journey, all on the 21st of the month.

The Summer Solstice (June 21) and Winter Solstice (December 21) mark the longest day and the shortest day; the height of the sun, and its lowest power. The Spring Equinox (March 21) and the Autumn Equinox (September 21) mark day and night at equal balance; Spring Equinox on the rising tide of the year, and Autumn Equinox on the falling tide.

This makes a four quartered circle which matches the familiar ritual circle. Already some of the teaching shows up. Spring/ Air is a time for mental matters, plans, new ideas, new ventures. Summer/ Fire is the peak of energy, so is a time for personal assessment, for the greatest possible power to be seen, and the larger picture - the whole of our society. Autumn/ Water flows down into steady effort, to bring in the deeper, fuller harvest. Winter/ Earth brings rest, and careful nourishment before we begin again.

A BOOK IS A BOX OF SUGGESTIONS:
PICK WHAT YOU WANT

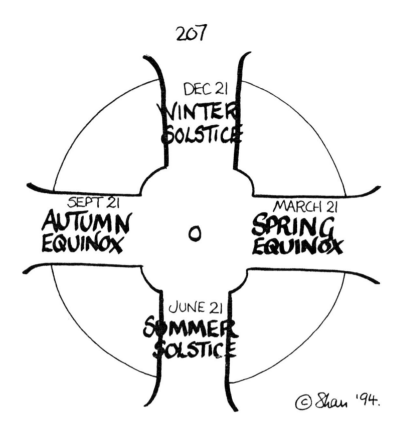

These four, the Solstices and the Equinoxes, being about the sun, are universal across all peoples of the world (except the Southern Hemisphere is a mirror image of our pattern).

The other four festivals are local British festivals, about midway between the first four. They are descendants of the ancient Celtic fire festivals, when bonfires were lit to encourage the sun's journey. When once the fires were lit on the tops of hills across the land it must have been a fine sight.

These 'cross quarter' festivals are all held at the change over points at the end and beginning of months: 31st October Halloween (our New Year), SAMHAIN

1st or 2nd February Candlemas, IMBOLC

1st May May Day, BELTAINE

1st - 7th August Harvest, LAMMAS or LUGHNASADH

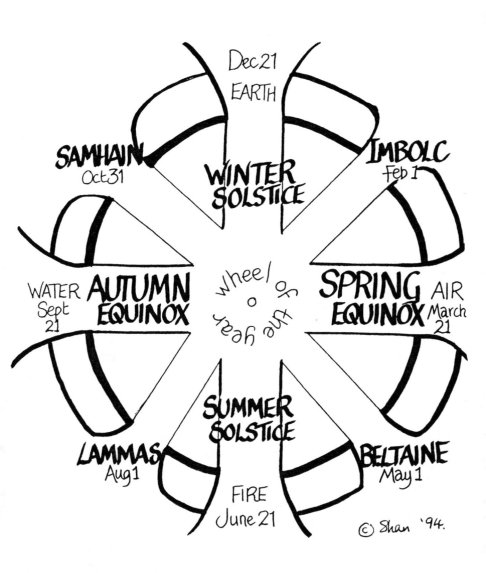

Wheel of the year

Dec 21 EARTH
WINTER SOLSTICE

SAMHAIN
Oct 31

IMBOLC
Feb 1

WATER
Sept 21

AUTUMN
EQUINOX

SPRING
EQUINOX

AIR
March 21

LAMMAS
Aug 1

SUMMER
SOLSTICE

BELTAINE
May 1

FIRE
June 21

© Shan '94.

You can see how most of the old festivals have survived the Christian takeover, because their natural, long established places in people's lives just couldn't be shifted. In fact the date of Christmas had to be moved from the summer to mid December because for Europeans this had always been the birth day of the god.

People often ask me about the exact right time to celebrate a festival, often because the actual date falls mid week which can be awkward in an employed life. First of all the custom is to observe Pagan dates on the evening before, because the older Pagan calendars counted in moon cycles and nights.

Secondly a truly precise timing is arrived at to the minute, by careful astronomical calculations, which might result in a point anywhere within three days of the guide dates I have given. If it suits your personality to be extremely precise you need to consult an astrologer, or an astrologer's ephemeris. Nautical almanacs or observatories like the big one at Greenwich can tell you when the Equinoxes and Solstices are, but not the cross quarters.It is easy to assume that real Pagans faithfully celebrate all eight festivals; in practice one has times of upheaval or preoccupation like anyone else, so some festivals may not get done every year. However, when beginning the Pagan way, it is an essential part of the learning of it to follow the great Wheel round a full circle, if you can. If one festival gets messed up by circumstances it just makes it a priority not to miss that one the following year. This means that by the third year you've done the complete cycle, and have taken each of the eight different messages into your life.

Another common assumption is that proper Pagan celebration takes place in groups, covens, lodges, groves etc. Nothing could be further from the truth. We are proud of our free, independent community, where each goes their own way, and it's a pretty pathetic Pagan who can't create their own Sabbat or Festival.

One of my pet hates is newcomers who want to be directed to the nearest coven or lodge (not more than half an hour's journey please) where they can be taken into a circle for the next Festival as an introduction to our ways. Please consider that any newcomer, however mature and sensitive, will be unsure and stiff; will need explanation; many things need to be slowed down or simplified for one to participate; and the host group just can't relax fully to enjoy themselves with a stranger in their midst. A group event takes a lot of work and preparation; it seems unfair for someone new to expect it all to be laid on just so they can 'see what you really do' like a spiritual tourist.

I can't see how a newcomer without a few months experience of their own Circle can get much out of it either, beyond a kind of powerful entertainment. But our festivals are not performances for an audience; they grow out of those celebrating them.

You can make a Sabbat for yourself: you don't need a group of adepts to show you how. Once you have done it for yourself once or twice, you are likely to be much more welcome at others' gatherings.

Your festival need not be complicated; or if you want it to be elaborate, then go for it. This can be a time for masks, costume, acting out drama, strictly patterned ceremony, leaping round bonfires, feasting, drinking, drumming, singing, dancing, special recipes, all night extravaganza. It's just as much about quiet reflection, going within, respecting your own hearth and your own company. It could be bits of both kinds of power.

What you choose may be entirely around your own personality; you may feel that quiet retreat is a special blessing, or a crashing bore - which rather settles your overall approach. If you've done some circles at home, you may like to go outside (see Outdoor Circles). Your own back garden, if you have one, could be wonderful, lit by garden flares. A problem that often occurs is when you are really enjoying the Circle, and the sense of connecting with the old ways of the earth, but your lover, parents, spouse, best friend, or children just don't share your enthusiasm. It would be so nice to share your pleasure a little, especially at celebration times like these.

It won't help to push and persuade. You can leave books around openly, leaving them to pick them up and flick through or browse. It's best not to suggest they read one, more than once. People like to decide their level of interest for themselves in their own time. Any slight pressure, even affectionate suggestions, looks like those awful bible people who come to the door.

If they're going to get interested, then they will, in their own time - might be a long time. They're actually more likely to get curious if you don't talk about it much. But if they're not interested, they're just not interested, and there's not a damn thing you can do about it. It's called free will, unfortunately.

However, there are simple things you can ask them to do with you which do express the spirit of each festival, allowing them to feel they are staying independent of your interests, but making you feel you are sharing some of it. In my descriptions below I put these things in brackets.

OCT 31 New Year: **Samhain** pronounced Sow -aine.

First frosts. Festival of the old year's ending so time to honour the elderly and the dead. Mementoes and photos of those gone before. The Crone. Completing and letting go.

Considered an excellent time to read the Tarot, Runes etc and to make personal resolutions. Children's games.

(Lighting an orange candle, or pumpkin lantern, at dusk or suppertime to pay respect to anyone loved and lost. A visit around now, perhaps with a gift for any elderly friend or relative. Have a Halloween party.)

DECEMBER 21 Winter Solstice: **Yule**

Family gathering. Festival of the death and rebirth of the Sun. Mother and Child. Put out all lights, if possible turn off the electrics at mains: then after meditation, relight everything, starting with one candle. Dark and light, young and old in conflict, the light and the young win. Children celebrated with gifts and family solidarity. Feeding the body against the coming cold: feasting. Enclosed comfort.

(Yule tree of life. Gifts. Feast. Drinking. Family.)

FEBRUARY 2 St Brigid/ Candlemas: **Imbolc**

Cold, bare earth; but the seeds first movement below. First births, the lambs (Imbolc means ewes milk). First flowers - crocus, snowdrop. Festival of faith in the unseen (good time for divination again), female renewal, purification, conception. Celebrate small babies, young children. Hopes and dreams, plans, ideals. Care for skin, hair, nails and general health, thorough self nourishment; winter fat, not diets. (Small candles on supper table in a pretty pattern to encourage the light, or cheer us up. Can be lit with a wish - children love this. Massage, sauna, hairdo, bath oils.)

MARCH 21 Spring Equinox: **Eostra**

New life. Birds, nesting, eggs, buds, leaves, flowers. Winds, rain, storms, as the year re -balances. Festival of the Return:Maiden and Young God. Cosmic Egg, Eostra was a goddess of the Egg. Housecleaning, sprucing up, new clothes. Short trips, moving. Diets, more exercise. New projects, new start, courtship, excitement. (Day or weekend of Spring Cleaning with an easy instant or takeaway meal in the evening. Dinner out? A new shirt, T shirt. Country excursion, or walk on the park. Daffodils.)

MAY 1 May Day: Beltaine, BELTAIN, BELTANE

Outdoor life, good health, sexuality, flowers, bonfires. Festival of freedom. Love union of Goddess and God, celebration of both female and male beauty. Sex Magic, Lovers Blessing. Passionate love, struggle, conflict, testing of vows and partnerships. Making and breaking contracts. Frustration at limits. Art, dance (maypole), music. Travel. (A weekend/ day in the country, a party in the garden, a barbecue, a picnic with garden flares, flower woven crowns, lovemaking with flowers, wine and candles).

JUNE 21 Summer Solstice: Summer Solstice

Abundant fields, summer fruits, vigorous bodies, large gatherings. Festival of power and strength. Night vigil till dawn. Conflict of light and dark, light has his day of splendour, but the dark quietly begins his rule. Bare skin, sweat, holidays, long journeys, exercise, dance, music, ambitious projects, green politics. Taking risks, letting go. (Visit a large camp, a crowd event around this time, feel the power of community. Make a special breakfast. Any enjoyable challenge.)

AUGUST 1 Harvest: Lammas, LUGHNASADH

Fresh food, local produce, golden fields, sensuality, laziness. Long days of light, playtime. Festival of thanksgiving. The Green Man gives his life to feed us, the Lady cuts him down as the sacrifice. Lammas means first loaf, Lugh was the Sun King. Uncertain moods, sharing yet lonely, creative and frustrated, up and down. (Visit a corn field, fetch corn stalks, mix with flowers for display on a harvest supper table. Say Pagan grace 'Thank you for the fruits of the Earth' or 'Thank you for giving your lives to feed ours.')

SEPTEMBER 21 Autumn Equinox: The Kore

Fields cut and ploughing, first hard winds speak of winter. Festival of mourning. The Maiden begins her Descent into the dark, we say farewell. Purification, bathing, healing. Letting go of the summer, getting out woollies, fixing roof, plumbing. Antifreeze. Focus back on work, projects. (Sorting out summer photos, toasting summer memories. Lists of autumn jobs. Assessing the year, looking at what's left to do. Mulled wine, mead, special drinks).

OUTDOOR RITUAL

Working ritual outdoors is a strong part of our Pagan tradition. Although a city Witch like me is actually more accustomed to working in a heated room, I do know the different raw power that comes from working out in the air, subject to rain, stones, mud, and darkness, yet still charged wonderfully by my friends the trees, and Mother Earth under me. Most of us become Pagans or Witches at least in part because of how strongly we feel about Nature, our powerful, patient Mother. Taking our rituals out close to her naked reality is necessary at least sometimes if we are not to be 'armchair Pagans'.

Outdoor ritual does not necessarily mean mud, darkness, out in the wild. I have worked lovely rituals in London parks, in bright sunshine on a Sunday morning. Passers by merely think I am eccentric as I dance round my tree, or if there's a group of us I think we look like a rather sloppy country dance group. Most ritual activities are quite unremarkable to observe on the outside; just people moving about talking to each other and having a picnic. Dogs rush joyously across the Circle on their own quests, and the occasional walker wanders close enough to wonder. People are too shy to stand and watch for more than a minute or two unless shown notice and invitations to stay, so I have never had any bother.

Outdoor work means a larger space with lots of room to run about, so it's popular with children. You have the vault of the sky, the touch of the earth, the warmth of the sun, or the silver of the moon and stars, the protection of trees, and sometimes natural waters. You also have the magic of found objects; sticks, stones, leaves, flowers, feathers.... which lie in your path waiting to help.

PREPARATION VISIT

It is essential to choose a site that is familiar; either go somewhere you have visited before, or make a preparation visit beforehand. Somewhere unknown and exciting can end in tears due to too much cowshit, nettles, broken glass, an unseen ditch in the dark, ritual workers lost nearby, or furious farmers waving shotguns.

Groups can rely on one or two members' knowledge of the site, especially if using my checklist here!

CHOICE OF SITE. The place needs to be quite close to a road unless you are all hardy trekkers; also what looks like an easy walk in daylight can be much harder in the dark, burdened with gear. Yet you also need some privacy, so high bushes, or a copse around the place, or a wall near the road, is desirable.

Make sure there's no pub visible from the site. If you can see it from where you are, yobbos leaving at closing time can see your lights, and harass you.

Well known sacred sites/ stone circles are attractive, but just because they're popular, they have their own problems. Their owners or managers can be touchy about wild invasions; also you are less likely to have the place to yourself unless it's a weekday night and not around a Sabbat date. For a first outdoor rite, remember all earth places are sacred, and maybe somewhere quiet and more ordinary will offer you a friendly and more personal welcome.

Choose somewhere no more than two hours journey away, so you're not too tired when you arrive to enjoy the ritual itself.

The strict technical position is that 'common ground' (woods, heath etc) and sacred sites are not available for parties or gatherings without their custodian's consent. The custodian is the local council, the National Trust, or English Heritage. This leaves the use of private property, yours or a friend's, or a broadminded farmer. A family party, presented by sensible sounding people, is actually quite likely to get a friendly response from a farmer; you may have to pay.

Otherwise, if you choose to use 'public land' do it with great care. Go somewhere unseen from the road. Consider posting a guardian watcher. Be very, very careful about fire safety; clear up very thoroughly before you go. Not only does mess left afterwards mean authorities become more restrictive about night events, but something dropped can identify you for prosecution.

WOMEN'S RITES A large group of women, seven or more, has little to fear. But small groups or solos need to be wary. Check extra carefully about being hidden, that there are no nearby pubs. Keep the ritual quieter; use movement to Raise Energy rather than loud sound.

If you want a reassuring crisis plan, have dark cloaks to hand, and be ready to dowse all lights, and hide in cloaks! Some well known Dianics have 'disappeared' like that and watched puzzled police look about and then go away.

My women's coven years ago had considerable success with attendant yobbos by sitting quietly, doing nothing, thinking very hard about how boring we really were. After a while of trying to get our attention (we didn't completely ignore them) they drifted off in a slightly frustrated fashion. But although it worked, it annoyed us we had to put quite a lot of energy into that rather than into our Harvest celebration, which is what we were there for.

HOW TO GET THERE It may be familiar to you but it won't be so easy for others; solo workers need as little to distract you as possible at the time when you've got a lot to remember. So carefully check the way at a pre-visit.

Driving: make notes on the route, listing easy landmarks noticeable on the way there (not on the way back, as they may be invisible coming the other way.) Select a gather point near the site in case anyone gets lost: a train station or motorway services are good places. Check where people can park near the site.

Public Transport: Check times of trains or buses. How are you getting from station/ bus stop to the site? What about last journey times? Have a gather point at the station or bus stop, or even better, at a pub or cafe near it.

Generally - make sure that instructions for others, or yourself later on, are so clear even someone rather stupid could understand them. It saves slips when nervous at the time.

THE RITUAL GROUND It's desirable but not always possible to have a flat or nearly flat piece of ground; otherwise moving and dancing is made difficult.

Check it thoroughly for nettles, broken glass, stones and big twigs, anything sharp or very lumpy. It's nice to have the choice of bare feet on earth; but even without this, a stumble can mean hurt hands or worse. If you can't clear the ground thoroughly, stay shod, and take care. Make sure others are clearly warned of stones/ glass etc. Don't on any account include toddlers or children on a ground that is not carefully cleared.

Check barbed wire, or electric fencing.

Also check any water nearby. Is it deep? Is there a slope where (drunken) adults could slip down? For child safety don't set a circle near water AT ALL. For the best ritual pattern, the ideal is water if any towards the West, higher ground to the East, and a big tree in the North or the centre. Not always possible! Find the directions by looking for setting sun in the west - or take a compass.

If there isn't a source of water nearby, note down that some water must be imported for Purification.

BONFIRES It is a criminal offence to make fire on land which does not either belong to someone present, or where no consent has been given by the owner.

It is a murderously stupid offence to start a fire after a long dry period with no rain; woodland fires injure and kill.

Practical details for bonfires are as follows:- Clear the ground of dry grass (summer) to an area about 9" larger than the fire itself. Or edge your fire with big stones, both to stop fire spread and help its draught. In an exposed place where you can feel breeze or wind move on your face, try to put the fire where a rock, some bushes or a swell of ground is between the fire and the main direction of the wind. To check wind direction, wet finger, hold it up; you'll feel it most from the direction of the wind.

Overhead branches in summer and autumn must be twice the height of a person Kindling is very dry grass, small bits of paper, small dry twigs. You need this to start a fire, because big twigs and logs don't burn right away. Like a ritual, or any important task, a fire needs to be built carefully step by step.

Get larger fuel from the ground itself if it's dry; if there's been rain bring wood with you. Make a pile in advance and cover it, to be really clever. Don't break anything off trees unless it's already dead wood, with no green growth on it. You need a pile about three times larger than you intend the fire to be, so as to last a couple of hours or so.

Use paraffin to get it started; don't be proud about this unless you have special training. Don't forget the matches; smokers with lights are a dying breed and rubbing twigs together is strictly for the movies - it's a skilled art.

A fire wants to aim upwards; it's the ambitious Element. So put sticks in a tepee, with ends resting together upwards. Stuff paper and dry grass in the centre, and dribble paraffin on it. Put the paraffin well away from the fire, then drop lighted matches on the kindling. When it lights up, poke more kindling in the centre, replacing the stick tepee if it falls over. Gradually put in bigger kindling, bits of dry bark, and twigs.

Once it glows good and red you've done it. Now it just needs frequent feeding, about every twenty minutes. You can avoid this by putting the end of a whole branch (dry) in it, make sure it gets well lit, then push more in as time goes on.

COUNTRY PEOPLE HATE ...The things country people hate townies for are gates left open, and cigarettes left glowing. So grind those butts well into the earth.

RITUAL KIT PREPARATION has to be more careful than usual, because once you're away there can be no last minute dash to the kitchen for something forgotten. So write a list of everything you're taking and do a final check off before you go. Once that's done be ruthless about switching off the worry, from now on you'll work with what you have or forage.

CANDLES won't stay alight so put them in large glass jars; even then they can go out. Use them mainly for their familiarity and colour. You can also get outdoor candles in coloured glass containers from garden shops. The garden flares made on long sticks are excellent; they give a strong flame and last well, giving a strong dramatic effect. One of my favourite rituals ever was on a beach and we used quarter flares, stuck deep in the sand; they looked magnificent against a dark sea and sky.

Think of other things to mark the four quarters; a tall stick for Air, something red or shiny at Fire, shells, or a big bowl with a little water at Water, a log, tree or large stone for Earth. I have had lovely altars with all our bits and pieces lying among the roots of a tree. Don't take beautiful fragile things like a glass chalice; or if you do, take only one thing like that, try to protect it, but accept it may get broken.

CLOTHES Check that your shoes are comfy, and that big warm black cloak of tradition is a very practical piece of gear. Witches' wellies are also required kit if your chosen site is anywhere less tame than the park. A spare pair of socks is lovely if you get wet feet. An extra sweater if you get chilled can be very welcome. This all sounds unromantic, but vamping it up as a fluttery dryad or silken magus may not suit the Elements.

If you raise good energy and get ecstatically warm, you can always discard layers to reveal glamour beneath. The reverse, warming a body that's got chilled, is quite difficult, even if other folk have layers to spare you.

I did once make a great outdoor robe of furry stuff, lined, with pockets to hold small gear. Practicality and elegance, one of my favourite marriages.

FIRST AID: Elastoplast, disinfectant for cuts and grazes. A stretchy bandage + safety pin, for twisted wrists or ankles. Witch hazel + tissues for bruise. Burn ointment. Insect repellent (summer dusk) and sting cream. Tweezers for splinters, and small sharp scissors are also useful.

CATERING Ritual catering outdoors needn't be a problem as fresh air makes very ordinary things taste good. It does so by sharpening appetite so you do need to make the food solid and plentiful - breads, rice, potato, cheese or meat. A good cheap and tasty standby is a rice 'n bean mess, with sweet corn, chopped ham, green beans, onion, mushrooms, tomatoes etc. Make a lot of it, and make up a bag of grated cheese. Sausages/ sausage rolls are popular though not of course with vegetarians.

Cakes and biscuits are welcome; best stick to fairly common types that everyone knows. After doing slightly challenging things familiar food is favourite. Fruit is good.

Stay away from anything runny: it makes a mess; but take paper towel anyway. Plastic spoons, paper plates are useful. They can feed the fire later.

Sausages, baked potatoes, burgers, mulled wine or hot cider in the bonfire are great, but they do take a bit of practice. A big hot fire, and four times the cooking time at home are basic.

Hot drinks are a must on chilly evenings. Use big thermoses, insulated hot water containers. Or take a kettle, tea bags/ coffee, powdered milk and sugar, as required to taste. A large plastic can for water becomes necessary; not expensive from hardware shops. Fill the kettle, and balance it on two large stones in the fire where it's red. It needs a lot of time to boil (about 20 mins), so do it well in advance of need. The ones with the whistle in the nose are good so you don't get preoccupied, forget it, amd boil it dry.

A camping gaz stove is not expensive and a very useful investment.

For warming people up a few mouthfuls of strong liqueur is a great help eg cherry brandy or mead. Helps when arriving cold at a site, and in the Communion chalice.

FINAL CHECKLIST
Maps & instructions for getting there.
Torch. Matches. Paraffin for making bonfire.
Kindling for bonfire.
Socks, sweater, blanket? sleeping bag? waterproof sheet
Wellies or solid shoes, cloak.
Food and drink. Bottle opener. Paper towel.
First aid.
Ritual kit with outdoor flares & water for Purification.
Drums, drumsticks, rattles.
Black sacks for clearing up.

RITUAL PLANNING
Generally it's best to plan the actual ritual before getting to the site, at least until you've done a few and got used to what it's like.

THE MAJOR DIFFERENCE between outdoor and indoor work is that you can control the situation far less outside. Other people can appear, and may have as much right to be there as you do. Costume is frequently dominated by comfort, although long thick robes can be colourful and dramatic; try fur fabric, or felt. Small delicate things like paper can blow away; all sorts of things get dusty, muddy or wet. On the other hand, the land itself will help you, bringing you close to what is real with fewer props than you need indoors. Trees, waters, rocks, ancestral memories speak to you. And the smaller personalities of twigs, leaves, small stones etc will reach out to you and join the party.

WIND BLOWS WORDS away, so dramatic dialogue needs action to keep it alive. Even without wind, spaces are larger outside, so speech can often only be heard by the nearest person. This affects a Purification a lot; in uncomfortable weather it may work better to do a full Purification before setting off, in cars or in a sheltered place nearby. The lesson seems to be that working indoors we are weaving power between ourselves: working outdoors, we are weaving power with the place. It has its own magic, to speak in privacy with the Elements, even though others are nearby.

HONOURING THE PLACE Try not to make a ritual that could be done anywhere. The place is giving its hospitality to you; return the courtesy by working with its nature. Build certain parts of it into what you do: make the circle round a tree; touch a rock in quiet communication; hide in a bush, cave, or crevice; use the water there to Purify. Plant seeds or bulbs. Make a doll, crown or mask from things you can find there. Decorate a bush, tree or rock with ribbons etc. Bury a gift, or a symbol of something you want to grow. (I buried a cover from the first edition of this book.)

Keep the plan very flexible, and be ready to improvise if weather or other events interfere.

WHEN YOU ARRIVE Unload all the stuff and give it a quick check. Get the fire going, or if you're not having one, get in a circle for a hug, or a drink, or both. This is especially useful if it's chilly.

If there's time, have a while to wander and get to know the place, then come back to the centre.

You can mark the Circle by furrowing the earth with your Wand or a stick you find at the site. This is very effective, and helps other people notice the privacy and distance you want them to respect.

Lay out all the necessary gear for the ritual. Your altar can be on the earth, on a cloth, on a log, on a rock. Other stuff like blankets, first aid, extra clothes are best kept together in one place.

Food and drink looks wonderfully cheerful and inviting arranged at the Earth altar.

Drums will need to be warmed up at the fire, unless it's a warm day - in which case they might need damping. Keep sticks, small pipes and athames in pockets or at a quarter; they get lost easily.

PURIFICATION Purification in a larger space, maybe with a breeze, means you don't hear what everyone says so clearly. This feels odd when you're used to the cosy intimacy it creates indoors. But this has its own magic of each one of us speaking in a strange privacy with the Elements. You may like to Purify before you leave, with everything else planned and put ready.

A walking meditation is fascinating barefoot on cleared earth - as long as it's not too cold, and clear of anything sharp like glass.

CASTING THE CIRCLE Candles can be kept going in jars but they do take extra trouble. Light them by standing with your back to breeze or wind. Incense is also awkward and needs a partly closed container to keep it going, but it's still unreliable outdoors. Either have it going to pass round once only, or dispense with it for outdoor work. After all we go outdoors to work with natural sights and smells.

RAISING ENERGY This may take longer because of the unfamiliar place and the greater size to fill. It is easy to feel puny and insignificant, compared to the hot full container of indoor work. But outside we are there to honour the powers of the Earth, and not so much to honour our own power. The power of tree, sky, earth and light will more than compensate you. Embrace the tree. Talk to her/him. Lie face down or face up on the Mother and talk to her. Whirl back and forth at each of the quarters, watching the branches wheel in your sky overhead. Run silly. Sing proud and free to those who made you.

Use lots of movement to Raise Energy at intervals if it's cold.

COMMUNION Your Communion may have to be passed standing if the ground is muddy. If it's cold then brandy or other spirits may be more than welcome. Staying still for long may be too chilly so at a pinch, pass the Chalice once and then get back to shelter to enjoy a feast. On a pleasant day, or summer evening, however, there is little to compare with lying on grasses, with a full Chalice, surrounded by sweet air and living creatures.

OPENING THE CIRCLE When Opening the Circle, be mannerly, and thank the Spirit of the Place as well as the rest of your Elemental friends. Before you go, show your thanks by leaving no wrappings or bottles, candle stubs or other remains.

Remember that other people have intense fears of Witchcraft, and fears are always stronger at night, as all feelings are. So it's best to be discreet on your way to and from a site at night. Keep 'Witchy' objects out of sight in bags and don't brandish your broomstick! What is to you innocent, sacred, and fun, can be terrifying to others, because of all the centuries of christian propaganda. What people can pass over in tolerance in daylight provokes them to anger at night, especially if they've been drinking or are already in an unhappy state. So even a very upfront Witch like me goes modestly! at night.

After all the practicalities and warnings, night time outside is absolutely wonderful. With full moon and stars overhead, silhouetted trees around me, and the rustling earth under, then I am an old self who has known this many times before.

IN THE CIRCLE YOU CAN'T DO IT WRONG

ECO - MAGIC
WORKING WITH THE WEB

It is one of the fundamental teachings of Paganism that we are the children of the Earth, not its masters. The Earth is our Mother, and we are part of her living Body, together with all other creatures. This has to affect how we treat other beings: they are fellow spirits, not packages in a grand supermarket to take and use as we wish. 'Living lightly upon the Earth' means living modestly, taking not whatever we can get, but just what we need, and giving back in return.

The ancient magical law of karma is not really about past lives; that's a detail. It's about how we have to live with the consequences of what we do.

Western society is one of the most vigorous and inventive the world has ever known, but it snatches and gobbles like an insecure, badly behaved child. Everywhere the warnings are flashing at us that our collective power to shape the world is steadily destroying the very envelope of life we need to survive. Yet we are foolishly arrogant if we claim the Earth herself is in danger, for the planet is a tough old lady who is quite capable of waiting a few millennia and creating another form of life. It is we ourselves who are in crisis.

Modern people who work for the Green lifestyle movements like to take inspiration from older tribal peoples, with their shamanic beliefs. This is where we get the 'living lightly on the Earth' guideline. However, we need not buckle completely under Western guilt. Many traditional tribal societies lived just as greedily as we do, only their smaller numbers meant that it didn't do as much damage so quickly.

Our society is so huge, so complex, made up of so many millions of people, with powerful organisations like international corporations, banks and governments. We quickly feel powerless and frustrated about changing what they do. The very warnings of crisis supposed to stimulate us to action, can batter us into depression and passivity. What can I do? after all.

Exhausts The urgency of it all exhausts us at the same time as we get involved. After a first, heady passion of commitment, we find out more about it, and the sheer awfulness of what is going on swamps us into despair.

There's the massive size of the problem - our whole way of life; and the blinding emergency - act NOW, before it's too late. If I can just get my breath back after that, I might maybe take one item and get started. But even this sensible attitude gets me into a whole tangle.

For example, petrol for my car burns lead off into the atmosphere, which is poisonous. Unleaded petrol doesn't put lead into the air, but it takes 10% more of it to fuel the car, so that puts 10% more of a lot of other poisons into the air. Then a high tech filter gives an almost clean exhaust, but one of its main parts is platinum. Getting platinum means strip mining, and production methods that heavily pollute the atmosphere. So what on earth is a Green driver to do? Give up the car some would say.

Try another: heating the home. Coal or oil releases sulphur dioxide into the atmosphere, which causes acid rain that kills vegetation. Smokeless fuel is not pollution free to produce, and a fire needs a lot more of it. Gas is quite good, but there are now mutant fish round the rigs in the North Sea. Electricity means nukes, or is based on coal or oil. Even using heavy insulation to cut fuel consumption means pollution in the production of the insulation materials.

Is there any point in even trying? It is mostly impossible not to pollute; there's just a careful weighing up of what pollutes a bit less. (In this case, insulation is a one off act of pollution to set against years of lower fuel use; and gas is the low pollutant fuel.)

Facing such a mass of complication, and feeling desperately urgent to heal the hurt at the same time, is a highly effective package of pain. We spin into panic, and either back off in frustrated guilt, or swing into overdrive, trying to save the Earth overnight. Saviours of the Earth all too often become bullies, preaching and nagging until they actually put people off the very things they're supposedly trying to get people to do. It took me much longer to use eco- products in my kitchen because I automatically avoided the kind of people who tried to guilt trip me about it, so I avoided the subject too.

Panic, the cause of our reactions, is ironically the dark gift of great Pan, lord of the Wild and the Beasts. When we panic it's best to let it run its course, and only then return to the task. In considering meditation, I suggested that it is more productive not to judge or criticise myself for getting distracted, but to accept it each time it happens as a natural event, and just gently return to the task.

Panic, given its head, brings out active survival hormones, to sharpen us. So sooner or later, in spite of the delay to wait for calm, we can get back to the knotty problem of how to unravel our ecological tangle. Taking more time to look at what is going on, and thinking through just how to work on it, seems crazy in face of the shrieking sirens of disaster all around us. But when caught in an accident, we act much more sensibly if we take time to breathe, calm down, and check the possible results of what we can do.

Taking time to think things through, and waiting for a sense of clear, sure confidence, is rather like giving a lot of precious time to Purifying before a ritual. But once our fog of fears and anxiety is soothed, we can get ten times as much done in the time left, after all.

People in a state of calm don't waste resources, don't fall over their own nervous feet, or make mistakes generally. In a state of urgency, we can't really afford not to use our own goodwill carefully and respectfully.

Theodore Roszak in 'The Voice of the Earth' tells us that the recent decades with ecology movements and personal development movements are actually the same movement. In learning to love and honour our own needs, we come to love and honour the needs of other life forms, and the Earth itself. As we gain the courage to really feel our own hurts, we become more aware of the hurting Earth. Alternatively, in working in the Earth's service, we have to learn to nourish our strength so as not to fail her. We may come to know our own sacred being because of being part of hers.

Theodore was impressed by a recent survey on car drivers in Los Angeles. Those interviewed overwhelmingly talked of the drive to and from work as a valued personal retreat for private thought and reflection, time out from busy lives. Each thought this was their own solitary reason for clinging to car ownership. He comments that Green goals cannot succeed unless they work with real personal needs in people's lives.

When I finally got round to using eco cleaners in my kitchen I expected them to be second rate. I prepared for extra scrubbing and trouble. To my delighted surprise, I found eco cleaners were much better; they cleaned stubborn grut quickly and easily;

things even stay clean longer. Later my eco educated husband told me that ordinary cleaners rely heavily on bleaching the dirt, while eco cleaners actually clean it better.

As a result I have stayed faithful to my green cleaners, even when it means an extra shopping trip, or a bit more money. If they'd been as awful as I expected I would probably have lapsed often, and maybe even given up the effort while I was ill or under stress.

A similar pattern of idealism and selfishness is important in healing work. Over fifteen hardworking years as a healer, there's no way I'd have coped with the constant sharing about broken love, self hatred, rape, incest, misery, confusion, depression and nastiness. Sweet kindness and 'I want to help people' just isn't enough.

Sometimes I do it from pride in my skill. Often I can hold to it because people are fascinating in their patterns. Some days when I'm tired and fed up like any other worker, I think of the money to pay my bills. Of course I am kind too. But sweetness and light evaporate under strain, so other, less pretty needs of my own have to underpin the proceedings if I am not to give up and burn out.

If we are going to genuinely change the way we live to a harmony with the earth, we need more than a year or two's passionate love affair with what we have to do. We need to slowly and steadily, step by step, build the changes into our lives so solidly, that they become quietly taken for granted as our way of life. That means sticking to it when the great global principles are far away and our everyday individual concerns appear to be everything.

Trying to do it because we're guilty might help a bit, but in the end guilt diminishes me, makes me feel unimportant because I am unworthy. Being so unimportant makes my silly efforts pointless, so I'm likely to give up.

The power of the Circle is essential medicine, to build us up into a sense of our power, to key us into our individual power to change reality.

Small If it is the massive, international organisations that are blindly destroying our life web, then it needs the small, individual caring of people locally to heal it. Children learn not to drop litter by seeing us use rubbish bins. Of such tiny pieces the jigsaw can be remade to a new picture. Individuals can tackle small, specific tasks, and the combined power of millions of pairs of hands and feet is the triumphant message of our times. At Lammas, or Harvest, we can make our chosen vows, not to solve everything, but to care for one corner of land, OR to use the new local bottle bank, OR to stuff some envelopes for an eco charity.

Small is beautiful, said Schumacher, and he had something to say. But so is the mighty web of life itself, of which we are all part. In waiting for clear thinking, in taking time to go step by step, in the way that suits us best so we can keep it up, we are also giving the web time to work on us. For we don't just sort out the best balance of non polluting behaviour by intelligent thought. We don't discover the best place for our particular shoulder on the Wheel through common sense. We need time to dream, asleep and awake, over many nights, so the deep self can softly fold together the guidance we need.

This is not just the next few months, this project. It is not even the next three, or seven years. It is the whole of our lives we are being asked to redirect. Doing that with some slow seeming preparation works with the great, slow Web itself. Afterwards, it's the result that matters, not the wait. When I moved house the weeks and months I waited to do it seemed to take so long. But once done, that all faded and what matters is the years I have lived here.

It can seem petty, these little things we can do. For some of us the comfort is that many are doing them too, and added together we make an impact. Big demonstrations, or focus days for action and ritual give us a powerful boost and make our united power manifest. For others who live in isolated places, or who do not flourish in groups and organised activity, the question is what can one, or a few achieve?

The occult teaching of the sown seed is ancient, and persistent. Reading the rites of Dion Fortune who worked in the first decades of this century, I am struck by how her visions are identical to commonplace ideas about women and men today. The circleworker who casts deeply felt hope into the great web sends an influential quiver through it. The seed can grow into a great tree of life.

However, just because this gets results from the sheer quality and intensity of the few, it must come from a deeply real attitude: single focus. It cannot work well when we think things should be like that, or because it's politically correct, or because it's high minded and spiritual. A whole, undivided will can make miracles happen. A set of needs which don't agree with a layer of shoulds above, is a divided mind.

Need I worked a successful temple and clan into being because I was plain lonely; genuine personal need and passion reaches deep into the web in a natural way. So build your chosen contribution from real needs in your own life. You understand those better than anyone else can. And as you carry out these small tasks, these humble bits of the great pattern, do not get too humble. For your chance will come.

One day, there will be a meeting with someone who can influence the bigger picture. Perhaps you can give them the kindness and support they need to keep going. Perhaps you can tell them something you have learned that helps them understand what is needed. Perhaps you can even rebuke them, shake them a little.

One day, you could come across a project that needs a skill you used to use, and could brush up. You could find someone you get on with, and together your resources add up to something exciting and possible. You can gradually improve your skills until you amaze yourself with what you can do. Once upon a time someone asked my younger self to help organise a conference about something I cared about. I was completely freaked at the very idea - who, me? I had no idea what they'd want of me, and backed off with excuses. But years later I became an organiser of big, national events. If you'd told me then, I'd never have believed you.

With patience, accepting what you are now without contempt, you can grow bit by bit, into a 'mover and shaper.' Perhaps you wish to do that kind of thing only once or twice in your life, to make your mark, and do your bit. Or perhaps you'd frankly like to do it a lot. Offer yourself in the Circle, in service, do whatever practical tasks you can, and the tools for key action will be put in your hands. When it happens, take a deep breath, admit you're scared, do it. And if you run away like I did, grow some more, and you'll get there next time.

Activists! If you're already in the thick of it, working on mailshots, petitions, committees, demos, digging out canals and rescuing animals: don't forget that other important endangered species - you. Seriously, caring people are valuable, so maintain yourself well. You may even be working to save or cherish something to prove you're not worthless. Work on your self respect; take time to pamper yourself, and you'll have so much more to give your ideal. Burned out activists are ten a penny, while those who manage their own health and needs caringly are rare creatures of great value to their campaigns, and to their companions.

As you become more productive, your struggle can be to stay linked in respect to those less aware than you are of what's going on. You have speeded up, and others can seem slow. You can still trust them to get there in the end though, even if they fumble and muddle on the way, as you once did.

Priest/ess of the Earth

It is a beautiful teaching of the Craft that each woman who casts a Circle, is a priestess, and each man who works one, is a priest.

Now spiritual work, at its most basic, is about meaning, about finding hope and sense when things are dark. Some of us find it in art, some in social ideals, some in children, some in clean houses or service, and some in nature. Some have a core myth, belief or philosophy.

What use are our pretty myths and legends, our spells, our graceful or passionate rites, if they wilt away under the scorch of misfortune and despair? Yet in facing the colossal powers that eat the forests; that cruelly torture and exterminate animals; that crush the native peoples; that poison the very four Elements that sustain life; and damage the delicate lungs, skin and blood of our children who are the future for our race; in facing all these agonies it is hardly surprising that we crumple.

To be a priest/ess for yourself takes strength and responsibility certainly. But you can falter, and fall, and stay in collapse for as long as you need, grieving your despair and helplessness. You should do so, for as Starhawk says 'Where there is fear there is power.'

To be a priest/ess for a community means not only keeping hope going for myself but for others too. It becomes a job to guard the eternal flickering tiny flame of freedom and meaning. What else are people asking me under all their varied problems or ceremonial rites of passage, but 'Reassure me there is a point to all this. Tell me it can all work out.'

In this role I can have moments of doubt, moments of uncertainty. I can spend several hours under the duvet, sweating and quivering, at times. But these can only be brief retreats. For the letters and the telephone don't stop, and I have accepted the job. A priest/ess must renew meaning and hope, not just for oneself, not just for a while, but steadily, for whoever needs it, for life. (One fails such a huge job, as parents all fail theirs here and there, but one keeps on trying.)

Being a priest/ess for the Earth is not so different. When you take it on, if you do so seriously, it means 'for better or worse.' It means somehow squeaking through on a thread of hope when it feels really rough. It means failing one battle, resting, and taking on another. The vision of an Earth Mother loved by her children is not a hobby.

One of the great comforts, which means sources of strength, is to look away from the dominant voices. The TV, the newspapers, radio are a highly impressive web in their own right. Our ancestors would not have known about war in the Middle East, or Africa, or Central Europe. News was local. So what seems to us like a universal tale of disaster has a lot to do with how good the technology is that brings us the news from far away. We just get a lot more information about troubles.

The selection of what we are told is obviously important. For even on a local basis we still hear about a lot of pain and violence. Most news is bad news, because we naturally react strongly to crisis, and those reactions make us buy papers and watch news bulletins.

Housework One day years ago, I stopped at a zebra crossing and watched an elder person hold a lollipop sign out for children to cross. I can remember when this scheme started, twinning unoccupied pensioners with much needed safety work to protect children. Millions of children have quietly benefited, and the pensioners self respect as well, with not one headline.

In getting miserable about disaster and cruelty and stupidity, it is horribly easy to overlook the real nature of goodness. It's like housework: you only really notice it when it's not done. The housework of the world adds up to a staggering pile of little cleaning up jobs.

In resisting the loss of hope, to better serve as a priest/ess of the Earth, keeping the vision alive can unfortunately slip into the frantic, pushy efforts of a fanatic. Your job is to keep your own hope alive, as an example and a resource, but not to force it on others. Your enthusiasm can push others away from what you love, unless you bite it back, and let others come to it in their own time.

It's a cosmic balancing act: keeping the fire going, yet not making it blaze so high it's too hot for others to come near. Such a balance is not only difficult, it's impossible. We can get it almost right, most of the time, if we try.

'I am the beauty of the green Earth, the white Moon among the stars, the mystery of the Waters, and the desire in the heart of each one of us.'

Rite for the Earth

PREPARATION Put things at the four quarters to represent those we want to protect. Air is the ozone layer, and clean air. Fire is endangered peoples, including Western people living near nuclear power stations. Water is the oceans and her creatures. Earth is the forests, and the many land species at risk.

You'll need some things for your treat or special indulgence towards the end of the rite.

A drum, a drum tape, a tape with a steady beat, a 15 -20 mins tape of a single drum beat (just bong, bong, bong) you make yourself would be very helpful. You can also practice beating a drum with a steady, monotonous beat yourself. It doesn't need to be musical, just simple bong, bong, bong steady.

PURIFICATION Make especially sure this is very personal, about your own very individual everyday matters. Don't waft away into idealism, and only care for larger patterns.

CASTING THE CIRCLE Honour each of the things at the quarters as you go. Tell them of your love and care.

RAISING ENERGY Hum and chant to each quarter in turn offering the energy you spin to its creatures and its element. Focus using the sphere, perhaps as the Earth itself.

WORKING 1) Trance: The drum beat would help here. Use a tape, or do it yourself. Relax thoroughly. Let yourself sink down through the floor. Look up and see it moving upwards above you.

Sink down safely through earth, past roots reaching down. Go down through dark rock, until it lightens, and warms, and glows.

Go into the fiery chamber of her heart. Hear the thud, thud of her great heart. Let her fire cleanse you, strengthen you. Wait and listen in case she has instruction.

Rise up again, as you went down, back up through the floor.

2) Vow 1. Make a personal vow to do something very real, something you quite definitely can manage to do, in your everyday life. You may decide beforehand what this is to be, or it may come to you during therite itself. Be ready to be flexible if a prepared vow to be overset by another that makes itself felt in the circle.

After making your vow, meditate once more. Visualise, or get the clear feeling of the hurt, neglected thing you want to help, actually being strong and clean and flourishing. Don't bother with just seeing how you're going to put it right: go for the goal, find it where it exists, already happened.

3) Vow 2 or present action. Give yourself some kind of treat, or make another vow, equally serious to the first one, to make a treat happen to reward you as a healthy selfish person, for your efforts. Do not brush this aside lightly; this is the fuel for your engine of dedication. Self indulgence is a Pagan virtue.

COMMUNION

OPEN THE CIRCLE.

FROM MY BOOKSHELF

NATURAL MAGIC Doreen Valiente (Hale '75)
Classic book on the magic of the Craft by the greatest living priestess today. Gentle, clear, wise.

THE SPIRAL DANCE A rebirth of the religion of the Great Goddess Starhawk (Harper '79) The American witch whose practical handbook fired a new generation of Paganism with her burning feminist, ecological vision. A personal, everyday style like mine.

MAGIC FOR THE AQUARIAN AGE A contemporary textbook of practical magical techniques Marian Green (Aquarian '83)
One of the finest British teachers of both Craft and High Magic; for her complete list of books correspondence courses and workshops send SAE to BCM SCL Quest London WC1N 3XX see A Witch Alone, & A Calendar of Festivals here.

A BOOK OF PAGAN RITUALS Herman Slater (Hale) Originally published USA by the well known proprietor of 'Magickal Childe' who recently died. Clear, useful and practical.

A WITCH ALONE Marian Green Delightful, practical course of solitary training month by month through the great seasonal wheel of the natural year. Based on the traditional Craft rather than the more modern systems of interpretation, but presented with careful relevance to modern (city) life.

MOON MAGIC and THE SEA PRIESTESS Dion Fortune
Novels, but containing a great deal of powerful ritual material, especially about Goddess and God, women/men.

THE MYSTICAL QABALAH Dion Fortune Qabalah meditations explained by one of the foremost magicians of the century.

THE SHINING PATHS Dolores Ashcroft Nowicki (Thorsons) a helpful series of pathworkings expressing the Qabalah.

(The next four are the main classic sources for High Magic work; this is more formally structured than mine. It aims to shape the self towards a higher purpose; mine accepts the self as wisely doing so anyway. Two streams of the river.)

1) MODERN RITUAL MAGIC: The Rise of Western Occultism Francis King (various publishers since '70) A classic of High Magic plus others by the same author.

2) THE FOUNDATIONS OF PRACTICAL MAGIC An Introduction to Qabalistic Magical and Meditative Techniques Israel Regardie (Aquarian '79)

3) TEMPLE MAGIC: Building the Personal Temple, Gateway to other worlds William G Gray (Llewellyn '88)

4) THE MAGICIAN, HIS TRAINING AND WORK W E Butler (Thorsons) One of the clearest and most sensible introductions.

WRITTEN DOWN STUFF LOOKS
MORE IMPORTANT THAN IT IS

THE PSYCHOLOGY OF RITUAL Murry Hope (Element '88) History, psycholgy and therapeutic uses of ritual in the Western Mystery tradition; Atlantis, psychism etc.

PRACTICAL CELTIC MAGIC/ PRACTICAL EGYPTIAN MAGIC/ PRACTICAL GREEK MAGIC Murry Hope (Element) Scholarly exploration of each cultural tradition with examples.

FIRST STEPS IN RITUAL Dolores Ashcroft Nowicki Very nice selection of simple recipes from various cultures, Greek, Celtic, Egyptian, Atlantean etc - but not the step by step training the title implies.

THE FELLOWSHIP OF ISIS have a remarkable collection of research booklets on Goddesses of world cultures, and their own carefully designed rites for all occasions. For intro leaflet and list send SAE to the Fellowship of Isis, Clonegal Castle, Enniscorthy Eire.

THE HOLY BOOK OF WOMEN'S MYSTERIES Zsusanna Budapest (Airlift) Dianic Craft, or the women centred way, which has so powerfully redrawn the sexual map.

(For more books on women's mysteries and the new men's work contact The Goddess and the Green Man, Glastonbury, Somerset for their catalogue - it's excellently comprehensive and up to date.).

THE WAY OF THE SHAMAN Michael Harner (Bantam) Short classic on shamanism, with details on drum trance. (American)

THE CEREMONIAL CIRCLE Shamanic Practice, Ritual and Renewal Sedonia Cahill and Joshua Halpern (Mandala '91) Lots of practical guidance to American shamanic work.

CEREMONIES FOR CHANGE: Creating Personal Ritual to heal Life's Hurts Lynda S Paladin (Stillpoint USA '91) Gentle work for healing sadness and loss.

THE ART OF RITUAL: A guide to creating and performing your own rituals for growth and change Beck Metrick (Celestial Arts '90) Detailed analysis, with excellent analysis and lists. Jungian psychology approach, language a bit academic for my taste.

BY RITE: Custom Ceremony & Community in England 1700 -1880 Bob Bushaway (Junction '82) Sociological book about peasant society using festival customs to moderate class inequality.

EIGHT SABBATS FOR WITCHES Janet & Colin Farrar (Hale) The festivals as practised by Wicca; a classic.

A CALENDAR OF FESTIVALS Marian Green Fascinating collection of rites, customs, recipes and myths throughout the year. Lovely interfaith calendar of all faiths major festivals including Pagan roots.

PASSAGES IN TIME: Ritual Today James Roose Evans (Element)

New out this year by an innovative theatre director who is also an ordained Anglican priest, but includes Goddess and God rituals.